STYLES OF RUIN

Recent Titles in
Contributions to the Study of World Literature

STYLES OF RUIN

Joseph Brodsky and the Postmodernist Elegy

DAVID RIGSBEE

Contributions to the Study of World Literature, Number 93

GREENWOOD PRESS
Westport, Connecticut • London

Library of Congress Cataloging-in-Publication Data

Rigsbee, David.
    Styles of ruin : Joseph Brodsky and the postmodernist elegy /
David Rigsbee.
      p. cm.—(Contributions to the study of world literature,
ISSN 0738–9345 ; no. 93)
    Includes bibliographical references (p.) and index.
    ISBN 0–313–30419–X (alk. paper)
    1. Brodsky, Joseph, 1940– —Criticism and interpretation.
2. Elegiac poetry, Russian—History and criticism. I. Title.
II. Series.
PG3479.4.R64Z86   1999
891.71′44—dc21   98–26454

British Library Cataloguing in Publication Data is available.

Library of Congress Catalog Card Number: 98–26454
ISBN: 0–313–30419–X
ISSN: 0738–9345

First published in 1999

Greenwood Press, 88 Post Road West, Westport, CT 06881
An imprint of Greenwood Publishing Group, Inc.

Printed in the United States of America

The paper used in this book complies with the
Permanent Paper Standard issued by the National
Information Standards Organization (Z39.48–1984).

10 9 8 7 6 5 4 3 2 1

Writers (Baltimore: Johns Hopkins University Press, 1992). Reprinted by permission of Johns Hopkins University Press.

Excerpts from Peter M. Sacks, *The English Elegy: Studies in the Genre from Spenser to Yeats* (Baltimore: Johns Hopkins University Press, 1985). Reprinted by permission of Johns Hopkins University Press.

Excerpt from Jahan Ramazani, *Poetry of Mourning: The Modern Elegy from Hardy to Heaney* (Chicago: University of Chicago Press, 1994). Reprinted by permission of University of Chicago Press.

for Jill

Contents

Preface

Death was our first sublime. It was the first dawning of a vastness tied to our contingency, even as it will be the irreversible ratification of that contingency. To elegize is to sing about the ends of things, apocalyptic matters both global and local, even as it is about memory and legacy. At the same time, as its song borders upon silence, to elegize also suggests something about how poets, as language users, devise beginnings—often ironic—in the face of discontinuity.

This is a book that examines such songs in the case of an important late twentieth century Russian-American poet whose career may be tracked against a grid of apocalyptic assessments. Therefore, it is as much talk about death as it is talk about the songs of death, because talk about elegy is, among other things (but first and foremost), talk about death. Yet no less a sage than Wittgenstein assures us that we enter upon such talk naïvely, that there is nothing to be said about death ("Death is not a part of life"). Wittgenstein's objection to talk about death is situated on the realization that this is an experience about which we can neither develop knowledge nor have shaped an informed opinion. Of course, such cautions founder on the ubiquity and something like authenticity of just such opinions and shapings, including those that poems shape. Therein lies much of the (re)generative—if plainly and generally plaintive—conflict that fuels poems in the first place. Wittgenstein's dictum is mainly a warning against arrant theorizing about the untheorizable. Be that as it may, the universality of death and its consequences, or, to be more precise, mortality, is the central crux of conscious human life and the fact upon which most of our thinking about values is founded, from aesthetics to morals. Certainly, Yeats thought death one of the two considerations worthy of the thoughts of "a mature man" (the other being sex).[1] If we cannot talk about death, as per Wittgenstein, we can certainly talk (endlessly) about our mortal condition and summon the aid of myths to lend texture and density to the otherwise unthinkable.

But how to do so without appearing, in some fashion, both to speak emptily and to dilate upon the obvious? Elegies offer, or try to, one of the categorical and historically recognized ways imagined to fit meaning to death. Or to put the matter the other way around, poetic discourse is itself a species of meaning founded upon death, and our understanding of the business of poetry is therefore inseparable from it. Certainly, there are other ways to fit meaning to death, notably religious ones, and religion has had a distinctive role to play in the composition of elegies too, providing that note of *consolatio* that enables formal closure and affective farewell, which often seem the occasion for the elegy's structural and stylistic version of what Freud called "the work of mourning."

Luckily for the poet, of course, every poem, regardless of its generic assignment, already constitutes a meditation upon closure, just as every stanza—indeed, every line—suggests measures taken to keep an eye on (and often to forestall) closure's inevitability. Closure renders us historical; the reconfiguration of time that poiesis manifests promotes the individual at the expense of history. But, contrary to Marxian and similarly ideological criticisms, poetry has never sought to promote the individual (e.g., the poet) as such. In fact, it would be virtually impossible for such a poetry to survive unless it were carried forth on the shoulders of something like a cult of personality, and poets in this century are highly aware of where such maneuvers lead (an awareness that goes double for Russians). In this sense, poetry was "romantic" *avant le lettre,* for the individual is offered as deserving of transcendence, a worthiness that grounds itself originally in the desire to confer "fame," but later extends, as Jahan Ramazani has shown, to include less public, but no less mourned, *lachrimabiles,* such as family members. In embarking upon this reformation, the poet extends the elegiac machinery to encompass not only those whose works qualify them as worthy but potentially all—a poetic grace that is the result of our mortality only. Thus, it is not the subject's worthiness for transcendence that is any more the ground of elegy, but his or her very contingency: It is the condition of this contingency and our acute awareness of it that legitimizes a self, which would otherwise mutely disappear in its material destiny. Allen Grossman distinguishes between private and legitimate selves in order to locate, heuristically, the poetic subject:

I am in effect saying . . . that poetry has a destiny not in selves, but in persons; and that, whereas selves are found or discovered, persons and personhood is an artifact, something that is *made*, an inscription upon the ontological snowfields [*sic*] of a world that is not in itself human. I view the world, and I think poetry by its very structures calls attention to the world, as not human; and in the presence of that world not human, the world that lies in the white spaces upon which our words are inscribed—on that world poetry writes the name of the person. And the distinction between person and self is that *person* is value-bearing. (20)[2]

The transcendent structures of poetry are purchased always at the expense of the self's desires. Good poets, no matter how actually worthy the example of their own selves may be, understand the economics of this exchange. The "self," like the Freudian Id, has no legitimate claim to partake of the transcendent linguistic apparatus that constitutes public discourse. In fact, it is inherently antithetical to our notions of what make up the adjective "public," for the self's (like the Id's) agenda is a deafening monotony of self-aggrandizement: Nothing of interest comes across to others, for whom the linguistic sphere mediates, precisely, the otherness into an intersubjective thisness. But this description is not to suggest that the self does not try, nevertheless, to advance its objectives at the public expense. In fact, poetry's abuse at the hands of amateur nightingales, to say nothing of its reception by insensitively schooled readers, has led to a common misconception that poetry exists, at least in part, to allow the self to murmur its wood-notes without the shame of public censure. However, as far as public discourse is concerned—a medium predicated on transformation—the stress is on the facilitation of linguistic interchange. The issue goes to the heart of the still-ongoing debate between materialists and transparentists: Those who wish to believe that language (and therefore poetry) is a transparent medium have no problem in conceiving of poetry as a stylized linguistic vessel that encodes and transports selves' effusions across time, delivering them in the same condition in which they were set forth—that is, ahistorically. Their enemies, the materialists (such as "language" poets), insist that no such "product" arrives and that poetry must be reconceived sans traditional subjects, which they take to be one of the chief entailments of the transparentist legacy.

The elegist must come to terms with the many ways in which poetry can fall afoul of its most popular myths because the genre is itself situated on the contingency of all speaking persons. As Harold Bloom says, following Emerson, "nothing is got for nothing," and since death is the condition of nothing directed to our persons, it is the something of the elegy that offers itself as a value-eventuating counter to death. In other words, far from distinguishing between fact and value, the elegist records the collision of fact (history, death) with value (language). In making these assertions, I am subscribing to the claim—well established as far as poetry is concerned—that there are no extra-linguistic truths: Poetry "discovers" no external truths that it brings back alive, neither in nature nor in "human nature." Language creates value, and truths are not registered in language after the fact: Language is itself value-bearing. For Brodsky, language is equally fact-creating: There are no facts about which language "refers." But this is not to deny that there is something that language denominates as "reality" or "nature." Nor is it to deny that poetry is a "transcendent" enterprise. How could it not be, as it joins times and persons? To use the term "transcendent" is simply to picture a poem, which is above all a species of language, as engaged in the mediating process between mutually interesting dimensions.

It will be obvious to some that the notion of "transcendent structures," to rearrange, slightly, Justus Lawler's phrase, is at home with an artist of Brodsky's classical nostalgias.[3] This lover of Virgil understands that myths of transcendence (e.g., Aeneas meeting the dead in Book VI of the *Aeneid*) serve to enforce the notion of mutually sustaining and perpetuating texts—in short, "tradition," a transcendent structure if ever there was one. The transcendent impulse that is native to the elegiac project connects up nicely with translation: One is, after all, transcending the lexical base. By the same token, the translated poet's desire for the perfection of signs (what we shall later see, following Valentina Polukhina's useful phrase, as "the cult of the word") becomes diffracted among alien signifiers, perhaps ironically underscoring, in one important sense, the impossibility of ever attaining the poetic Ideal (that, for example, poets don't write their poems in math—a cause for regret in a poet as radical as Velemir Khlebnikov), even as it goes about achieving its minimum success—a poem that travels across barriers. Perhaps it is a sign of its capitulation to the material nature in which we are incarnated that all poetic transcendence comes as cold comfort to the elegiac subject, who has relinquished precisely that consciousness that distinguished him or her in the first place. Perhaps, too, this is a reason that the traditional elegist has sought to stretch the canvas of religious solace onto the frame of poetic consolation. But here again is the opportunity for a trade-off, for while translation queers the intra-linguistic poetic Ideal, it gains a compensating transcendent power precisely by underscoring its own derivative status. In other words, translation underwrites transcendence, providing an additional venue for the poet's self-estrangement—that exile merely literalizes in the person. As Brodsky has suggested, these are felicitous developments, and it is the aim of this book to take him at his word, reading him against the grid, not only of Russian poetic tradition and practice, but most especially of Anglo-American. For to the extent that "exile" is home and translation, the poem, this ratio-intoxicated poet has predicated an impressive body of work upon structures of transcendence whose springboard is the one universal to which even the most jaded relativist will acquiesce, namely death. I hope it goes without saying, therefore, that this is not a book whose aim is to preach to a choir of Slavicists nor, indeed, of Brodsky novitiates. Neither does it pretend to any extraordinary, intramural knowledge about Soviet literature. I hope it will, if anything, be taken as a meditation upon contemporary American poetic practice as it engages the state of its own postmodernist metaphorics by means of an illuminating hybrid poet.

Before beginning this meditation, we need to dispel what is otherwise likely to be a term of confusion by attempting to distinguish between two types of transcendence. The first type belongs to what we might call transcendence proper, an impetus that the Romantic breed seized from religion and appropriated for itself at the advent of the modern age and that is characterized by the overflowing of the self (or the escape from the trap of the ego) into the "other." Much postmodernist theory, in disallowing "the metaphysics of presence," also forecloses on this kind of transcendence, demoting it to an illusion. Indeed, to the extent that such a thing as a metaphysics of presence must be critiqued, the impossibility of transcendence comes as an entailment of the enterprise. There is no "transcendence" because, roughly, there is no traditional place to transcend *to*: no transcendent realm, God, or Platonic Universal—any of which would qualify as a synonym for "metaphysics." There is, on this now familiar view, no place to hang one's hat. Following the postmodernist *Zeitgeist* with brio, Brodsky finds such schemes of transcendence both *passé* and inappropriate: they don't fit with what we know of the historical realities of the modern world (and not just the modern world). Which is not to say that such schemes are or were not laudable: They simply do not offer the poet the solace they once might have, and he rejects them. All the same, he looks upon the solace of religion, particularly, through a nostalgic lens, and this fact was once seen as evidence of the poet's active belief, rather than his disposition toward the spiritual. It did not help matters that the early Brodsky was identified so closely with the aims and beliefs of T. S. Eliot, for whom the poetic (aesthetic) dimension was to be eventually conflated with the spiritual one. But Brodsky's man of sidewalks, insofar as he entertains notions of the ineffable, prefers to stick with Kierkegaard's aesthetic man (although allowing for the possibility, however remote, that he may wander upward into the ethical category). A well-known early poem, "Nature Morte," illustrates the ease with which a misreading can support the case for a religious Brodsky. The "still life" in question is the crucifixion, and Mary approaches the Son, asking, "Are you my son?—or God?" Jesus' answer ("Whether dead or alive, / woman, it's all the same— / son or God, I am thine"), by its very ambiguity, refuses to commit to a religious interpretation of the scene it depicts. Indeed, as the title indicates, the whole matter is presented aesthetically. Brodsky's Christ declines to answer to his own divinity, as if to suggest that this much is a secret, or at the very least a matter unsuitable for human consumption, for it would become just another fact, just another phenomenon whose main feature turns out to be its own contingency. As a route to transcendence (and its analogs), it is therefore disallowed.

The other route, however, remains open, and that is an equally traditional route that assigns a transcendent purpose to language, especially poems. As we have seen, the hard-core postmodernist critic may argue that Heidegger's "metaphysics of presence," as it relates to linguistic representation, makes any transcendence a dead issue: words don't "correspond" to reality; hence the transcendent quest never gets underway. It simply spins its wheels, meanwhile ironically invoking the vocabulary of journeys. Moreover, subjectivity itself is compromised, "constructed," and not intentional in the manner that it purports to be. Brodsky has no truck with the latter problematic ("consciousness is on its own"), but as for the former, he heartily agrees, to the point that words not only don't, but shouldn't "correspond": They merely take their cue from a reality no correspondence ever favored, to trudge thence into a paradise of their own making. This homemade linguistic paradise, the poem, stands both as a rebuke to reality's capacity for life-long depredation and as an illustration, if illustration were needed, that it (paradise) lies elsewhere. It is this elsewhere that sanctions all the poet's moves and will constitute the chief heuristic device of this book. For it is an elsewhere to which humans are, unfortunately, heir, owing to their penchant— particularly vivid in our own century—for collusion in their own mortality.

I first met Joseph Brodsky in 1972, the year of his exile from the Soviet Union. Freshly graduated from the Writing Seminars at Johns Hopkins, where I had submitted some translations of Brodsky's work as part of an M.A. thesis in poetry, and living outside New York, I received a call from my undergraduate poetry teacher, Carolyn Kizer, who was then serving as acting director of the Writing Program at Columbia: "The Russian poet you translated is in New York and reading at Barnard this week. Why don't you come?" I did and met Brodsky and translator George Kline through Kizer's kind intercession. Although it occurred at the high-water mark of theatrical recitations (à la Yevtushenko), the young Brodsky's reading aroused enthusiasm and respect in a mixed house of Russian and non-Russian speakers, who witnessed a departure from the now-predictable fare of thundering Slavic bards. He had afterward adroitly fielded questions both from aficionados and, more conspicuously, from a press of Russian literature specialists, most of whom were themselves *in exilium*. I knew the type: intense, declamatory, themselves standing in elegiac relation to various venues behind the Iron Curtain. But underneath their index-jabbing ardor and clotted academic idiom was a less problematic relation to literary expression than was the case for other students of poetry. Indeed, banished from their home cultures, Russian academics had constructed a discursive community in which no words could be allowed to be taken for granted, least of all a poet's. In a sense, words, sealed off from their natural environment but thriving in the hothouse of New York intellectual life were all many had brought with them. This scenario was quite different from the innumerable other poetry readings I had attended, at which the poet's performance was greeted with the cool gentility of creative writing majors. Not that there was anything fundamentally wrong with this, but the premises of what constituted a "reading" seemed in this case to have changed and grown more consequential, as though a reading was not so much a recital of written poetry as a ritual devised to provide an intersection for Logos and communicant. For one thing, he had gotten his poems by memory. For another, he intoned the words in such a way as to suggest a distinction between their ends and those of ordinary speech, which by contrast fell short. It was as though, in the stylized enunciation, he had drawn attention to the sacred aspects of words in the midst of their general commodification. This was a dimension at the time new to me and one that underscored a sense of urgency to which I was not then privy.

Afterwards I happened to meet Brodsky on the steps outside, one hand pocketed—as it had been throughout the reading—the other attached to what came to be the ubiquitous cigarette with which he managed to envelop himself in a gray nimbus, and found a person different from the literary performer of the previous hour. Seemingly smaller, affable, anxious to downplay the excitement of the reading and its aftermath, he accepted my introduction and overlooked the youthfully impertinent simplicity (I was 23) with which I rose to his question, "Do you write poetry too?" From that moment, I sensed that he was already engaged in discovering the tenor of the culture into which he was thrown, for though I had used the fact that I had translated his poems in graduate school as a calling card, he was as interested in getting his balance for the *terra incognita* of American poetry as any young poet fresh from the hinterlands. We began visiting each other in New York, Massachusetts, North Carolina, and later Michigan. Brodsky was keen on the idea of securing a poet-friend whose credentials included the adjectives "young" and "American" so as not to rely solely on the kindnesses of assorted professors of Russian Literature, not the least formidable of whom was Professor George Kline. Professor Kline had translated the 1972 *Selected Poems* and, without benefit of advanced ear-training in American poetry, had brought Brodsky's poems to an American and British public in unprepossessing, workmanlike English. For Brodsky's exodus was followed by masses of untranslated poems, and he was anxious to redistribute the burden of Englishing his output more impartially. He was equally keen on securing a holistic view of *ars Americana* and, more broadly, of American popular culture. During the course of this period, he gave a novice's preference, perhaps in gratitude, to American things rather than their European equivalents, though in doing so he would find these did not always square with the preferences of many liberal, educated, brie-and-Volvo Americans. Speaking of cars, I can still remember his friends' bemusement at his proud purchase of a gargantuan AMC Matador, from behind whose wheel he would crush, better than any Marshal Zhukov, the feeble resistance put up to his domination of the passing lane and emerge, curiously refreshed, at the houses of poet friends, already talking about the poets he was reading—Kinnell, Simic, Lowell, or Wilbur—poets who were frequently synonymous with people he had visited but days ago in this same Matador. He was always keen to test American poetry against the grid of opinions he had formed while a protégé of Akhmatova, and heated arguments would be required to overcome these divinely inspired prejudices. Of course, such dismissive reflexes are the prelude to advocacy, and Brodsky's later admiration for a poet like Robert Lowell, whose poetry no doubt strikes the outsider as a sectarian matter indeed (as it did for Brodsky), reveals the transformation that he has undergone not only to ascertain what is alive in American poetry on its own terms, but, more importantly, to turn himself into a poet of dual citizenship.

It was during this period also that I came to see Brodsky's sometimes notorious views not as examples of blind stubbornness but as instances of self-assertion, enterprising but self-correcting. The assimilationist must guard his integrity by insisting on a past that already exists and is his. Assimilation, after all, encounters the twin dangers of capitulation and forgetting: two enemies of the poet. Moreover, I came to see the poet's self-assertion not as a matter of right or wrong opinions, but as the force of this past entering the alien present, which, so to speak, constantly checks the other's credentials, and not as a matter of psychology, but of culture. That the key to Brodsky's poetry is the elegy should not be taken as a suggestion that nostalgias are to be contained, nor survival a thing in need of expression—an impression likely to be accelerated by circumstance. The key to elegiac success involves the poet's redistribution and redeployment of poetic forces from prior conventional and nonce objectives to, essentially, one: that past and present be brought within troping distance of each other and so provide a model of mutual accessibility within language. The successful elegy, therefore, always comes close to comprising a performative genre in which the past escapes mere assessment and memorial to undergo, suitably transformed, the transcendent task of "locating" continuity. Thus spatial and temporal dimensions are both involved, and each acquires the power to stand for the other. Brodsky's "healing needle," therefore, is twofold: as an image of continuity management and as a metaphor for the transcendent machinery by which poetry provides the parallel life of art, whose mission is to rise in contrast and comparison to the contingent lives of people. In this Brodsky's poetry, like all serious poetry, orients itself in relation to some imagined Good, of which it is itself the symbol, even if it is not, precisely, an instance. But this is not to suggest that all serious poetry swallows Plato whole. Far from it, for there is some generosity to be imagined in setting one's artistic ambitions in orbit around such a faint Good, even if that concept only serves to stand—as Brodsky's does—finally devoid of people and in reproach to history.

It was a long time before Brodsky would bring himself to speak of Russian literature in our meetings. Brodsky was right in not allowing himself to be "fixed" in the middle of his journey, and such as I learned from his example I learned very specifically by his example. This was the lesson of *faute de mieux*, embodiment, the lesson that Yeats tried to teach with regard to truth. Thus, I was not entitled to take, as objects of cognition, aspects of the Russian experience with poetry. Rather, I was being invited to forego my commitment to understanding in return for some nearer, if unconceptualizable, relationship to language—and to the silence in which it is embedded and into which it will eventually merge. This book, as with all communication with the silent and the silenced—the elegist's territory—is thus necessarily replete with examples of my failure to take the lesson to heart. It is also, I hope, an expression of appreciation for some lessons learned.

In spite of the fact that in translating Brodsky I came face-to-face with the elegiac nature of his task, it was not until my much later doctoral studies with Jahan Ramazani that I began to see, as if anew, a possibility for expressing some of the considerations bearing on Brodsky's poetry that had haunted me for nearly two decades. To put it simply, Professor Ramazani showed that it was possible to play Aaron to another's Moses without losing track of the magnitude and complexity of the message. For Ramazani, interpretation and appreciation are interchangeable terms, and he therefore suffers no anxiety of reception, nor offers a reductive account of the poetic art to make his case. Working in the best spirit of criticism, he has patiently sought to locate the implications of elegiac convention as they relate to contemporary and Modernist practice and uncovered the vital points at which convention expands or yields to circumstance. He also introduced me to the useful discourses of such key figures as Adorno and Heidegger and led me back to the sources of our century's enriched appreciation of elegiac thinking, by way of Sigmund Freud and Melanie Klein. Richard Rorty likewise clarified many points relating to Nietzsche and Heidegger and the writers following after them who have contributed to our means of thinking about poetry and the tasks of language and its wonder-child, metaphor. An exemplary and humane thinker, he has also been the source of much moral support. Mark Edmundson has been most helpful in pointing up many of the connections between philosophers and contemporary poets, as well as introducing me to many of the theorists whose work bridges the two worlds. All three of these men, each of whom has the generosity to entertain poetry's imposing claims about itself and who reads poetry with an unmatched degree of care and sympathy, helped me to see how it was possible to demilitarize the tensions between postmodernist assumptions and contemporary poetic practice. To these three in particular I owe thanks for helping me to articulate my own renascent sense of the compatibility of poetry with "theory"—a notion that still receives more resistance than it deserves by both poets and theorists.

I am also grateful to my late friend Carl Proffer, who with his wife Ellendea, changed the landscape of Soviet literature for American eyes and provided me, through many stimulating conversations over a number of years, with a sense of the milieu out of which Brodsky arose. Daniel Kinney illuminated many relevant passages in Homer, Virgil, and Dante, whose connections with the "classical" aspect of Brodsky's poetry, while generally acknowledged, have also been generally taken for granted. Professor Kinney's keen eye for nuance helped me to focus more closely on this aspect of Brodsky's work.

For discussions about W. H. Auden, Brodsky's closest thing to a complete poetic role model, I must thank my wife, the artist Jill Bullitt, whose understanding of the thoroughly literary character as a species of artistic character reflects her own acquaintance with the poet during the 1960s. I wish also to thank my comrade-in-pens, the poet Marilyn Chin, for the pleasure of many speculative, late-night conversations about poetry and the issues taken up in this study. My greatest debt, of course, belongs to Joseph Brodsky, whose stamp upon the thinking here is unfortunately occluded by my reliance on academic jargon and my own unwieldy recourse to theoretical concepts that he himself, like his mentor Auden, would never have the bad taste to commit, but whose loyal generosity, now joined with his silence, nevertheless allowed him to overlook.

In quoting from Brodsky's works, I use the following abbreviations:

SP—Selected Poems
PS—A Part of Speech
U—To Urania
SF—So Forth
L—Less Than One
W—Watermark

NOTES

1. Quite apart from the metaphors that the language about death has contributed to language about sex, the two share another similarity: Each activates fantasy in the sense that it provides a constantly available matrix for speculative meditation.

2. We should add that, because such persons exist courtesy of language, words alone inscribe the values to which Grossman refers—a position that Brodsky echoes, with particular vividness, in his elegies.

3. By "transcendent structures," I refer to those linguistic and formal genres, conventions, styles, and modes that, roughly, translate private into public discourse (where there is, vitally, no end to their potential "discursivity").

1

Introduction:
"Words to Nonexistence . . ."

From the 1980s on, it became an increasingly acceptable shift in the critical shop talk of contemporary poetry for critics, no less than cultural commentators and journalists, to focus their attention on the "meaning" of Brodsky, rather than the meaning of the poet's work. This shift in focus became even more strikingly the case after the poet's 1987 award of the Nobel Prize for Literature. Seamus Heaney, for example, felt moved to a defense of the award by writing an article entitled "Brodsky's Nobel: What the Applause Was All About"[1] as if the "meaning" were somehow not only distinguishable but also detachable from the poetry it honored. While Heaney was a personal friend and is a thoughtful partisan of Brodsky's work, it is not insignificant that on this occasion he sought to set the record straight by pointing not to the poetry but to the poet as the embodiment of it. Indeed, the very notion of a poet as embodying *something* of his or her poetry seems to lie at the source of much discussion and contention—at least opinion—vis-à-vis this poet's work. Why is this so? In a way that is uncharacteristic of the usual perspectives brought to bear on contemporary poets, particularly those whose feet have trod on North American soil, Brodsky appeared somehow to live in the sleeve of his own poems, themselves seamed with a history out of reach to most of his peers. At the same time, from the beginning of his tenure in the United States as one more political and artistic exile until his death as a globe-spanning literary lion, Brodsky went to considerable lengths to register himself as an American poet—and with predictably ambiguous results. In doing so, he declined many of the more customary tributes offered to the celebrity dissident, whether as a symbolic martyr—with the subsequent honorific of the "survivor," who lands in the bosom of the nearest academic community and pens his memoirs—or as an after-dinner moralist who could be counted on to lecture us on the comfortable theme of our middle-class ills. Indeed, the lecture circuits remain perpetually clogged with just such glamorous exiles. Those who persisted (and persist) on placing Brodsky in these lights have run a continual risk of getting him wrong in an essential way, for time and again he insisted only that we mind the business of poetry—indeed, the business of language generally, and that is the problem. Though well-meaning, Heaney's praise of the poet's dedication to the art carries with it the uncomfortable suggestion that when we honor the writer, we do so at the expense of the work.

Others lacking Heaney's degree of respect for the enormous difficulties of the art—that is, cultural cheerleaders more or less of the cultural right—saw in the Nobel award a confirmation of some vague, neo-Augustan position, based on their belief that Brodsky's association with W. H. Auden made him appear an avatar of the hyper-civilized Mid-Atlantic Man and therefore as a cosmopolitan antidote to the darker-browed Solzhenitsyn. Meanwhile, another, equally misguided camp sought to combine a growing suspicion among Brodsky-watchers—that the poet was often too much the personal maverick to hew to ideological correctness—with a reproof to the effect that the master on whom they had pinned their hopes might be guilty of having unfortunately drifted, from time to time, into a facile, gnomic mannerism. While these supposed champions attempted to join in high-minded, if not high-handed, encomia (like the Russophile John Bayley[2])—often, by shouldering the term "poetry" onto the broader shelf of "culture," others had decided they no longer liked what they saw and meant to say so. For instance, John Simon, reviewing Brodsky's third collection in English translation, *To Urania*, provided a case in point of a cultural journalist pretending outrage at what he felt were the poet's solecisms and general sloppy craftsmanship. In this volume, Simon found "opaque maunderings in tormented English" and "worse yet, doggerel." Accusing Brodsky of coasting, he found much of the volume to consist of "wit writing," which he obliged his readers by defining as intellectually engaged but emotionally dry versifying, presumably implying a missing center, which had something to do with expressiveness and affect. He even indulged in a *faux pas* of his own: When, roused from his boredom at the award of a prize to which he gave small credence and smaller homage, he imagined calling on the Nobel committee to take the honor ("epaulets") back, concluding that "the muses appear to be forsaking him."[3] A number of influential American poets had also begun to grumble well before the Nobel award. The poet Robert Hass, whom we might expect to be an otherwise interested party,[4] had shot his own warning across the bow in 1983, expressing perplexity that the reputation seemed so in excess of the accomplishment. But he wrote off his disappointment to the possibility that Brodsky's poems struck Russian ears with less dissonance than they did their American counterparts, which had to hear the poet's voice through the thick and haphazard intermediary of translation or not at all.[5] Sam Hamill likewise advanced the suspicion that for the workaday faction of American poets, Brodsky had come to been perceived as a mannered, opinionated crank, mass-producing knock-off classicism, an imperfect Auden clone, ironically devoid of the master's most divine gift, his matchless ear.[6] If Brodsky was liable to the wrong kind of praise, he was equally liable to the wrong kind of blame.

To Brodsky's most astute readers, such notes could only—against extensive evidence to the contrary—warp the sense of what they regarded as most important about their bard. Instead of encountering a fiery, truth-bearing dissident turned apostate and bourgeois (or noble and symbolic), along with his poems, they took Brodsky at his word: "He" has been translated into his work. They wished to draw our attention away from the outer, contingent manifestations of a career— that part subject to the poet's own suppression—and toward the systematic, career-long deployment of a poetic project. In other words, they wished the objective critical scrutiny that we would accord any poet not caught up in matters extraneous to his stated purposes. Such critical receptiveness would, according to this view, be simply a matter of courtesy. But for his devotees it was a courtesy never fully extended to a poet about whom commentators spent an unusual amount of energy trying to pigeon-hole within largely irrelevant, but in any case ineffective, contexts.

It is through such a supposition of continuity and coherence that I wish to view one particular thread of the poet's work, the elegies. Looking back to the beginning of this work of more than three decades, we see a young ironist precociously beginning a bold poetic undertaking that set about steadily unpacking the riches of its original inferences to an astonishing, even extravagant degree. Like a reverse Beckett, Brodsky sought to complicate the drama of his poetry, which is the drama of the twentieth-century displaced person, homeless, contingent, but not without resources, the most engaging of which is a full-blown Apollonian wit. This wit, like truth, has its home in language, and if truth is language's missionary arm, wit is its defender, patrolling the perimeter to deflect any opposition to its freedom- and world-making. Most importantly, wit can turn the tables on determinism, if only in the short stretch, and while it comes up empty against the natural conclusion of contingency and exile, it also incorporates it—death—into its project. Wit has one stylistic imperative: It must not end up as a self-completing diversion, but must reinforce the stylistic cordage of verse, as Uncle Wiz knew, because whatever else it is doing, it is also always moving to engage the most fundamental nemesis of consciousness, namely, the terminal structure of the abode of consciousness.

Poetry understood and experienced in this way is not language reduced to rhetoric but, on the contrary, language promoted to it. But Brodsky departs from older, and perhaps more familiar, varieties of the poetry of wit in the realization that he shares with the poetically un-witty Yeats: the idea that the only salvation for our embodiment in three dimensions lies in our ability to acquire means to shed one. In short, the human must imagine the self as becoming not merely literary, but literature itself. Brodsky's poems suggest that a life guided by the light of aesthetics guarantees that the dash between life-dates will not be seen as an abbreviation of the mereness of the journey, since that dash symbolizes the bone of contention between history, which would shrink it on principal, and memory, which would prefer to stretch it until its outline began to make a figure.

If in spite of the above-mentioned caveats, Joseph Brodsky became one of the most visible elegists of our time, this elegiac dimension has seemed to arrive *tout court* with the fact of his exile to the West in 1972. Elegy for Brodsky was always a congenial poetic genre, one that performed yeoman's work for social, metaphysical, and satirical purposes, as well as for the "work of mourning."[7] It was also the kind of poetic work that appealed to the classicist in him (it is "the most fully developed genre in poetry" [*L* 195]). In a sense that has been misconstrued as a Kafkaesque irony (and Brodsky was himself perhaps partly, though inadvertently, to blame for the misconstruing), the fact of his physical exile seems precisely to have lent the advantage of spatial disjunctiveness—to go with the elegy's traditional temporal disjunctiveness. Brodsky seized on this added dimension's tropaic possibilities, and by combining these with a general elegiac disposition (which, as we will see, has roots in autobiographical and metaphysical sources), worked toward a thematic complexity that not only has added to the store of elegies per se but also has imparted an ambiance for improvisation to a form that history had already left ironic in the face of its own layered conventions.

Brodsky has observed in connection with Constantine Cavafy that some poets in fact sound better, more themselves—more *estranged*—in languages other than their native tongues, their poems being lent a certain authenticity by the ventriloquism of translation and taking on a certain pathos, thanks to their fate, inspired or indifferent, at the hands of translators: "Every poet loses in translation, and Cavafy is not an exception. What is exceptional is that he also gains" (*L* 55). Although the art of the translator involves ferreting out or even inventing equivalencies within a different register of codes and signs (to say nothing of the slants and biases by which we register the presence of style) that are the enabling features provided by the largesse of any particular linguistic tradition, even the freshman of languages knows that there are no inter-linguistic *quid pro quos* and that translation is, at best, a means of austere linguistic deputation. At worst, it becomes a grotesque cloning of atmospheres in meta-languages that exist only to harry the poem to the reader's consciousness before a merciful silence envelops it again. In either case, this state of affairs sometimes puts the translated poet in sight of the strategic advantage hinted at by Brodsky's remarks on Cavafy, for the translated poem always produces the sign of its own absence as a poem and hence arrives in the foster language as an honorary elegy already. In this sense, it is likely that the translation will go the poem one better by, as it were, embodying this absence in the same form as the original, whereas the original poem's only absence belongs to the signifieds it purports to evoke. One might even say that a translation takes that absence to a higher power by submitting it, by default, to a more rigorous emphasis on formality.[8]

Cavafy was, incidentally, at home with bureaucrats, and Brodsky is no doubt being slightly, playfully disingenuous in his discussion of the Alexandrian poet to the extent that he is also writing autobiographically. For the condition that obtained for Cavafy, or better, the condition and career of Cavafy's poems bear striking resemblances to Brodsky's own, irrespective of their quite different stylistic achievements, and Brodsky's poems in translation, where fame dictates that they largely repose, can only stand to gain from such a discussion. The point to be made about Cavafy in regard to "translation," however, differs slightly from the one to be made about Brodsky. The thing to understand about Cavafy stands upon this crowning irony: that exile, distasteful though it is, is not simply a new theme, even a paramount one, but the necessary condition of his accomplishment as a poet. Brodsky's estrangement, for the most part only authenticated anew by means of a new geographical dimension—his involuntary exile to the West in 1972—is central to an understanding of the growth of his accomplishment. The point to be made about Brodsky is the one he has made about himself: that consciousness equals estrangement.

Although the following assertion is virtually unprovable, its truth should impress itself upon readers instantly: namely, that most readers encounter most major poets in languages other than the original. Most readers have encountered Brodsky's poetry in translation.[9] Indeed, the Swedish Academy read Brodsky in English in considering him for the Nobel Prize. This linguistic prerequisite is, of course, also the case for his peer poets, including some, like Heaney and Walcott, about whom it may be said that the fact of their translations into other tongues scarcely seizes the common reader's mind as a dimension of their importance, though this same importance has imposed the necessity. Obviously what is "lost in translation," as the cliché goes, pertains to matters of linguistic complexity, style, allusion, and so on, matters of context that stand to be shed when the poem crosses into another language. In their turn, further problems of reception arise: How do we know that this translation gets a poet right? Is it fair to say, given a poem stripped of its native richness, we can get it right? Further, what does it mean to "get it right," anyway? The case of Brodsky's wide acceptance (as for Paz, Neruda, Herbert, and others) suggests that the poem not only loses something in translation, but also, as with Cavafy, gains a compensating power.

In Brodsky's case, it would not be unjust to observe that much of the power generated by his elegiac channel is conditioned by extraordinary particulars, thanks to which our praise and regret are inextricably bound up. Brodsky was quick to minimize the impression of symmetry between his life and his works on the grounds of our making a biographical fallacy, meanwhile alluding to this very symmetry, albeit in satirical terms. Brodsky's advice to Mikhail Baryshnikov ("Earth's flat all over: try the States") contains more than an iota of the sly truth that assimilation to America and its language provides access to a *lingua franca* that stands to compensate in initially unpredictable ways for the losses that attend the arrival.

Nevertheless, Brodsky's enterprise, like Cavafy's, begins with the simple and familiar Archimedean principle of de-centering:

Because civilizations are finite, in the life of each of them comes a moment when centers cease to hold. What keeps them at such times from disintegration is not legions but languages. . . . The job of holding at such times is done by the men from the provinces, from the outskirts. Contrary to popular belief, the outskirts are not where the world ends—they are precisely where it unravels. (*L* 164)

To put this another way made explicit and familiar by Viktor Shklovsky and others: For the poet, the degree of articulation becomes a function of de-centering or "defamiliarizing." What is being "de-centered" here is the poet's language itself, a fact that provides the master-trope: The poetic subject is de-centered by virtue of his estrangement, alienation, exile (and translation). This, essentially, is the point Brodsky has driven home in his encomium for another poet of exilic turn of mind, Derek Walcott. For Brodsky, Walcott has under-stood the strength of his own marginal perspective as a post-colonial black, for whom "instead of reductive racial self-assertion, which no doubt would have endeared him to both his foes and his champions, [he] identifies himself with that 'disembodied vowel' of the language" (*L* 168). Brodsky is, by implication, even more to the point about himself, for who could be farther from the center of a language than one who, having dived into the dividing seas, at last pulls off his frog mask and crawls ashore, receiving the greetings of the natives in words not his own? Thus, too, the poet tropes his situation by means of such praises as his own for Walcott, and it is but a short step from the fellow-feeling of encomia to the elegy's task of consolation and reconstitution through inheritance, which is, in turn, the inference of similarity (as of poetic power) derived from past time, instead of from geographical distance. It is by such twistings that we arrive at the traditional territory of the elegy:

> Preserve these words against a time of cold,
> a day of fear: man survives like a fish,
> stranded, beached, but intent
> on adapting itself to some deep, cellular wish,
> wriggling toward bushes, forming hinged leg-struts, then
> to depart (leaving a track like the scrawl of a pen)
> for the interior, the heart of the continent.
>
> ("Lullaby of Cape Cod," trans. Anthony Hecht)

In Harold Bloom's terms, our poetry wars are backward. We are forced, spinning against the way we drive, to slide into the field of Oedipal struggles. By contrast, Brodsky's poetry, strategically armed with the legacy of European and American attitudes and postures, struggles against the future, or at any rate, against *a* future; for as any Russian will tell you, one does not undertake lightly to do battle on multiple fronts. For one thing, the struggle with the future necessarily carries with it a variety of elegiac implications. I say "necessarily" because from a poet's point of view every future tropes the present and thus involves itself with the business of memory, which is to say culture, and this, for the poet, manifests itself in language and what may befall that language. Poetry is *inter alia* the rhetorical structures of such turnings: It is both the turning and the turned, as it were, and in being both displays an essential ambivalence—a desirable ambivalence, however, for it avoids the over-determination that would otherwise be its lot. This is another way of saying that the poem relies on the "double-playing" of its temporal dimension. It is at once a thing to be taken in and a thing that can only be "taken in" in time. If we bring to mind this business of the poem's duration, we become aware too of the quick complexity of the poem's transactions with time. It not only manifests itself in duration; it refers to duration, and this double timeliness becomes vexed to the degree that a poem attempts to achieve "timelessness." Its status as another bit of material is equally complex, but it is not my concern here to attempt to unravel its complexities on that score. However, as concerns the duration to which it refers, we can say roughly that this equals some portion(s) of the past. Much of the ambivalence arrives when a poet tries to play one of these time senses against the other. As we will see, this sense of double-playing (what I am referring to by the more familiar "ambivalence") marks Brodsky's poetry to a considerable degree. Memory's part in this ambivalence is well known: Every trope is a selective operation upon memory, just as every memory is a trope upon a past state of affairs. What is noteworthy is the degree to which Brodsky deploys the elegy's dependence on past time in the service of questions relating to the future. That, too, is part of the double-seaming, the ambivalence.

Traditionally, the elegy is a genre directed, on the occasion of a specific death, toward questions of our mortality. The "work of mourning," however, is complex and, until recently, has been subject to complex traditional patterning. More modern offshoots of the elegiac stock have been cultivated out of a sense of greater, if vaguer, loss (predicated in large part on secular demystifications), and themselves trope and ironize the generic tradition from which they draw. One of these offshoots is the disposition of an elegiac stance, a feeling that runs through much modern and contemporary poetry and one that cannot be accounted for simply by recourse to an acknowledgment of our mortal status or indeed to poetic myth-making, but one that suggests a more historically determined cluster of causes. It seeks to pose the question of what it is like to live in a condition of metaphysical and historical loss, of what it is like to live in a culture that is no longer called on to pose the question of its losses in terms of the generic at all. Thus what the elegy proper sets out to do is supplemented by a broadened wavelength that sends its signal out across the entire spectrum of poetry.

For a poet of Brodsky's *weltanschauung*, this way of putting things is rather a cliché. What it may mean in terms of his poetry can only be elicited by ironic approaches in that the condition of loss registers itself prior to systems and mythologies intent on coopting loss—including personal loss—for their own legitimation. In fact, it registers itself not as a matter of terminus but as terminability itself. Thus loss is always a means that we honorifically denote as change. Because there is change at all, because poetry itself is an instrument of duration, all poetry contains the inherent potential for being elegiac. In *The Sighted Singer*, Allen Grossman brings out this aspect of poetics:

I have always been attracted to those accounts of the function of poetry which specify the keeping of the image of the person in the world as its principle outcome. The most ancient poets are found making possible the recollection across time of the images of heroes. The most passionate advocacies for the art of poetry in sophisticated late periods, such as the period of Horace, turn upon the function of poetry as keeping alive, across the abysses of death and of the difference between persons, the human image. (6)

Insofar as poetry is referenced to memory (including language as memory—the memory of other poems, for example), it deals with absence; but how exactly does it "deal" with this abstraction? Generally speaking, most postmodernist criticism makes the case that in trying to recapture "presence," poetry is doomed to fail for the reason that words are neither essences nor signs that correspond to reality but differential "marks and noises" (to use Rorty's and Davidson's term). If, however, we shift the emphasis from poetry's supposed attempt to recapture presence to its attempt to deal with absence—a prior matter altogether—we find that a poem is not just the sign of an absence it wishes to mark in language; it is itself the sign of its own absence, a phenomenon only made extravagant, as we have seen, by translation. That is to say, poetry features its own "constructedness" in the first place by virtue of being manifest in a poem, as opposed to some other arrangement of marks. So-called language poets have seized on this queer ontological aspect of poetry, preferring to omit the pretext of a "subject" that exists extra-linguistically out in the world—some thing or state of affairs to which a poem "refers." Insofar as our present language game is concerned, however, it seems that the pretext of recapture is still a desideratum for most poets, even if we have become knowing and indeed some- what cavalier about the bars of our linguistic cage. Nevertheless, it is arguable that the battles being fought over the issue of language's materiality versus its supposed transparency carry with them the suggestion that we can extend the feeling of disillusion, getting as much of it as we can bear, perhaps in the hope that our wounds, like Jacob's, will mark the degree of our betterment.

Brodsky seems to favor an aestheticist position when he suggests that art is a substitute for life. For those of us who have been schooled in Wilde, Yeats, and Mallarmé, the idea is hardly new. In spite of that, the assertion still has a nice epigrammatic appeal. It is also easy to misunderstand. What is most of interest is neither "art" nor "life" but the principle of substitution. What Brodsky suggests, and seems to have arrived at as a belief early in his career, is that the bridge between these two terms does not carry essences, that the process of sub- stitution admits absence as its precondition, both in the meanings of words and things and in the "content" or "subject" of a given work of art. The equation betrays no illusion as to what it is that is being transformed, nor to what we might be able to say about the resulting substitution. As Brodsky writes in his essay on Osip Mandelstam, "Writing is literally an existential process; it uses thinking for its own ends, it consumes notions, themes, and the like not vice versa. What dictates a poem is the language, and this is the voice of the language, which we know under the nicknames of Muse or Inspiration" (*L* 124-25).

Thus, once the thematic quibble is dispensed with by such a candid acknowledgment, we can have business as usual. One of the usual things about elegiac poets is that sooner or later they get around to writing elegies about themselves or, at the very least, give in to the impulse to direct the occasional elegiac ray toward the first person. Whatever else it may have done to this poet's work, his exile provided an added (and ideal) occasion for such self-elegizing. Self-elegy differs from other-directed elegies in the obvious sense that the self that is elegized is subject to "elegy" only in a manner of speaking. Even so, for the poet to suggest that he or she is undertaking the macho feat of posthumous address is tempting. Brodsky solicits his reader's attention to such "posthumous" voicings, for these would imply an escape, not just into rebirth (and, perhaps, self-begetting) but also from the life hedged in with its two main existential mainstays: nothingness and boredom: "Boredom, after all, is the most frequent feature of existence, and one wonders why it fared so poorly in the nineteenth-century prose that strived so much for realism" [*L* 30]). Brodsky is, however, aware of the dangers inherent in succumbing too completely to this temptation:

Every "on the death of" poem, as a rule, serves not only as a means for an author to express his sentiments occasioned by a loss but also as a pretext for more or less general speculations on the phenomenon of death per se. In mourning his loss (be it the beloved, a national hero, a close friend, or a guiding light), an author by the same token frequently mourns—directly, obliquely, often unwittingly—himself, for the tragic timbre is always autobiographical. In other words, any "on the death of" poem contains an element of self-portrait. (*L* 195)

Much of the work on elegy today, when it does not center on specific poets, has come from studies of the genre qua genre or, increasingly, from psychological perspectives, the latter seeking to explain the workings of the elegy in terms of "the work of mourning," poetic inheritance, and the like. What these approaches must of necessity skimp amounts to this: that the elegiac complexion can spread from the occasions of specific deaths and be put to use manifesting more abstract, and yet nearer, facts of absence. These facts constitute nearly the entire contents of consciousness and all of memory. The intra-poetic nature of elegiac dynamics lends itself to certain kinds of philosophic thinking as readily as to psychologizing, and this thinking is by turns ontological (asking why "being" stands in contrast to all that is not, especially including the dead) and epistemological (asking how I know my words, already compromised and subject to deconstruction as soon as written, will be able to possess the requisite power to initiate a discourse with and about the dead, will indeed both substitute and suffice for that which is gone).

In spite of, or perhaps because of, the autodidactic nature of Brodsky's poetic education, he swerved equally from the academic's understanding of elegy as a form and from the professor's intimacy with Freudian and post-Freudian hermeneutic models in favor of a more broadly understood conception of elegiac thinking. To put the matter another way, going to school with Eliot seemed a better idea than going to school with Freud. As a result, his poetic models were, by and large, not mediated by any imported theory of the sort that one is almost sure to detect in university wits, although he himself was notorious as an ad hoc theorizer, often drawing unusual and instructive inferences from poems.

Even when it comes about out of necessity, the fact of being self-taught, as Brodsky largely was, is a vexed matter for most who would arrive at the poetry hauling conceptual "tools" provided by traditional academic training. But the poet, powered by an eclecticism that circumvents committee-inspired curricula and, by corollary, their reading strategies, comes up with its own perfectly helpful, perfectly personal canon. In other words, Brodsky declines to enter the debating hall through the front door and yet insists on debating nonetheless, though with a different set of texts. Such an approach is likely to be the source of perplexity for poets schooled in the universities with their even now wide assumptions about the poet's calling. This is so especially in the United States, where most poets are trained to warble their wood-notes in writing programs, right next door to the new historicist Miltonist, the feminist reader-response theorist, and the psycholinguist. Ironically, such training is apt to harmonize with Brodsky's trial judge, who professed amazement that Brodsky would presume to call himself a poet without the sanction of the Writer's Union, to say nothing of a university education. The record of the trial makes good reading, and lest the cautionary tale it unfolds slide from conscience, it should be stressed that such a commoditized view of the poet's licensing to practice poetry continues to stand behind the regnant academic skepticism toward scribbling gypsies who have not seen fit to pursue their degrees, only the punitive consequences for the Russian poet were greater, because the Russian public of course takes its poetry more seriously than does the American public.

The general air of suspicion evinced by the Soviet authorities took some time to descend on Brodsky in this hemisphere, owing to the glamour Westerners have attached to dissident heroes, and it had a good deal less than a total damning effect thanks to the divide that separates academic and literary culture. Whether one was reckoned a hero or simply an opinionated émigré became all one to the poet, though. I would suggest that it was neither to the MLA nor to the East Coast literati that Brodsky wished to hook up his poetry connections (though the latter claimed him by virtue of his residency in New York and the former belatedly devoted some attention to his work). His real connections completed private circuits, and his personal grid of literary antecedents (e.g., Virgil, Donne, Pushkin, Tsvetaeva, Mandelstam, Akhmatova, Montale, Cavafy, Eliot, Auden, Dostoyevsky, Shestov, and Berlin) has seemed all the more personal for appearing to exhibit no obvious internal coherence, as if a "higher" and "more coherent" assemblage were not equally or even more contingent for applying to no one in particular. The benefit of Brodsky's list follows from its being personal and thus not subject to the artistic irrelevance of explanations that go into the making of academic canons of literature. We can charge Brodsky, then—just as we can charge any number of strong American poets—with producing a canon that has no other objective than its usefulness, and not a general usefulness, but a personal one.

Many of Brodsky's poems are implicitly "dialogues" with the dead, although as we consider the absence of the great dead, or the sudden nothingness that stands in their place, we realize that these dialogues look more like monologues and partake of the monologist's improvisations. Although improvisation may come about as a result of necessity, it promises, even threatens, to reach a point of diminishing returns in proportion to it. The improvisation begins to harden into *schtick*. Aware of this phenomenon, Brodsky has spoken of it in connection with Tsvetaeva's "New Year's Greetings":

But the further a poet goes in his development, the greater—unintentionally—his demands are on an audience, and the narrower that audience is. The situation oftentimes ends with the reader becoming the author's projection, which scarcely coincides with any living creature at all. In those instances, the poet directly addresses either the angels, as Rilke does in the *Duino Elegies*, or another poet—especially one who is dead, as Tsvetaeva addresses Rilke. In both instances what takes place is a monologue, and in both instances it assumes an absolute quality, for the author addresses his words to nonexistence, to Chronos. (*L* 200)

In Brodsky's poems, improvisations often yield a strange speech, cluttered with a thinginess and wordiness that ought, by rights, to exhibit contempt for the absent and is rendered ironic by the fact that it does not, as it finally seeks to accommodate itself to its own contingent nature. If poetry can come to be seen as a vehicle that draws attention to itself and its subject, even as it must also deplore the fact of its own contingency, it has the quantum nature of words to thank, since they can capitalize on their material status as marks subject, in brotherly fashion, to historical forces (e.g., their own oblivion) and on their ability to carry the image across remote temporal frontiers, an ability denied to most things. Brodsky identifies the vehicular quality of words as proportionate to their engagement with death:

For all our cerebral progress, we are still greatly subject to relapse into the Romantic (and, hence, Realistic, as well) notion that "art imitates life." If art does anything of this kind, it undertakes to reflect those few elements of existence which transcend "life," extend it beyond its terminal point—an undertaking which is frequently mistaken for art's or the artist's own groping for immortality. In other words, art "imitates" death rather than life; i.e., it imitates that realm of which life supplies no notion: realizing its own brevity, art tries to domesticate the longest possible version of time. After all, what distinguishes art from life is the ability of the former to produce a higher degree of lyricism than is possible within any human interplay. Hence poetry's affinity with—if not the very invention of—the notion of afterlife. (*L* 103-4)

Words are ambivalent, which feature is another way of claiming them as personal, and Brodsky is eager to establish this claim, not only for his own words, but for those of other practitioners of his language ("Ambivalence, I think, is the chief characteristic of my nation" [*L* 10]). And yet Brodsky is aware that ambivalence is not the most desirable feature of general language games bent on coherence. This is not to say that his or any other poetry is therefore by nature incoherent; simply, coherence is a project that usually implies a large general aim, one of whose features is that its terms can be paraphrased in other terms. As we have been taught and as poets themselves are fond of telling us, poetry is best paraphrased by repetition, which directs the spotlight to words, not the larger paraphrase, not the idea that will "clarify" a problem by retrieving reality, rescuing it, so to speak, from its concealment by language. In Brodsky's terms, the fact that poetry is unparaphrasable is as it should be, for "no poem is ever written for its story line's sake only, just as no life is lived for the sake of an obituary" (*L* 47).

For the dead, words are all that is left. The poet knows that to paraphrase the dead is, in some sense, to make them even more dead: Rather, "Death is something more than human loss. Above all, it is a drama of language as such: that of the inadequacy of linguistic experience vis-à-vis existential experience" (*L* 198). Thus there is a moral and ethical component to the elegist's task that far exceeds "the work of mourning," though it in no way adjusts the feather in the poet's cap, since it is not a component that is cobbled into any particular elegy ("As a theme, death is a good litmus test for a poet's ethics" [*L* 50]). The strain of elegy that runs through Brodsky's poetry is an acknowledgment of a surrounding *néant*; of our being rounded with more than a little sleep. He identifies a similar strain in the poetry of his mentor, Anna Akhmatova:

It's not that she tried to "immortalize" her dead: most of them were the pride of Russian literature already and thus had immortalized themselves enough. She simply tried to manage the meaninglessness of existence, which suddenly gaped before her because of the destruction of the sources of its meaning, to domesticate the reprehensible infinity by inhabiting it with familiar shadows. Besides, addressing the dead was the only way of preventing speech from slipping into a howl. (*L* 49)

Therefore, a poet's particular cluttering of things—which is to say words—acknowledges a solidarity with the dead, even if no especial dead are in view. At the same time, the poet acknowledges the ambivalence of the enterprise, both with respect to its aim and to him- or herself as poet. Not to do so would be to lay claim to a power that undercuts the very contingency that is the source of poetic power. But the acknowledgment of poetic ambivalence is liable to misinterpretation, to charges of aestheticism, of "failure of nerve," while it is in fact the very opposite. Brodsky speaks of an ambivalence that inheres in the Russian character as a survival device ("There isn't a Russian executioner who isn't scared of turning victim one day" [*L* 10]), a device that suggests "wisdom": "This kind of ambivalence, I think, is precisely that 'blessed news' which the East, having little else to offer, is about to impose on the rest of the world. And the world looks ripe for it" (*L* 10).

Brodsky's project, as I see it, is in one sense an extension of the project of Yeats and Mallarmé, namely, to transform life into literature, working out along the way the implications and entailments of that transformation. (For example, to what extent is the transformation also an attempted escape? Isn't this escape but another instance of the elegist's ironic complicity with death?) But Brodsky goes Yeats and Mallarmé one better in asking, in effect, where this literature is then headed. Such a project seems to play down the former (life), under the aegis of the latter (literature), which it in turn treats as a greater, if ironic, good. Note that the same project that looks like heroism in Yeats looks like mystical aestheticism in Mallarmé (it is possible to reverse the attributes, but they remain incompatible qualities).

The problem, as Brodsky knew, is that the very thing that is at issue here is the thing that is insufficiently understood. If we take the metaphysician's tongs, we can extract something like "words alone are certain good," and that would alert us to the prestige of the poetic art, an art that is frequently in the painstaking business of pursuing Platonic Ideals beyond language. Alternatively, we can take the same tongs and hold up a self blighted by mortality and consciousness, ambivalently engineered and standing in need of something like salvation. Then it is a more or less simple matter to put the two together and compliment ourselves on identifying both the need and the aim of transformation. This is to play both ends against the middle, however, and the middle is, alas, something we loosely call "process" and does not lend itself to the kind of extraction—and abstraction (paraphrase)—that turns a perfectly good idea into a literary cliché.

Brodsky departs from the Yeatsian model (which I will refer to in preference to Mallarmé's) in subverting our wish to seize the metaphysical tongs on behalf of some idea, either to grasp the self or the literature. He accomplishes this subversion by placing the self on the level of a thing and literature on the level of another (albeit special) thing. He sums up this position as follows: "Art is not a better, but an alternative existence. . . . It is a spirit seeking flesh but finding words" (*L* 123). Instead of expressing ideas about poems, he talks about the sounds of words as they inform memory and consciousness in, for example, the memorization of poems ("If there is any substitute for life it's memory. To memorize, then, is to restore intimacy" [*L* 150]). There is therefore no "meaning" to Brodsky in the sense that would satisfy either the old-style academic critic or the journalist, except on an extra-poetic basis. Nor, on this view, is it the job of the poems to "mean" something that exists outside them. It is arguable that the teacher's role of tasking poetry with such assignments contributed to

Brodsky's disillusionment with his own schooling and helped to bring such a pugnacious aestheticism into being.

As we know, exile introduces the element we have identified as necessary for elegy, namely, absence. What is absent in this case is not simply friends and family, but one's own previous self. Exile underscores one's contingency and "thinghood" because it reveals the extent to which any self is constituted of the agglomeration of these others. Of course, in a sense that parallels poetry in translation, the prior self is always what is absent, but geographical separation obliges one with metaphors of actual spatial absence that prove more dramatic than comparable temporal metaphors because they can be presented to the eye, though, to be sure, temporal metaphors also figure importantly—and increasingly so over geographical distance, which, unlike time, remains a stable fact. Like the self that it constructs and that it conveniently allows to stand in its place, language also becomes aware, as it were, of its unstable nature; for exile stands ready to lock it into a time capsule, and thus every subsequent utterance elegizes it.

The recourse to a bookish *parole*, such as Nabokov overmastered and used to pledge allegiance to his paradise lost, did not seem to have befallen Brodsky in his more-than-two decades' residence in the United States. Indeed, instead of regretting the inevitable colloquially unrefreshed Russian that he arrived with, he relished and embraced the accented English that can only be an adopted tongue, suggesting, again, that translation somehow suits the circumstance better than the original. In this, he is speaking of the need to rethink our instinctive reaction to the presence of substitutions, toward a sense that abolishes the poet's usual distinction between original and translation. Nor does this mean that he renounced the authenticity of words and their privileged place over ideas. Quite the contrary, it made his insistence on literal and total translation look quaint or a touch pedantic, for "the sad truth is that words fail reality as well. At least it's been my impression that any experience coming from the Russian realm, even when depicted with photographic precision, simply bounces off the English language, leaving no visible imprint on its surface" (*L* 30).

I would not wish to suggest that the elegiac dimension in Brodsky's work is all that there is to see. Rather, I would suggest that here is case where the poet made of necessity a high virtue and ramified a fact of division far beyond its status as a biographical transition, important as that was. As for the predisposition toward elegy, Brodsky has made it plain that the feeling of estrangement, which is the consciousness of exile, stands prior to consciousness:

A writer's biography is in his twists of language. I remember, for instance, that when I was about ten or eleven it occurred to me that Marx's dictum that "existence conditions consciousness" was true only for as long as it takes consciousness to acquire the art of estrangement; thereafter, consciousness is on its own and can both condition and ignore existence. (*L* 3)

The KGB, we might say, merely literalized his metaphor, thinking it would have the last laugh. The fact is, there is no last laugh, for even with the armature of wit, the development of this essentially elegiac career was not simply about last things. Here there is no personal eschatology, no settling scores along the way, no putting things to right ("In spiritual odysseys there are no Ithacas" [*L* 97]). Wit's job, which is tantamount to that of the literary itself, is to provide the ballast that keeps the elegiac mind from being overwhelmed by the doubling of absences and from the awareness that to have lived two lives is to owe two deaths, with the added opportunity to express ambivalence at this state of affairs. This consideration would seem to bring us full circle from another direction, so to speak, to Brodsky's natural love of all authentic literary manifestations of wit, since wit, being antiphonal to mourning, is therefore its natural elegiac partner.

If Brodsky's poetry is informed by often inconspicuous elegiac conceptions of what poetry can and should be about, we might rightly ask what this has to do with the earlier assertion that the poetry is future-directed. Part of the answer lies in the fact that the future, like the completed fact of literature, stands over against the life that is being lived. As Yeats knew, the future bears down on us to inquire of the words that will provide its furniture. The future, then, takes the form of an inquiry in that it manages to solicit the answers to our becomings. It stands in the mind, therefore, as a speculative field that requests definition. In this regard, it is similar to the past—similar, too, in that both are characterized by real absence and thus answerable only in metaphor. Indeed, the similarity is so striking between these tenses that are not actually present to us (separated by the difference between "anymore" and "yet") that to perform a deed in terms of one is to demand equal time for the other. Insofar as it is a variety of imaginative labor, the "work" of poetry consists, in this light, in making the "right" (or the likeliest) words that will redeem the time. This fact bears importantly on the naming function of poetry, its so-called Orphic dimension. The productions that result—the "works" in the plural—help to give birth to the future. The natal metaphor is deliberate, for a poet's work is also that poet's self-description, one not providing a complete figure, either, until death or debility stop the flow of description. It is the illusion that in the completion of life, one has created a person, a creation whose efficacy and "accuracy" can be vouched for only in reference to the other persons and selves that went into its making. The writer of elegies exteriorizes a process well known to all poets—that of attempting to monitor the progress of this self-creation. Again, we see the temptation to "get outside" the whole project, to look back posthumously. Quite apart from reasons of "inheritance," of which Brodsky was supremely aware ("A significant part . . . of every poet's endeavor involves polemics with these shadows whose hot or cold breath he senses on his neck" [*L* 95]), we can also add to this temptation the "professional"[10] obligation to write the elegy for the specifically literary precursor—the dead poet:

For some odd reason, the expression "death of a poet" always sounds somewhat more concrete than "life of a poet." Perhaps this is because both "life" and "poet," as words, are almost synonymous in their positive vagueness. Whereas "death"—even as a word—is about as definite as a poet's own production, i.e., a poem, the main feature of which is its last line. Whatever a work of art consists of, it runs to the finale which makes for its form and denies resurrection. After the last line of a poem nothing follows except literary criticism. So when we read a poet, we participate in his or his work's death. (*L* 123)

Such speculations would lead us to believe that the exile finds greater cause to advance the claim that self-monitoring is desirable, being able to divide his or her life into mutually exclusive phases, the first of which is, like a life, complete and thus also looks suspiciously as if it included one's death. In Brodsky's terms, to write elegies is to join the great dead, and this is another way of saying that one joins literature, that one meets what one has determined the future to be.

Brodsky was ironically fortunate in undergoing a circumstance that yielded a past ripe for transformation, just as it seemed to authorize the kind of present he adopted. I am aware that in saying this, I seem to have merely reformulated a rather heartless opinion held by some American writers to the effect that imprisonment at least had the advantage both of spiritually deepening and underwriting the moral authority of Russian writers. I would, however, while admitting—heartlessly—to the grain of truth in this claim, put forward the suggestion that Brodsky presciently understood the literary and perspectival advantages of his "case" and undertook to realize its multiple implications with respect to his own poetry, perhaps with the knowledge that such undertakings must manifest themselves at the expense of any sort of life that might have been lived. This is simply another way of saying, to work the ocular metaphor he loved, that he set about improving his sight to the point that he could peer soberly into the midst of hopelessly contingent events and nevertheless find in them—as he presumably would have found in others—conditions sufficient for the production of art. This is the only heroism that anyone should claim on his behalf. To think of the circumstances of his forced exile from home and loved ones as "tragic" only diverts our attention onto the instruments of polemic. Brodsky, though thrust into the public light, aspired only to illuminate a private space. As he claimed in the Nobel lecture, "If art teaches anything (to the artist, in the first place) it is the privateness of the human condition." Be that as it may, the emphasis on the solitary is in no way meant to suggest that "private" equals solipsistic. On the contrary, as I hope to show, it is through the necessarily private encounter with the fact of death that the strands of our desire for continuity sew together such civilization as Westerners have been able to cloak about their individual destinies. If we accept the premise of this book, namely, that there is something both proper and significant about considering Brodsky's poems under the sign of translation, it follows that its appropriateness is consistent with the fact that translation, in its haste to debase the original poem by offering its virtual, paraphrastic version (one of countless possible) as worthy of equivalence, also submits it to nature, naturalizing it. This process of naturalization is in keeping with Brodsky's thinking with respect to the career of the elegy in general, in his insistence on the fate of words as similar to the fate of anything else: no transcendence, but like Beckett, one has no other recourse other than to try for it.

NOTES

1. "Wholeheartedly dedicated to his vocation, Brodsky has established personal relations with not only Russian poetry but also the whole of the classical and vernacular literatures of Europe and the Americas. He is a successor to two great poetic traditions, but he has also incorporated the demands of the literature of the past into his own mentality; the stylistic consequences of great poetry can be felt in his actions and his interpretation of the world" (1).

2. Bayley's assertion that Brodsky is heir to Auden as an arbiter of civilized literary discourse may seem to some a *tertium quid* in the ongoing tensions between the kinds of discourse represented by nationalist and internationalist proponents on the British literary scene.

3. Simon's review summarizes right-wing disenchantment with the course of Brodsky's work.

4. Hass is one of Czeslaw Milosz's American translators. Milosz has himself been a strong supporter of Brodsky's poetry, stressing the exile's imagination as characteristic of much twentieth-century writing and exile itself as the condition preferred by the modern ironic Muse.

5. "It is a book to have looked forward to, not only because Americans have grown accustomed through writers like Nabokov and Czeslaw Milosz to the haunting literature of exile being made in our midst, but also because Brodsky has lived in both faces of the mirror world of the cold war; and the rest of us, affected daily by its subliminal pressure, want his testimony. There are a handful of poems here to justify that hope, but for the most part reading *A Part of Speech* is like wandering through the ruins of what has been reported to be a noble building" (135).

6. Hamill's review also raises eyebrows by leaving the suggestion that there is suspicion to be had for the poet who attempts to graft or impose himself upon the cultural family tree.

7. See also Peter M. Sacks and Jahan Ramazani for full discussions of how elegy serves to engage in such a work.

8. A specialty, too, of the modern bureaucratic state, as Brodsky himself has surmised in the essay "On Tyranny":

The goal [of political parties] is to accommodate . . . numerical expansion in the non-expanding world, and the only way to achieve it is through the depersonalization and bureaucratization of everybody alive. For life itself is a common denominator; that's enough of a premise for structuring existence in a more detailed fashion. (*L* 121)

9. As John Felstiner sees in a fine critical biography of Paul Celan, to arrive "under the sign of translation" is to arrive, as it were, with full credentials as a twentieth-century poet. Translation is the sign of elegy, too, as Felstiner recognizes in a discussion of Celan's "Todesfüge," a celebrated death-camp poem that seizes and changes incrementally the chief instrument of the Reich: language. In that text, poetry itself is able to

locate the safety not accorded to Celan's camp-mates only by passing through a host of tongues, to say nothing of the wider cultural net that his cross-linguistic allusions casts. The anonymity of the polyglot records and underscores the scarcity of personal (read: historical) safety.

10. David Bethea reminds us, by way of Lawrence Lipking, that the professional elegy is a *tombeau*, both an homage to a precursor and a declaration of differentiated resolve (94).

2

The Healing Needle: "The Great Elegy for John Donne"

My dream thou brok'st not, but continuedst it.
—John Donne

In the mid-1960s, Brodsky had found a job translating the English Metaphysical poets for an anthology, a task even then congenial to his temperament, if not to his level of fluency.[1] One result of this project was his youthful masterpiece "The Great Elegy for John Donne," a poem that already hinted of the ways in which the poet would soon go about modifying the traditional elegy, even as he would pay respect to many of its conventions. Brodsky's admitted attraction to the Metaphysicals was not merely a personal footnote to a serendipitous discovery, either. More to the point, he was drawn to their systematic elaborations of what it is to conceive of experience as "literary," both as a means of artistic self-determination and, by extension, as a species of self-creation. While critical tradition distinguishes Donne's inventiveness from, say, Ben Jonson's Horatian classicism, to the poet these are more likely to seem intramural niceties than descriptions of poetic kinds. Obviously, in its veneration of classical authors, Brodsky's conception of poetry does not reveal a departure in spirit from Donne's. If Donne rebelled against anything, it was not the past as embodied in tradition, but the future as it came, willy-nilly, over the horizon. In this, an understanding of tradition only stood to strengthen him. Brodsky, too, at this stage, found himself working out the implications of his own tradition to an unusual degree. By his "own" tradition, I mean not only the poetics of twentieth-century Russian poetry, as represented by Tsvetaeva, Mandelstam, and Akhmatova, who may indeed be seen as representatives (Russian division) of the international artistic renaissance that goes by the catchall "Modernism," but also of the poetics of such English-language Modernists as Eliot, himself the subject of a major elegy. Brodsky was equally aware of the oft-claimed affinities of the

Moderns with some aspect or other of John Donne and company, although it appears that instead of becoming aware through Eliot's essays, he was simply able to intuit as much from the preponderant interest in these poets through anthologies. Most important, perhaps, by seizing on Donne, as did Eliot, as one of his poetic forefathers, Brodsky early on sought to give his poetry a distinctive stylistic profile. In other words, John Donne functioned to allow him to uncover and map a course in modern, international poetry between two positions: one a polemical—even doctrinal—position represented by Eliot; the other, an aesthetic position embodied by W. H. Auden.[2] "The Great Elegy for John Donne" and "Verses on the Death of T. S. Eliot" thus also mark something of a necessary monumental farewell to these poets, and Brodsky raises both honorifically, if only to return them more decisively to their graves.

Be that as it may, we may generalize for a moment in noting that a poet's elegy for an earlier poet (what has been called, not without a knowing hint of sarcasm, the "professional elegy"[3]) is almost certainly to be a site at which we may witness that moment when, it is imagined, the dead forebear cedes his mantle to the ephebe. Whether that moment qualifies as Dantean or merely Darwinian depends, of course, on a host of variables, but the later poet will, in the course of the homage, inevitably, if unconsciously or implicitly, raise the touchy subject of the poetic inheritance. Moreover, the poem itself will seem to stand as a first instance of that inheritance. One inherits poetic power not only from the dead but also, so to speak, at the expense of the dead, who are not in a position to grant anything. It is, after all, the very silence of the dead that in some sense opens the space one's own verse will fill, and whether this is done in the name of the dead poet must remain a vexed matter indeed, since an inheritance can usually lay claim to no other sanction than the elegist's own account. That account must include something of the contextual matrix out of which the earlier poet, in turn, arose. Whether we call that "tradition" or "history" is a matter of quibbling vocabularies, but the fact remains, as Eliot himself has not been the first to note, that every addition requires a realignment.[4] Indeed, every addition must have already been about the task of realignment in the first place in order to be an addition.

The occasion of a poet's death, connected as it is with the plain fact of that poet's completed life, promises stony, unforeseen difficulties. The same may be said a fortiori for that poet's poems, which stand staunchly in their otherness. Although here it may sound as if we are confusing death with, say, mere absence or an otherness brought about as a result of differing uses of language (or for that matter, of different languages), it is helpful to bear in mind that all these difficulties become so thanks to the interplay between identity and difference, itself the hallmark of language as such.[5] Subsidiary, but no less present, is the problem of decorum. The fact that one is called upon to write of the dead, to give voice to absence, perverts, we might say, the natural course of things, substituting the special case (voice) for the natural one (silence). Fleeing the natural, the elegist is driven in the direction of aesthetics, which is to say idealism, perfection, and the restructuring of time from linear determinism to an ideal circularity or repetition that intends to confound both time and its effects, not only with regard to the personal object of elegy, but just as certainly with regard to the elegist. Of course, since the elegist demands the very death (and time, its medium) that aesthetics would restructure, it is difficult as a result to dispel the impression that the poet is attempting to have it both ways: Requiring death to facilitate the scene of the elegist's own reception of power, the same elegist then appears, thanklessly, as it were, to mitigate the power of that death. Indeed, we might simply say that there is a sense in which the elegist is hopelessly in complicity with death all the way down, for which reason the guilt attaching to one's transactions in the face of a specific occasion of death (and mourning) is all the more prevalent and in need of cloaking.

Brodsky would seem intuitively to minimize many of the effects of this complicity and skirt the problem of decorum in choosing as subject a poet long dead: The effect of proximity is subtracted. Indeed, subtraction supplies Brodsky with one of his chief stylistic devices, namely synecdoche—the less that stands in the place of and implies the more—and while it has often been remarked that this is a poem curiously replete with objects—an elegy that proceeds by way of revealing a plenum in the midst of death—it has generally escaped notice that the poem is also one that can offer its own saving plenum only after the gambit of subtraction has been made. Death itself, at least as we perceive it as a kind of experience, has been removed. We might add that inasmuch as death is removed from the elegy, the poem elegizes not only prior life but death itself, and in so doing, it calls upon the poet (and subsequent poems) to reinstitute death to its rightful place.

John Donne provides an interesting subject on other grounds as well. Like the earlier poet, Brodsky is fond of comparing disparate and dissimilar objects and ideas. Both poets seem to find aesthetic satisfaction in the piecemeal removal of objections to the comparison, and both seem fond of reconciling the differences by means of installing in the place of the ordinary eye a greater light-gathering lens: for Donne, the lens is God; for Brodsky, language. Brodsky then updates Donne in that the resolution of his lens includes God, not as resolver—but as an additional, albeit special, spectatorial entity. Donne's procedure is often propositional ("Let man's soul be a sphere"); Brodsky's is photographic, often cinematic, following the path of an eye to form an argument often by triangulation, rather than following the path of an argument with the eye.[6] For Donne, thought or, rather, imaginative thought in the form of "what if . . . ," creates both the terms and the procedure. Donne's frequent recourse to the propositional style stands between Renaissance delight in invention and the Enlightenment's wish to subsume all to rationality. Brodsky senses this dual motivation on the part of Donne, and his is a playful send-up of rationalist tactics, while having in his own right the historical opportunity to parody modern rationalist pretensions. At the same time, Brodsky is mindful of an additional plenum— namely, Donne's spiritual realm—that for the English poet provides, among other things, an authenticating and generative function perhaps often unavailable to a modern poet, who must pretend not to be peeling away the corn silk of nostalgia. The purpose in Donne, it might be argued, is the reconciliation of things to vision. The poems therefore stand as an example of a unitary procedure. With Brodsky, comparisons rather point up our indebtedness to language and our dependence on it to give local habitation and name to what passes, wrapped in its contingency, across the optical nerve. These are two variants on the theme that asks what organizational principle we can induce from the flux, against the apprehension of chaos and powerlessness, of which death is the common touchstone. There is obviously delight in discovering that language (or God) can so sustain us against the chaotic backdrop of the ordinary. But in "The Great Elegy for John Donne," not God but language is in the position to sustain us. And not Donne's language, which is asleep, but Brodsky's. Donne himself, in his twin aspects as the man-of-experience and the man-of-spirit, nicely embodies his own material for comparison, and Brodsky will exploit this felicitous difference as part of his Metaphysical procedure.

The poem also stands as an early and flamboyant example of the poet's Anglophilia. Not only does it elegize the English poet, but with a certain prematurity, it also suggests both a culmination and a farewell to some of the conventions associated with Donne, such as dialogic self-and-soul meditations and devotional verse generally.[7] The twin, competing aspects of Donne (Wild Jack Donne versus the Dean of St. Paul's) are far from mutually exclusive: They prefigure the familiar, later divorces (and rapprochements) of self and other, subject and object, and so forth—in short, the fragmenting of all notions of wholeness, a procedure that has attended the onset of scientifically derived modernity. More specifically, Donne stands as an early example of one for whom the body authorizes at least as much justification as the soul toward a poetic facility. That Donne does speak in terms of the soul, however, provides Brodsky an opportunity to suggest the possibility of a bird's eye view ("that point from which, to him who downward stares, / this dread Last Judgement seems no longer dread"), and it is this imagined feat of omniscience, *per impossibile*, that charges the poem with Brodsky's own nostalgia, not for exercising a spiritual option, but for proposing a seemingly credible synoptic vision.[8]

While it is the synoptic vision to which the poem aspires, its design is situated on two contrasting movements: The first is the unfolding of a list enumerating objects in a world asleep, where those objects—nouns—stand to be counted by virtue of their discrete inanimacy.[9] The second movement begins with the identification of the consoling figure of the poet's (Donne's) soul, which breaks through the suspended animation of his (and the world's) "sleep," and in a dreamlike speech of (self-) justification, offers to provide the "healing needle" that will sew up the dichotomies—secular/religious, sinning/redeeming, death/resurrection, artistic salvation/Christian salvation—that have rent the poet's conscience (and consciousness), as well as, ironically, fueling the engine of his poetry. The poem ultimately questions the price of drama and power generated by these contraries.

In an incantatory voice that seems to strive toward both hypnosis and self-hypnosis, the poem begins its enumerations in John Donne's house and proceeds to widen the perspective by means of the ripple-effect brought, not just by the plethora of objects, but by its own insistence at making additions:

> John Donne has sunk in sleep . . . All things beside
> are sleeping too: walls, bed, and floor—all sleep.
> The table, pictures, carpets, hooks and bolts,
> clothes-closets, cupboards, candles, curtains, all
> now sleep: the washbowl, bottle, tumbler, bread,
> breadknife and china, crystal, pots and pans,
> bed-sheets and nightlamp, chests of drawers, a clock,
> a mirror, stairway, doors.
>
> (*SP* 39, trans. George Kline)

If, as we have seen, the early Brodskyan elegy begins with so familiar a task as confronting the detritus of nostalgia—the poet's prerequisite assignment—so too the method of this poem begins in something as simple as inductive gathering. Paradoxically, while the motion of gathering is that of containment, a taking-in, the movement of the poem is that of widening, a spreading-out. Yet both motions characterize the same idea, namely, that perspective is all. Yet in spite of the impressively energetic cataloguing of things, there is discovered no unwobbling pivot. In its absence, we get instead the poet's hovering consciousness, conventionally symbolized at the end of the poem in the poet's stellified remains, that is, in a star. The paradoxical quality that the poem registers invites the inference that this hovering—the equipoise of language—makes a substitute (on Brodsky's view, a more than adequate substitute) for transcendent guarantees of the sort that Donne, as Christian bard, ostensibly sought. There is a further inference to consider: As Donne's avatar, Brodsky confers a retroactive redemption upon the questing Donne, as the consciousness of the later and the dream of the earlier poets (both of whose desires are deputized by language) converge; thus Donne's Christianity is seen as a mythological expression for language, specifically poetic language, and so, in a way unanticipated by Eliot, Donne appears as a modern (or indeed postmodern) language-worshipper *avant le lettre*.

If such first attempts as "The Great Elegy for John Donne" strike us rather more as forced encounters than organically resolved specimens of the elegy, it is because meaning seems at first sight a superimposition onto the stubborn, aboriginal essence of things.[10] Night, as it sets about denying any customary perspective on life, to say nothing of what it is like (itself the poet's universalizing push to metaphor), triggers a paradoxical clarity for the poet scouting for essences. For example, we are driven to consider what the Kafkaesque point of a *jail* is "in sleep" ("All jails and locks have lapsed in sleep"). It is as if all ordinary purposes are neutralized—or further, are made to seem somehow beside the point of existence. Moreover, it seems as if the things surrounding us are, in Goethe's words, "merely derived phenomena . . . in which we live." Be that as it may, Brodsky would like to render a condition from which even in the "dead of winter," which is of course another way of speaking of one's own death, one can nevertheless "rise" transfigured from a hibernation or super-naturally deep sleep. To be sure, activity as such is disabled by sleep, the *imitatio* of death's inanimacy. The fact that there is something called a "point" is only entailed by and in a world that manages to stay awake.[11] We are led to surmise that the only perspective appropriate to the irony of night is a godlike one, *sub specie aeternitatis*, and such a perspective, in turn, is made available not by any actual or visualizable point of view but by language, wherein nouns (the names and pictures of things), for instance, can pass in review, even as they themselves manifest the general somnolence.[12]

The availability of such a perspective is not merely a product of the private, verbal legerdemain of Brodsky, either, and it would be graceless to argue that the poet intended to exercise propriety over this characteristic of language. Rather, as "Night [is] everywhere," so too is the language that makes of night a means of "clarity."[13] Not only is night "everywhere," in the context of the poem, it is, of course, also everywhere in the sense that it is constitutive of "thing-ness" itself.[14] Nevertheless, in spite of the poet's implicit claims on behalf of language, claims that will be reiterated and elaborated throughout his career, there is a sense in which "The Great Elegy for John Donne" marks a change of key in the way we may hear the classical music of elegiac meditation. Brodsky's updated classicism consists here in an investigation of the possibilities of positing something we may again call the "literary" as an equivalent term for something we may call "order," since there is an orderliness to language that is not subsumed or victimized by the darkness (as, for instance, history, another map of the search for orderliness, most decidedly is). When Brodsky writes:

> His verses sleep.
> His images, his rhymes, and his strong lines
> fade out of view

and

> The swarms of books,
> the streams of words, cloaked in oblivion's ice,
> sleep soundly

as well as

> Night everywhere,
> night in all things: in corners, in men's eyes,

in bed-sheets, in the papers on a desk,
in the worm-eaten words of sterile speech,

we observe not only the image of words cast into darkness but those same words located and, as it were, extracted by quotation marks, into the present reading. Again, the elegist, faced with both a real and a metaphorical silence, and knowing he has recourse only to translation, sets about reviving the earlier poet in a drama of reconciliation in which Donne's poetic mission is joined to the expediency of translation, just as his dichotomies of body and soul are promised eventual redemption by more traditional means. It should be obvious that Brodsky is here capitalizing on the synonymous connection of tradition to translation, and nothing could underscore the personal nature of poetic transmission more emphatically than the fact that John Donne, the English poet incarnate, is made to plead the case of his soul in Russian.[15]

"The Great Elegy for John Donne" includes, at length, an imagined panorama of seventeenth century England, but despite the stay-at-home's predictable recitation of landmarks (e.g., St. Paul's, white cliffs) this is no tour.[16] For all its sweep, the poem takes place completely—we might even say resolutely—at night. Not only does the poet summon forth the names for things under the ironic anonymity of night and sleep; he also conveys a further blankness with the description of winter and the elegiac blanket of snow. Nor is there a sense that the house or the living community in general is in any way exempt from winter's reach:

A roof-slope, whiter than a tablecloth,
the roof's high ridge. A neighborhood in snow,
carved to the quick by this sharp windowframe.

These things, enumerated against the blankness of snow, are like words upon the page; indeed, they *are* words upon the page. Inasmuch as Brodsky draws imagistic attention to this connection, he begins to suggest not just the similarity but the identity of living things—living and inanimate—and words. As a result, he will make no distinction between the lyric and the real; for him, they are the same. As he puts the matter elsewhere, "The sea, madam, is someone's speech."

The sleep of the poem is so profound as to be inclusive even of death, as opposed to serving merely as its place-holder: "the dead lie calmly in their graves and dream"; "All birds / and beasts now sleep—nature alive and dead." Not only is the sleep profound, it is general, spreading beyond creation to the realm of the immortals, revealing the extent of John Donne's tribulation in life—and the eventual solution, which is hedged in all the more with uncertainty, since the merciful Creator's entire system of rewards and punishments seems now to be suspended in the general narcolepsy:

There high above men's heads, all are asleep.
the angels sleep. Saints—to their saintly shame—

have quite forgotten this our anxious world.
Dark Hell-fires sleep, and glorious Paradise.

Only dreams—human dreams—can provide a world controverting the nighttime, snowbound world of these inanimate things, and it is only through a dreamlike, even phantasmagoric medium worthy of Dostoyevsky that John Donne meets his angelic soul and the sign of his redemption. That this is so suggests not a real victory, for such a victory is available not to John Donne, who is dead, but only to "John Donne." In other words, it is a lyric victory, and such a victory in turn suggests both the appropriating power of elegiac (and lyric) rhetoric and, more cautiously, its tentative nature (while words seem to be constrained by some hypostasized allegiance to realism—they are themselves part of the reality from and to which they cleave, making the very phrase "lyric victory" smack of tautology). The lyric victory, as Keats foresaw, stands to "tease us out of thought." Brodsky resists this temptation on the strength of his belief, consistent with a view that language confers that very sense of the real from which we derive our sense of reality, that a lyric victory *is* a real one. Again, his poetics leads him to the view that distinctions drawn between the lyric and the real have no actual interpretive force.

Brodsky's procedure is not to tease out these implications but simply to gather more and more within his ken, to note and pass on, at length raising the perspective until its scope reaches all creation (or "creation"). Unlike the procedure common to Donne, there is no dialectically driven argument hurtling toward a surprising conclusion, and indeed the second half's dialogue between John Donne and his soul fails to account for the particularity with which the first half is set forth. Nor do we assign an especial meaning to the soul's assuaging speech in the second half of the poem; it seems old-fashioned. Rather, it is the amassing of things before the eye, despite oblivion, that is most memorable in the poem.

From an inventory of the poet's house, one that extends down through the Chain of Being to the level of mice, we move to the historical neighborhood of London, England, and finally to the sea, which is likewise quelled by the ubiquity of slumber:

> The salt sea
> talks in its sleep with snows beneath her hull,
> and melts into the distant sleeping sky.
> John Donne has sunk in sleep, with him the sea.

In the course of this nominative process, Brodsky subtly counts among the things of the world not only objects and creatures but also concepts and abstractions, as if, like a skeptic, he had gotten certain about the reality of some prior world by sheer counting and had arrived independently at the Wittgensteinian conclusion that the world is indeed everything that is the case, including snow, sleep, mice, lines of poetry, the Devil, God, and "Anxiety and sin . . . [sleeping] in his syllables."

The consciousness that perceives these things, which has no direct role in the poem, is yet the poem's only "actor." It is meanwhile difficult to avoid the impression that the poet has performed a conjuring act in getting behind the very creation of which both he and the contents of his elegy are a part. While other poets have had the Miltonic ambition to create a god and then to give him the sacred and creative words by which they are supposed the eventual effects, Brodsky is the only poet—certainly the only contemporary poet—who has also, by suspending animation whatsoever, effectively neutralized that god and substituted his own poem as the sole witness, guardian, and mediator to creation. Only the poet is not "asleep," but his exclusion from the poem (which is to say, his role as elegist) is a necessary precondition for the consciousness to govern at all. This, the lepidopterist's creed, is something that stands behind all of Brodsky's elegies and is made explicit in his 1975 poem "The Butterfly." The paradox on which this feat is situated can best be resolved if we understand the central importance of language as a means by which life both succumbs and triumphs under the rule of substitution. This John Donne is a poet only in, and by virtue of, his imagined likelihood. But for Brodsky, this is, in fact, a poet's cardinal virtue. He changes, and yet no change that proceeds from his language wholly undoes the likelihood of his identity. Such a flexibility is, of course, related to Brodsky's own characteristic ambivalence, and it is even possible to argue that Brodsky's pronouncements on this score are somewhat preemptive, even as they seem to be statements of belief.

All elegies elegize, despite protestations to the contrary, by lamenting their subject's escape, not only from life, but also from the real and actual. It is the business of life, after all, to maintain the actual against incursions of the virtual and the unreal. Brodsky goes this one better by finding no useful distinction between actual and virtual, just as there was none to be found between real and lyric. Hence, there is no point here in arguing, as some have done, that the elegist lies against history. As a twentieth-century Russian, Brodsky found history at best troubling and at worst cruelly parodic of the poet's attempts to address time in the interests of human continuity within a framework of literate conversation.[17] Hence, "The Great Elegy for John Donne" is situated on a dream, and it is to that dream encounter that we now turn.

Although Brodsky has shown that the connection between sleep and darkness is both natural and close, he does not maintain that it is automatic, and the poem is careful to distinguish between the two. Roughly speaking, darkness is a natural attribute whose very ubiquity inclines it to acquire a second ground of abundant metaphorical possibilities; and though sleep provides a similarly rich ground, it (sleep) is also a state antithetical to waking behaviors, desires, and struggles. Once he has expanded the inventory of facts that go into constructing a world to include both the mundane and the metaphysical, the speaker turns to "stitching" these considerations—John Donne, things of the world, night-winter-sleep-death—together. He will later explicitly take up the metaphor of stitching, a metaphor that is native to the elegy, since it depicts a material means of mediation between the living and the dead, the material and the immaterial, body and soul, the made and the unmade, and presence and absence, while secondarily allowing the poem to establish an affiliation with the tradition of elegiac rhetoric (with all the appropriate connotations of "carrying over").[18] The poem stands as an instance of that to which the tradition, represented by Donne, finds its recipient.

To the visual quietus, we can also add silence as the foundation against which these objects, the poem's words, and a fortiori the soul's argument struggle to establish a meaningful domain. As we have seen, silence is inscribed in the poem and permeates both its things and its words in such continuous and equal measure that we are invited once again to equate things with words on some level. To the object of this inscription is added the figure of John Donne himself, who as a sleeping being becomes, in Polukhina's words, a *tertium* (i.e., a "man—thing—word").[19] While the poem manifests this triad in terms of inertness, indeed thanks to its emphasis on inertness flattens, as it were, the triad, it does so as part of a strategy the poet will employ with increasing sophistication in subsequent poems—a democratic flattening that eases discourse and dispenses with the need to pay ideological lip-service, while at the same time opening the way to a reverence for language itself.[20]

Aside from the poet's voice, the only other voice we hear is that of the "dreaming" John Donne and his soul.[21] In his dream, the poet is first aware of a "sobbing" sound, and Brodsky presents this fact between two images of stitching:

> There someone stands in the dense gloom.
> His voice is thin. His voice is needle-thin,
> yet without thread. And he in solitude
> swims through the falling snow—cloaked in cold mist—
> that stitches night to dawn.

If stitching suggests a connection between the living and the dead, it also reminds us that Brodsky is not only stitching (both sewing and versing) John Donne into something more than a sleeping figure but also stitching the earlier poet to himself (and perhaps with an equal hint that a new, poetic shroud for Donne is necessary as well).[22] Donne, awakened to the presence of someone in this dream world, begins a dream version of the elegy's traditional querying of the other ("is it really you?")—what Sacks refers to as "reality-testing"—only here, it is not the elegist but his subject who requests reassurance. The "who goes there?" quality of the passage is also reminiscent of the opening of *Hamlet*, where the dreaded ghost, as Freudian Superego, mandates another quest for a son that will, it seems, resolve his dualisms. Donne encounters equally demanding figures: an ordinary angel, a cherub, the Apostle Paul (the patron saint of Donne's church), and God—and challenges each as candidates, before

realizing that "my thought runs wild." His last candidate, Gabriel, extends the
extremity of his inquiry by introducing an eschatological note, which stands as
the omega point for Donne's queries by raising the possibility of his end (as one
who has made the conversion to words)—indeed, of the end of history itself:

> "No, it is I, your soul, John Donne, who speaks.
> I grieve alone upon the heights of Heaven,
> because my labors did bring forth to life
> feelings and thoughts as heavy as stark chains.
> Bearing this burden, you could yet fly up
> past those dark sins and passions, mounting higher."

The soul's complaint is peculiar: An immaterial being itself, the soul maintains
that its earthly mission paradoxically consists in eliciting something like a sense
of moral gravity, and it seems disturbed by the fact that the poet "could yet fly"
past "sins and passions," rather in the manner that Brodsky's perspective has,
to the religious mind, taken him past such affronts to Christian *gravitas*. In
either case, it seems that the poetic mind has little use for such a soul, and John
Donne's soul, at least, knows it. The soul's lament, though, is a warning about
perspective, suggesting on the one hand that this specifically poetic desire to
soar can perhaps be realized only at the expense of moral responsibility. Thus
poetry, or imaginative freedom, stands to imperil his soul by getting the world's
scale wrong. Scorning the structure of creation and its ground rules, the poet in
some sense fails his own humanity: "From there our Lord is but a light that
gleams, / through fog, in window of the farthest house."[23] Yet John Donne has
not succumbed completely to this temptation:

> And you did soar past God, and then drop back,
> for this harsh burden would not let you rise
> to that high vantage point.

The soul seems to suggest that although John Donne has been rescued before,
the surrounding oblivion is such that prior rescues make no guarantee with
respect to the present. That is, there can be no guarantee with respect to the
soul's disposition at death, especially since heaven, once vigilant, is now asleep
(just as Donne, who once watched over the flock at St. Paul's, is "asleep"). At
this point in the poem, we begin to see clearly the nature of the surrounding
snow, darkness, and sleep: They are, in one sense, a scrim upon which the
future—specifically the future where a similarly tempted poet named Joseph
Brodsky lives and writes in a place called the USSR—is projected. If the temptation
toward soaring is the temptation toward freedom, it is also the temptation to flee,
and the soul's own authority is at stake in seeing to it that the responsible poet,
despite the demands of his talent, does no such thing. Picking up somewhat where
the soul leaves off, Brodsky contrasts the image of the dangerous, soaring poet with
that of a bird, that traditional image for the poetic songster:

> Like some great bird, he sleeps in his own nest,
> his pure path and his thirst for purer life,
> himself entrusting to that steady star
> which now is closed in clouds. And like a bird,
> his soul is pure, and his life's path on earth,
> although it needs must wind through sin, is still
> closer to nature than that tall crow's nest
> which soars above the starlings' empty homes.
> Like some great bird, he too will wake at dawn;
> but now he lies beneath a veil of white,
> while snow and sleep stitch up the throbbing void.

In a manner that quite reverses Keats, the soul makes of this bird a responsible, if slightly stiff, being who seems unaware that his greater destiny might involve the exploitation of his powers of flight, and because he knows "his life's path [is] on earth," "his soul is pure."[24] Instead of trying his wings to their utmost, "he places trust [in] that steady star." For John Donne, the star represents not poetic ambition, but Christian accommodation. Yet in another sense, we can't help but surmise that for John Donne the poet, the star—unattainable, clouded—stands for something like Brodsky himself (hence "trust") and, moreover, for that reincarnation the elegy tries to undertake.

While we are clearly in the matter of poetic appropriation here, Brodsky's own ambivalent stance toward poetic ambition tempers what might otherwise be read as an outrageous claim not only on his own behalf but also on behalf of elegists generally: "Whatever millstone these swift waters turn / will grind the same coarse grain in this one world." Just as Auden had suggested that the poet's ideal world would make all poems and poets joyfully anonymous, so Brodsky would save John Donne at the price of Donne's anonymity and likewise that of his poems. Indeed, he has already done so with the poems, since here we "see" but don't read them—and that barely ("His images, his rhymes, and his strong lines / fade out of view"). Ironically in this noun-driven poem, the ability to impress one's name upon something is, for John Donne, what is lost in translation.

Any such linguistic transposition across temporal barriers is likely to be a necessary part of doing business in order to have any tradition in the first place. Brodsky's notoriously conservative pronouncements with respect to the tactics of actual poetic translation may be seen as a way of mitigating the dizzying effects of literary transmission in this larger sense. In terms of "The Great Elegy for John Donne," Brodsky attempts to console his forefather with the (modern?) understanding that just as that is how the world works, this is how poetic tradition works, for

> Man's garments gapes with holes. It can be torn,
> by him who will, at this edge or at that.
> It falls to shreds and is made whole again.

> Once more it's rent. And only the far sky,
> in darkness, brings the healing needle home.

The far sky, the far future, with its unknown compunctions and freedoms, both does and undoes, stitching with its graphic "needle" and penetrating with its doubts.[25] And just as one must repudiate one's more dangerous and dubious claims to uniqueness—one's impulse to solipsism—in order to believe that the future will unfold organically from the present, so one must trust the future's ability to read into the past a virtual reality that can both accommodate it and account for it.

NOTES

1. Once, when asked how he was able to translate these difficult poets with his limited knowledge of English, he replied that he first produced a word-for-word translation of the first and last stanzas of the poems, then "imagined what should go between." The point was not merely a jest, for Brodsky has frequently invited comparison with the Metaphysicals. As their avatar, he also stood, at the launch of his career, in a filial relationship to High Modernists like Eliot. Moreover, the Anglophilia with which this relationship is also infused marked the young poet as representing a departure, not only from the ennui of official verse but also from second-generation attempts to come to grips with the Modernist project within the tradition of Russian literature. In other words, it was a way of expressing a unique, cosmopolitan literary perspective.

2. Of course, Auden began his career as a socially conscious poet in reaction to Eliot and, at the time, seemed anything but erudite or "aesthetic," a self-redefinition that would require his own exile to the United States to accomplish.

3. The object of the professional elegy is the poet as the source of words, that is, the poet qua poet. It is therefore probably a phony distinction to maintain that the person of the poet is somehow distinct from the poet's role of word-giver. What it would mean to mourn the loss of the poet as if not a word-giver is not clear. When we read that Adonais is "not dead," we think of the fact of his (i.e., Keats's) words. Thus the intent to confound time is the intent to forestall the death of words.

4. Eliot's famous formulation in "Tradition and the Individual Talent" reverses the perception that tradition drives us: It is, rather, the present that directs the past in determining what constitutes it (the past). The elegist in Eliot surely realized that such a critical position, quite apart from the truth of its perception, both chastened and exacted a fare from the dead who would presume to make a claim on the living.

5. It is tempting to argue, for instance, that the elegist not only begins, in giving voice to the dead, to reclaim something from death, but also participates in that oblivion. Thus it is only by taking leave, even as he paradoxically identifies with the dead, that he begins to establish his own difference not only from the dead but from death itself.

6. Brodsky finds the eye's quest for surfaces to be a natural consequence of our evolution. For an extended use of this theme, see *Watermark*.

7. Although the poet's earlier work often suggests religious concerns and Christian themes, I would argue that the concerns center not on the dynamics of faith but on the condition of humanity in God's absence—a fundamentally modern elegiac orientation.

Certainly, the suggestion that Brodsky began as a "religious poet" in the mold of Eliot (vide Carlisle and Polukhina) fails to account for the existential bias the poems exemplify. The concluding lines of "Nature Morte" (1971), as we have seen, provide an instance of this emphasis on the human, as opposed to the superhuman. As a general rule, Brodsky quickly dispenses with nostalgia, although he—or rather the characters in the poems—begin in a condition that is close to the nostalgic, as though to suggest that all begin with the affect, but the poet moves briskly in the religious poems to substitute language for God and the literary for the religious to such a complete degree as to suggest that language is God, and conversely, the literary is religious.

8. "The cold eye of such poems [as 'The Convergence of the Twain'] became exemplary for modernists like Auden, who said of his 'poetical father' that he valued most his 'hawk's vision, his way of looking at life form a very great height.' The dispassionate stare of the Immanent Will would seem to be anathema to elegy: the genre had always depended on involvement, its pathos being born of resistance to death. To look on loss from a great height and see it as part of a fated pattern is to reduce mournful feelings to ironic twinges" (Ramazani 33).

9. Whereas many contemporary poets, following the lead of Whitman and others, offer their version of a worldly plenitude that locates the speaker in an unassailable quiddity whose chief benefit is to secure for the speaker an anti-skeptical occasion, Brodsky's poem, in the context of elegy and the "dreaminess" of non-being, constantly fights a rear-guard action against skepticism. One of the key tensions of the poem arises between the controlling consciousness (secured with the enumerations with which it tasks itself) and the slippage, from sleep to death, toward the uncontrollable. For an oddly illuminating comparison on this score with an otherwise completely dissimilar poet, see Allen Ginsberg's "What's Dead" (689).

10. Bethea sees this phenomenon as expressive of the gravitation from "pure 'feeling'" to "pure 'mind,'" where feeling—as lyricism—holds to the thematic pitch of events, as opposed to mind, in which the cessation of thematic underlining, as it were, is characteristic of its cloud chamber-like contemplativeness toward objects. Bethea similarly finds that this feature is consistent with the poem's presentation of "the sheer ontological 'thingness' of the world."

11. Similarly, the white of the snow contrasts with the darkness in poems leading chronologically up to "The Great Elegy for John Donne," and one might even say that, in the spirit of "it's all one," white (i.e. oblivion and nothingness, its abstraction) and black are equivalent. The problem then becomes the rising intimation that we can no more break out of oblivion than we can "break out" of consciousness: Nothing can escape the leveling (c.f., "The swarms of books, / the streams of words, cloaked in oblivion's ice, / sleep soundly"). Because the oblivion is one of sleep, all in the poem is a dream, as it were, an airy nothing that does not correspond to empirical fact. Curiously, we do not know what "waking" from this dream would be like. Waking, the disquotational motion, only produces another set of Nabokovian quotation marks.

12. Both the setting and end of sleep occur in silence, sleep's partner. Max Picard, the philosopher of silence, redescribes the situation Brodsky depicts: "Purposeless, unexploitable silence suddenly appears at the side of the all-too-purposeful, and frightens us by its very purposelessness. It interferes with the regular flow of the purposeful. It strengthens the untouchable, it lessens the damage inflicted by . . . exploitation. It makes things whole again, by taking them back from the world of dissipation into the world of wholeness. It gives things something of its own holy uselessness, for that is what silence

is: holy uselessness" (3). We may go on to note, in Picardian language, that the poem evokes both silence and sleep in spite of its plethora of images in the attempts to locate at last the "spirit" of Donne, in the sense that there is "no greater world of spirit than the linguistic world of spirit" (11).

13. In "The Great Elegy for John Donne," night is ubiquitous, thanks to language, and it may be noted that its ubiquity inheres, as well, in language. While this Heideggerian notion may seem foreign to Brodskyan aesthetics, it is important to note that in Brodsky's early poems, the complicity of darkness with language, beginning with the "dark of print" and extending to "darkness everywhere," is not merely a feature of the poet's "outlook" but a linguistically gnomic, inward-turning quality that infuses both the poetry and the prose. And while the Brodskyan style may show similarities to English Metaphysical poetry, it is with equal justice that we could say that because the English Metaphysicals brought language to the curve of thought, they opened the door to what is "dark" in language (and in thought qua thought). It is no wonder that the same neo-classicists who welcome the epigrammatic quality in Brodsky view with alarm his further push into the gnomic, nor that such a push, as in Heidegger, darkens the glass of "classicism" itself.

14. In Heideggerian terms, this constitution is the "phusis," the dark inanimacy—the very physicality—of physical things.

15. We might add that in "The Great Elegy for John Donne," Brodsky, as translator of Donne, is continuing the translator's task by other means.

16. As Brodsky metamorphosed from humble exile to restless globe-trotter, many of his poems took on the quality of literary postcards, with a postcard's attendant limitations (and, if Derrida is to be believed, freedoms). But it should be said in his defense that even postcard stylistics are reminders of both the body's rootlessness and its freedom with respect to space. This defense, of course, need sound none of the usual cautionary notes with respect to the psychology of traveling.

17. See Michael Oakeshott's "Poetry in the Conversation of Mankind" for an extended discussion of poetry's place as conversation, as opposed to goal-oriented uses of language. Oakeshott finds much to recommend non-teleological language games in the formation of a useful moral philosophy—a view very much in opposition to George Steiner's thesis in *Language and Silence* (1967) that the literary never has clean hands. In a manner that revises Oakeshott, Allen Grossman has recently argued that one aspect of poetry pertains to its cultural work in the control of violence (see *The Long School-room: Lessons in the Bitter Logic of the Poetic Principle*, 1997).

18. Because tradition is itself about crossing barriers, it therefore comes as little surprise that the elegy is a type of poem hedged in—and to some extent braced by—conventions that it is the task of the poet to transgress and revise.

19. Polukhina also takes up Brodsky's use of triadics.

20. This move to equalize God (good) and Devil (evil) or divine-human is common to other poems as well (cf. *Twenty Sonnets to Mary Queen of Scots* and "Nature Morte").

21. The association of death with dreaming, while hardly surprising, merits closer scrutiny here, for the death of John Donne is made to seem a dream—a way of approximating the evacuation of all activity not dissimilar from conventional ways of portraying the eternal and ineffable by means of the temporal and the spoken (indeed, the overwritten, where the silence of death is dealt with not only by the extreme irony of overwriting but also by being quite literally *written over).*

22. Obviously, a certain incompatibility exists between the metaphor of stitching and that of the carving or sculpting of sarcophagi. In the first place, the former ties together

that which is separate or severed, whereas the later represents; in the second place, stitching gathers the metaphysical aspect of writing verses together with the implication of domestic repair (i.e., that writing, while transcendental, is also a kind of domestic repair). The presentation of a recumbent figure of the deceased, in contrast, suggests the stony silence and obduracy of death—quite the opposite of the delicacy of the needle and its precise, busy tacking. Yet both occupy, in another sense, the same "plane of regard," to adopt a favorite Brodsky expression.

23. The secondary suggestion seems to be that even Christ, because of the completeness of his humanity, must partake of this aspect of humanity's obscurity.

24. Three features mark the traditional association of the bird with the poet: (1) freedom (flight), (2) perspective (the godlike perspective that the poem suggests is available), and (3) unmediated expressiveness. The second item is available not because reality makes it so, but because it shows not only how imagination and invention can manifest themselves but also that imagination and invention have, as it were, replacement value—which we may take to be, in one sense, the thesis of the poem: namely, the value of the trope. However, the claims that underlie Brodsky's tropes serve to assert a classic argument, fundamental to a generic understanding of the elegy. This is the argument that seeks to endorse and get a purchase on some means of continuity in the face of Sacks's term for death: "extreme discontinuity." Obviously, this is an occasion for not only commemoration but also anxiety, felt as usurpation or transgression in a weak poet, justice in a strong one.

25. By happy coincidence, "stitch" puns on the Russian and classical word for verse, "stich," one of the felicitous puns that befalls translators from time to time.

3

The Disseminating Muse: "Verses on the Death of T. S. Eliot"

> Words, after speech, reach
> into the silence.
> —T. S. Eliot

The elegy for Donne was followed in 1965 by another elegy for an English poet, "Verses on the Death of T. S. Eliot," a poem so closely patterned on Auden's elegy for Yeats as to shade homage into challenge.[1] By this time, Brodsky had undergone the nightmarish farce of his trial on the catchall charge of "social parasitism" and was banished to the Archangelsk region north of Leningrad for five years' hard labor (a term commuted to two years). Hearing of Eliot's death a week afterwards from friends (on January 12), he composed the poem in a matter of hours. Brodsky acknowledged his indebtedness to Auden for pointing him in the direction of a new kind of elegy. It is a kind of elegy that, far from stage-managing a general, literary consolation for the purposes of connoisseurship, engages and judges, as if to surpass consolation with estimation. We might note that such an elegy performs its own Reaper's task by removing a previously standing figure from the ground and returning that ground to its aboriginal flatness. In other words, in his character as stern judge, the elegist becomes a figure for death itself and so begins to undo (or at least complicates) his role as consolatory memorialist. In this elegy, Brodsky begins to assign Auden's triad of making, knowing, and judging to poetry proper and so turns away from—or at the very least assigns an inferior place to—the human sovereignty of emotion, about which it might be said that this sovereignty has been not just the object, but the target of consolatory practices whatsoever, including the poetic.

Brodsky has also mused on the question of poetic indebtedness in general in the essay on Mandelstam in a way that illuminates his own wished-for kinship vis-à-vis Auden, whose creativity, unlike Brodsky's, was carried out minus the conspicuous example of biological progeny: "One of the purposes of a work of art is to create dependents; the paradox is that the more indebted the artist, the richer he is" (*L* 98). In "To Please a Shadow," he has this to say about the contributions for which Auden was responsible toward his (Brodsky's) own changing approach to elegizing the great dead:

I was intending to read Eliot . . . But by pure chance the book opened to Auden's "In Memory of W. B. Yeats." I was young then and therefore particularly keen on elegies as a genre, having nobody around dying to write one for. So I read them perhaps more avidly than anything else, and I frequently thought that the most interesting feature of the genre was the authors' unwitting attempts at self-portrayal with which nearly every poem "in memoriam" is strewn—or soiled. Understandable though this tendency is, it often turns such a poem into the author's ruminations on the subject of death, from which we learn more about him than about the deceased. The Auden poem had none of this; what's more, I soon realized that even its structure was designed to pay tribute to the dead poet, imitating in reverse order the great Irishman's own modes of stylistic development. (*L* 361)

While "Verses on the Death of T. S. Eliot" surpasses the "The Great Elegy for John Donne" in terms of balance, tone, structure, and metaphorical thinking, its most significant advance over the earlier elegy occurs in its understanding of temporality. With the death of Eliot (to say nothing of that of his mentor, Akhmatova, who died in 1965), Brodsky had come to understand that to think in terms of temporal matters is already to think in terms of elegiac ones.[2] If time is the dimension that definitively separates us from the dead, then the "restructuring" of time, through poetry, would seem to be a step in the right direction, namely, the direction of literalizing structural tasks for what had before transpired largely under the aegis of metaphor.[3] This restructuring of time is what he discovered in Auden's elegy for Yeats, particularly in the strict prosodic ordering of the famous third part. In this regard, Brodsky notes that "prosody knows more about time than a human being would like to reckon with" (*L* 46) because "prosody . . . is simply a repository of time within language" (*L* 52). The third (final) part of Auden's elegy also contains the famous (and later deleted) lines,

Time that is intolerant
Of the brave and innocent,
And indifferent in a week
To a beautiful physique,

Worships language and forgives
Everyone by whom it lives.

Of these lines, Brodsky has commented in epiphanic terms that deserve to be quoted at length:

Auden had indeed said that time (not *the* time) worships language, and the train of thought that statement set in motion in me is still trundling to this day. For "worship" is an attitude of the lesser toward the greater. If time worships language, it means that language is greater, or older, than time, which is, in its turn, older and greater than space. That was how I was taught, and I indeed felt that way. So if time—which is synonymous with, nay, even absorbs deity—worships deity—worships language, where then does language come from? For the gift is always smaller than the giver. And then isn't language a repository of time? And isn't this why time worships it? And isn't a song, or a poem, or indeed a speech itself, with its caesuras, pauses, spondees, and so forth, a game language plays to restructure time? And aren't those by whom language "lives" those by whom time does too? And if time "forgives" them, does it do so out of generosity or out of necessity? And isn't generosity a necessity anyhow? (*L* 363)

Ideas that spoke of "restructuring time" were sure to appeal to a young man, even though youth traditionally militates against all but a pedestrian understanding of any such phrase. Be that as it may, Brodsky found himself armed with a mass of new ideas that would help him negotiate the leap from the young poet's romantic interest in the infinite by way of death to the mature poet's shrewder concentration on consonants and vowels as themselves vessels of time. Brodsky was in a good position to deploy these ideas the next time he picked up his pen *in memoriam*. Like Auden's elegy, "Verses on the Death of T. S. Eliot" is a sonatalike, tripartite work in which the opening, expository section yields to a meditational middle, culminating in a final section of marching quatrains that recapitulate the themes of the first two sections and also self-consciously infuse them with a more formal *melos*. Brodsky's poem departs structurally from the Auden model only in making the middle section a sonnet. The Eliot elegy is similar to the Yeats elegy in another key respect as well: the claims it makes on behalf of poetry. While Auden saw Yeats as "teach[ing] the free man how to praise," he acknowledged that "the words of the dead / are modified in the guts of the living." Brodsky's Eliot is a dead father-figure, yet it is not only the person who has died ("death chooses . . . / the poet, not his words, however strong, / but just . . . the poet's self"), but also his "house," a dynastic House of Eliot, where the "Black windowpanes [shrink] mutely in the snow." All that remains is poetry—words; and yet there is a sense in which that which is poetic transcends its means and becomes part of the living, not only modified in their guts, but in Brodsky's revision, also "splash[ing] against the eye, / sink[ing] into lymph . . ." This image of reincorporation is itself modified in the last section to "dandelion drift will make you known," suggesting that the final modification goes beyond the guts of the living to become a part of nature. Poetry per se is disseminated; that is, insofar as poetry purports to be a structure of specifically temporal transcendence, as here, what persists is precisely the will to (re)structure, a prosodic will, not "content" or message or anything of a more blatantly historical or contingent sort. It is, too, a dissemination of language, the means to restructure time; in that sense poetry is a gift, both from the dead poet and from the living elegist.

Certainly, Brodsky had not only Eliot, but Yeats and Auden in mind when he reckoned with the claims of poetry in the twentieth century (he would later add

Cavafy, Paz, Milosz, and others to this pantheon of poets who had achieved the authority to make general claims). This building of a core, a private canon of relevant poets, always carried with it the suggestion that if we were to take poetry seriously, we owed it to ourselves at some point to inspect the claims that this canon explicitly or implicitly put forward, for modern history had been such that even poetry could not cling to immunity from challenges to its assertions of permanence and ancient prestige.[4] Far from taking this as an injunction to reinvent the wheel, Brodsky undertook to justify a poetry that had become troubled in light of the very historical human events it sought to articulate. Eliot, therefore, epitomized the problem in that he stands as the poet most representative of the century's counter-drive from fragmentation to revisionary wholeness—ironically manifested in an embrace of fragmentariness itself. In fact, he is a poet for whom community (albeit of a somewhat cramped, sectarian variety) in a confused, bled, and violent century is a desirable idea, a community toward whom—and *pace* Auden—poetry should make something happen. Brodsky's elegy for Eliot, written in his own forced Arctic isolation, is thus in one sense a meditation of what this something might be.[5]

"Verses on the Death of T. S. Eliot" avails itself of its wintry setting to make—frequently ironic—use of traditional elegiac imagery pertaining to seasons in a manner similar to a very un-Eliotian poet, Thomas Hardy (whom Brodsky had also read during this period). Here, Christmas, with its hope of renewal and the new year with its slate-sweeping arc brought into play as contextual devices. As with Auden's "He died in the midst of winter," Brodsky's elegy begins, "He died at start of year, in January." Having underscored, as it were, his poem's connection to Auden's, even as he situates the poem along the fissure dividing irreconcilable states and tenses, Brodsky immediately recurs to his own voice:

> The cold's town-crier stood beneath the light.
> At crossings puddles stiffened into ice.
> He latched his door on the thin chain of years.

> (*SP* 99, trans. George Kline)

As is customary practice with much of his later poetry, Brodsky treats absence with the respect usually accorded to presence, engaging in hyperbole and tropes of substitution, as though testing the warp and woof of reality,[6] in terms of the actual death as well as in terms of his commitment to the action of words as adequate, in the first place and if at all, to undertake the task of substitution, since to do so implies both a moral and ethical move and as a feat of linguistic self-assertion—inseparable features in the act of elegizing. The "cold's town-crier" is substituted initially for the poet's (Eliot's) suddenly stilled voice;[7] perhaps ironically, he cries the time (which decries the poet's death), even as he traditionally calls the "all's well." The *cold's* town-crier [emphasis added] also substitutes for time, which is, in Brodsky's "Fourth Eclogue," cold ('Vremia est' kholod—"time equals cold" [*U* 77]). To the elegist, of course, there is another sense in which the death elegized *is* the "all's well" signal, announcing, as it does, a momentary clearing in the space of poetic possibility. It is also reassurance that the departed's biological muteness will not redound to his poems, even if they, as in "The Great Elegy for John Donne," have no other sponsor than the tradition the elegist is just at that moment annunciating. The stiffening ice, moreover, produces a cataract on the eye of the puddle. Both images are images of repetition as well as substitution: They represent the closing-down of the poet's life at the same time as they reconstitute parts of it (mouth, eye) under the aegis of the elegist's transformative license. Instances of repetition will themselves repeat in the poem, not only through images and echoes proper but also through the repetition of verse and rhyme. For example, in the second stanza we find

          poetry
  is orphaned, yet it breeds within the glass
  of lonely days, each echoing each, that swim
  to distance.

Literally this is "Despite its orphaned nature / Poetry is based on the similarity of monotonous days rushing into the distance." Not only does poetry have an "orphaned" nature (its poets are and will be dead—perhaps its parent texts as well); it is infinitely derivative in the best postmodern way. Such complex images that join abstractions at the level of things and in turn allude to classical antecedents (art derived from art rather than nature) become a stylistic hallmark of Brodsky's mature poetry. They signal both a recourse to as well as a restless extension upon the impulse toward mythopoesis,[8] an impulse, we might add, that looks toward central poetic constructs in the face of efforts on the part of major twentieth-century poets, including Eliot, to revise poetry-bound classical myths in order to stand in ironic and knowing relation to their artificial and ad hoc nature. Despite this, the elegist maintains that "the voice of poetry stands plain." Not unlike a New Critic, Brodsky thus seems at pains to separate the poet from the poetry, ironically rehearsing the act that death has already accomplished, so it will be possible to reinvest all the energies associated with fame into the remainder, poetry. At the same time, he wishes to do homage to the man, but not, presumably, to perpetuate something of his life; rather, to reinforce the sense of his vacancy (a reinforcement that would no doubt find Eliot's spirit in agreement), which reinforcement would, again, make his poetry stand in relief. While the elegist would bring forward an historical Eliot to this extent, he draws back from any condensed account of death:

  With neither grimace nor maliciousness
  death chooses from its bulging catalogue
  the poet, not his words . . .

While there is much in his poetic thinking that would incline Brodsky to historicize with the zest of a Hegel, he declines to go the historical route here and so parts company with much modern rendering-unto-history, in order to revert to poetry's most ambitious claim, its own immortality. In other words, he is willing to consign the poet to history, but he is less willing—at this stage, at least—to apply the same procedure to the poet's goods, his poems.

When we contrast Brodsky's elegies with Milosz's poetic memoirisms, Montale's spousal hauntings, Cavafy's homosexual nostalgias, and Larkin's *valses tristes* (to name work of but four modern elegists of international importance), it becomes clear that, for Brodsky, the form is always as much about its own internal operations, as about an external subject. But this is only to say that for Brodsky the elegiac situation often provides a pretext: Once we get beyond the occasions for mourning, we find that the elegy has been indeed a self-portrait, and not of the poet, but of the poet's language. Perhaps his importance lies in this difference, that he was always constitutionally willing to apply the pressure necessary for the form to declare its limits qua form. Specifically, he was also willing to work language into revealing its limits with respect to one of its most anciently revered—and hence mystified—conventions. He does so not only by persisting in the form, even when it is questionable that the occasion warrants (as if to suggest, again, that elegy is not primarily an occasional form of verse), but in diversifying that form's subjects, leaving behind the traditional elegy's emphasis on the work of mourning for the work of poetry, which to a poet of his way of thinking is to pose the matter in quite a more significant way. As Brodsky's elegiac work broadens into self-elegy, elegies for unlikely subjects, and even personal elegies that suppress the mechanism of grieving altogether, we perceive the almost Scholastic fascination (an adjective that always met with his approval—perhaps hinting, too, at the Russian love for analyzing intrigue) with the Byzantine implications of language as a transcendent medium. At the same time, it would not be inconsequential for us to observe that the choice of elegy bears on the weighty matter of poetic ambitions in still another way.

Unlike the members of his later peer group, Brodsky failed to be suitably impressed with the epic's place in the scheme of the old *curriculum poetae*. For an ambitious poet who was also an avowed classicist, this would seem to be a perverse, even somehow harmful, antipathy, not that the epic has spelled any first-order poet's marching orders after the miasmal achievement of the *Cantos*. Perhaps the way to understand its failure to attract lies in the fact that its seams and pressure points had become all too conspicuous after Pound. To deconstruct the epic, *pace* Walcott, seemed then and seems now an arid exercise. Sexist, militaristic, unreflective, its heroes inspire us with, to say the least, a vague obligation to loathe them, just as their totalizing philosophies and primping self-importance melt into abstractions of State and Religion. Nevertheless, to classical (or postclassical) eyes, the epic is still the *ne plus ultra* of the fully equipped poet. So why did Brodsky, who was no stranger to the long poem, quite simply avoid it? The answer may lie in his strong metaphorical disposition, which like the disposition of a commodity trader is never happier than in cashing in oranges for apples. Which is the point: To the *ancien regime* of the product-haunted world, the epic was ultimate, top-heavy, redoubtable; to the postmodernist wary of transcendent projects and synoptic claims, what we do is less important than that we do. As Brodsky's vision moved toward greater and greater naturalism, his Muse became less concerned in identifying significant end-points with epic words than with people (and the poems in their wake): hence, elegies. Hence, too, in that the elegy had already deconstructed the epic's chest-thumping obliquity and braggadocio. Moreover, the elegy, with its own end-point chiseled into the tombstone's announcement of permanent discontinuity, was as worthy a measure of modern (and postmodern) anxieties and psychic negotiations as the mind could come up with, since that same mind had no business believing it could unlearn its psychic and moral dodges on its way back to retroactively embracing a poetics of heroism. To Brodsky, then, the elegy was as fully capable in anatomizing and synthesizing our age, whose confederation with death's surrogates and media—with death itself—was no longer subject to denial.

All the same (perhaps all the more) a mechanism implying a special exemption from death—for instance, a poem—would seem either an ideal escape pod for the mind—or conversely another, as-yet-undiscovered arm of this protean death. Our understanding of Brodsky's aesthetic development might therefore stand to benefit from examining further the implicit claims surrounding poetry's "immortality," in light of the apprehension that words (or at least that part of words constituting their existence as "marks and noises") are themselves subject to the same historical and natural erosion against which they would offer the organism a unique requital from such an intolerable state of affairs. In light of such a reservation, any claim purporting to exempt words of the contingent nature of everything else would smack of sophistry and doubtless come to grief unless the poet were to articulate a conception quite different from what the ordinary reader has come to understand by the honorific, yet previously unambiguous term, "deathless." The origins to these problems, and indeed the framing of the problems in literary terms, are matters that pertain, as it were both within and without, to time's attempts to transform itself in the image of eternity, an image that is itself modeled on time. This inherent circularity at least has the advantage of allowing the young Brodsky to have it both ways: His poems can mimic commands issued *sub specie aeternitatis* when he wishes to support or advance a claim on behalf of poetry, or he can, conversely, underscore the perishable nature of words as a chastening maneuver against literary hubris. In elegizing Eliot, then recently dead, Brodsky is able to turn aside from the grand elegy, whose main feature is that it stands by poetry's self-proclamations, to an elegy that has shrewder speculation at its heart. This speculation takes into view the meaning of the virtually immediate imposition of words as a way of easing the transition from the fact of death to its impact. The elegy is also prospective in the sense that it aims as well to deal with the further career of the same words once the therapeutic mission is compete.

As a result, we may surmise the following ideas as they pertain, in terms of a radical poetic myth-making, to language and time. Although a human construct, language differs from other human administrative inventions in its ability, not merely to confer, but to create values—including values that are often mistakenly seen to be prior to, or independent of, language. This, as the poet implicitly argues, is a false perception, owing to a still widely held belief that language is a transparent medium, with the ability to disappear as a window disappears to the view it offers. Language is not a window but can be made to seem so, in which case the view that it offers (i.e., the "reality" to which it refers) arrives courtesy of the poet's invitation for us to participate in such a language game and depends on a reader's "willing suspension of disbelief"—in this case the disbelief that words offer something above and beyond their existence as marks and noises. In other words, we read as if in a "theater" of poetry and, as with any theater-going, we must resist the temptation to leap up on the stage because we don't like the action and intend to do something about it. Coleridge's phrase is in fact a prosaic description of faith, a faith that starts to crumble when prophesied miracles are not forthcoming and lyric victories do not stick any more tenaciously in the face of time's erosions than real ones do. Although, as we have seen, Brodsky would be the first to collapse the virtual into the real, he would be the last to offer the virtual as "superior" to the real, except where survival is tied to the ability to make the respective change. Yet in our era, the threshold for the miraculous is exceptionally high and the tolerance for prophcsying, correspondingly low. When the poet starts talking about death and the afterlife of words, he must exchange pleas for more and greater faith for the figure of himself and his poem, which suddenly finds itself encased in quotation marks. Must the same hold for the values implicit in poems?[9] In the case of Eliot, this is to ask rather more than one bargains for; in Brodsky's case, it seems just right, for if the whole of the language/reality dichotomy moves permanently to the level of metaphor, of "as-if," then so much the better for both: If we deputize language to act on behalf of reality—that is, to represent it—then we may come to suspect that there is something metaphorical about reality too, something that unhinges the materialist's clamp on truth. In this connection, Brodsky identifies the move as the culminating point in the history of poetry (and, indeed, of faith) in his essay on Cavafy. Here, we may substitute "reality" for "tenor" and "language" for "vehicle":

There are two elements which usually constitute a metaphor: the object of description (the "tenor," as I. A. Richards called it), and the object to which the first is imagistically, or simply grammatically, allied (the "vehicle"). The implication which the second part usually contains provides the writer with the possibility of virtually endless development. This is the way a poem works. What Cavafy did, almost from the very beginning of his career as a poet, was to jump straight to the second part. (L 56)

If we conceive of the poem as a theater, then Brodsky must act as a stage-manager, balancing the degree of theatricality against the "realism"—not reality—it supports. As "Verses on the Death of T. S. Eliot" is a formal elegy, many of the props arrive fully constructed. Brodsky makes much, for instance, of the wintry setting. At first, he seems explictly to deny nature's power to engage in pathetic expressiveness ("There was no time for nature to display / the splendors of her choreography"), but his denial is complicated by the fact that the "display" that time has prevented nature from making is one not of mourning but in fact of ostentation. The phrase, "there was no time" refers, not to some inconvenient lack of time in which to mourn the poet's death, but to the fact of the end of lifetimes—including nature's.

The achievement of the elegy for Eliot also depends on a series of complex images of opening and closing, emptiness and plenitude. The poem's opening gambit is to announce both the method and the theme. "He died at start of year, in January. / His front door flinched in frost by the streetlamp." Here we have both the matter of mortal fact and the first opening, January, which will separate the poet from his poems. The second line immediately produces a contrast (a closed door) and moreover separates the dimension of time from that of materiality. Without making too big a deal, we should nevertheless note that the door, an object of wood, substitutes for the traditional natural element in the pathetic fallacy, but it does so from its level as an inanimate thing. The pathos of nature (the so-called "pathetic fallacy") reflects the desire to control nature and hence time. By implying sensibility (the door "flinched") to an inanimate object, the poet is perhaps extending this will-to-control over things. Introducing a tactical distinction between the natural and the inanimate ("There was no time for nature"), which in fact overlap, Brodsky finesses the pathetic fallacy into a pathos of things; he will revert to the traditional use in the poem's third section. Just as the door flinches, "Black windowpanes [shrink] mutely." Again, the image is of an aperture in the process of closing, here a visual image that works in a characteristic visual pun, alluding both to the opacity of a dead eye and, synesthetically, to the muteness of the dead poet.[10] The muteness, however, occurs only so long as we stay among things. These distinctions, tactical though they be, prepare us for what develops at first between the poet and words but later later into a general imagistic fragmentation or dissemination as aspects of the poet are distributed among things of the world in a kind of Dionysian (and un-Eliotian) *sparagmos*. The first stanza contains another of these complex images: "At crossings puddles stiffened into ice." Stiffening is here a sensual image applied to the realm of sight; it also contains a suggestion that water's rigor mortis represents a transformation similar to that of "body" into "corpse" (and "body of work" into *corpus*), just as a stiffened puddle becomes a (slippery) stepping-stone. As with the door, an approach is closed off while another, transmuted, is offered in its place. Moreover, we are twice reminded of images within Eliot's work, namely, of water and the door. The constitutive and time-marking waters of *The Waste Land* and *Four Quartets* are embryonic in the puddles, which will later grow to the sea, and the door to childhood of "Burnt Norton" is reversed, at the end of life, as the door to death. Each of the related ideas ends in paradox: January, like its namesake Janus, faces two seemingly irreconcilable, but for Eliot redeemable, times (it contains, too, the moment of separation); the door of the house is frozen shut; the windowpanes are "black"; and the eye of the puddle has frozen into a cataract. Not only do these images themselves freeze in paradox, they seem to freeze in time by means of words. Thus at the moment of fullest expression, they are also most empty.

The second stanza is no less complex, for the elegist knows that paradox means stasis (and stasis is death, but more importantly, the cessation of time), and though death may be in some sense "pointless," it would be more pointless to let the poem subside in images of self-contradiction. As David Shaw reminds us, the purpose of paradox is to wrench thinking out of its habitual grooves by posing apparent contradictions, of which the close reader is intolerant (1-9). In this stanza, as we have seen, "Poetry is orphaned," and in this simple statement, we understand the explicit claim of separation that the elegist is making: The poems are separated from their author. In human social life, of course, separation from one's offspring creates the opportunity for plaintive, even sentimental circumstances. Yet the elegy does not extend the affective occasion, and the fact that now we have moved, perforce, to the realm of words obviates the need for such pathetic states as remorse. Words, to put the matter another way, have their own agenda, so that we should even feel the justice of the poet's death as a necessary event in the life of words. Poetry is orphaned, "and yet it breeds." Orphanhood, another sort of discontinuity, more specifically speaks to the question of sponsorship: when words are orphaned—unsponsored— they are also "free." The freedom that they acquire, however, looks dubious from the point of view of the poet bent on transcendence, for the destinies of words, particularly words that bring the dead back on stage, require something more than whimpered ends: The outsmarting of discontinuity counts as transcendence; pious memorials do not. Is there a middle way? The careers of words, certain words at any rate, land them in something like a trans-linguistic predicament—they must own up to the fact of their divergent natures. But because the constraints placed upon interpretation have been loosened by the poet's awareness of words' insurgent proclivities—thanks to their dependence upon the perspectival leverage—mere "ambivalence" (bad) becomes postmodernist "polyvalence" (good). Thus while ambivalence may upset our desire to be perspicuous with respect to the meanings of poems, polyvalency cheerfully lowers our expectations.

Observe, too, that Brodsky's announcement revises and extends Milton's "Lycidas is dead," a point of entry into the elegiac territory that doesn't require a Milton to effect. The thematic point here is not only that Lycidas is dead, but that the poetry has been propagated. Perhaps more conclusive is the statement we have already seen: "But in the rhyme / of years the voice of poetry stands plain." If the poetry is, after death, breeding, it will reconstitute itself "in the rhyme of years"—that is, another, vaster "poem."[11] We should equally note a feature common to elegiac dynamics, namely, the suggestion of "sexual" potency—specifically, of propagation—that has suddenly become part of the elegist's inheritance, not to mention the generative estate of future readers. By the same Freudian token, we would be remiss not to observe that the anxiety that would undoubtedly accompany the recapture of an original potency becomes prolonged in view of the potential number of its beneficiaries. It is perhaps the poet's version of the parents' quiet angst in the face of enormous, outranging children.

Brodsky moves, in the third stanza, to a consideration of the agency that enables the separation between poet and poetry, namely death:

> With neither grimace nor maliciousness,
> death chooses from his bulging catalogue
> the poet.

From the "perspective" of death, which is the perspective of a posterior nothingness, that untheorizable space beyond Terminus, a person has no special status and can therefore be the equivalent of a word in a catalogue; that is, man and word stand as equivalent.[12] Note that while death chooses the poet, the implication is that it could have chosen his words. Death "unfailingly" makes the choice that it does. In a sense, it appears as if death is on the side of words. It "has no use for thickets or for fields / or seas in their high, bright magnificence," since these belong to the elegy's affective and metaphysical consolations. Death leads in turn to an emptiness in time: "Used Christmas trees had flared in vacant lots, / and broken baubles had been broomed away." The emptiness of this time after the high significance of Christmas is both a kind of spiritual and intellectual gap, a "state space" in which to broom away reminders ("baubles") of a more salubrious time (i.e., this season). It is also a space of cosmic seriousness, seen *sub specie aeternitatis* as Brodsky subtly alludes to the "ancient women" who gather fuel in vacant lots in "Rhapsody on a Windy Night,"[13] only here, no such women—let alone Fates—attend any longer to the world-turning activity. Their role, if indeed they can be said to have one, has been reduced merely to that of other people in this person-less poem, which is to say the cold has driven them indoors, removing them from view. In this respect, "Verses on the Death of T. S. Eliot" resembles "The Great Elegy for John Donne," and the resemblance keys us into the thematic push to considerations of poetry's fate, once separated from its authors and auditors. In the Donne elegy, such separation prepares us for the privacy of dream world; here, we (and Eliot's poems) are prepared for reentry into the intractable hardnesses of the historical and natural worlds. In addition, both poems show us worlds in which contingency challenges our ability to control human destiny.

Time in the poem is not, therefore, the continuous river, the "strong brown god" of Eliotic imagery but a disjunctive force that supervises the separation of the poet and his poems. Seen this way, time is death's personal agent, and all the images of time are also the images of death and chaos. The sea, the image of all rivers *in extensa*, to say nothing of puddles, is a case in point.[14] It is the sea, too, it will be remembered, that divided Eliot's life into two chapters. Brodsky dwells on these images of division in large part, as we have seen, to describe or prophesy the transformation that death will bring about, but equally because they are central to Eliot's own poetry and thus constitute an intertextual homage to him:

> A Catholic, he lived till Christmas Day.
> But as the sea, whose tide has climbed and roared,
> slamming the seawall, draws its warring waves
> down and away, so he, in haste, withdrew
> from his own high and solemn victory.

Even the sea, like time itself, is subject to containment, and thus he, in his person, is subjected to containment in an image, which is, as it were, his own. On Brodsky's view, the poems are greater, the man lesser, thanks to language. The poet's "high and solemn victory," from which he withdraws (i.e., his life) belongs, in one sense, to the consolation of his Christianity. Yet Brodsky clearly hints that the withdrawal refers as well to his departure from his poetry. In any case, Eliot seems clearly implicated in a desire or movement to withdraw from poetry, although this hint of complicity (or perhaps, more tellingly, obedience) is situated in the same relation to the will, of which he may or may not be conscious, rather in the manner that a portion of oceanic material nearing the shore will suddenly find itself a wave.

If Eliot's consolation lay in his Christianity, such an assuaging thought for Eliot, personally, is therefore not our consolation (though Eliot, in his later orientation toward understanding as belief, would wish it so): "It was not God, but only time, mere time / that called him." Of time and God, time is here the more powerful, since anyone can, so to speak, reject the Deity's invitation. It will be Brodsky's project to deflect the brunt of this tyranny by calling it poetic advantage, thus making time serve, because it is an agent for death, as an agent for poetry too:

> Exuberant
> in strength, it laughs, a January gulf
> in that dry land of days where we remain.

The gulf, which alludes to Eliot's grave, is also the condition, the temporal remainder, in which we survive him. It is other things as well: first and foremost the space in which his poetry remains, and, we should now add, in fittingly inelegant jargon, the "space" of his poetic influence. The "dry land of days," the "waste land" in which we live deprived of the poet's life, is a matter of humorous irony and joy as far as time is concerned. Although the reference here remains deliberately ambiguous, we may see the "it" as time. Note that his rendering of time as a thing is quite literal, and we come close to confusing repetition with added emphasis in underscoring the fact that the reification of time is characteristically a metaphoric turning of time into a thing. We—or rather, "we"—remain, along with other things, especially words. Since these are no longer the "children" of the poet (i.e., they are "orphaned"), they enter the public domain on their own, and we can encounter them minus the anxiety attached to appropriating words that "belong" to others (as we shall see, a similar argument is made in the elegy for Robert Lowell). To put the matter another way, the words are common property, paradoxically all the more so, for having belonged to the great, dead poet.[15] The gulf hints at both the sea of time and chaos, the grave of the poet, and the void from which his words will issue, transformed.

The elegy's middle, sonnet section begins with a question, "Where are you, Magi, you who read men's souls?" As Sacks (22) tells us, the elegiac query (Milton's "Where were ye Nymphs . . . ?"), as a convention, masks a fundamental elegiac question: Why is it that no one can save us from death? Brodsky's version of this question begins by devaluing its affective and indeed pathetic aura on the grounds that it is an egoistical variant of what he regards as a more profound question: How is it that a part of us survives the body? His answer to this question is implied in the first line of this section, for although we may wonder at the absence of Magi, we nonetheless possess a term for beings for whom prophecy has become one of the possible states of language. When Magi "read men's souls," in this figurative language, they do so in terms of words. If souls are words, then there is a sense in which the depredations of time swerve clear of spirit, as these same words reform and inform the material world, "the dry land of days where we remain."

Brodsky's invocation of the Magi serves to establish a spiritual parallel to what has heretofore been a linguistic matter. Two allegorical figures (Adam and Eve, later England and America) who stand vigil by the grave site connect the spiritual to the cultural and historical. These figures (Brodsky's variant of the elegiac procession) suggest that the significance of the poet's linguistic (poetic) remains provides differing refractions depending on the audience involved— indeed, this is one of the poem's key contentions and the key, as well, to its implied assertion that poetry is a survival mechanism, a matter of more than literary interest to England and America. If we imaginatively dilate upon these figures a moment, it becomes clear that the "enormous" grave over which the allegorical figures incline is also in another sense the Atlantic Ocean, a figure for the gulf and the body both separating and mediating the dualities of nationality and culture for Eliot, Brodsky, and Auden, and to which we may add, for Brodsky, language. The sonnet section ends with a summary line ("But each grave is the limit of the earth"), suggesting that the grave—this containment—is also the limit of words,[16] in the sense that words are predicated on things ("the earth"), of which humans, as we have seen, are another instance. But this primary meaning is contrasted by the hint that there is also something "unearthly" in the fact of poetry's presence, for which the grave is not the limit; such unearthliness readily connects with poetry's self-description as a transcendence

mechanism and stands in contrast to the material ground through which humans
emerge (and end) and poems are inscribed. As Brodsky will discover (and we
will later see), this unearthliness and the transcendent possibility it intimates
powers elegy by the inch, but not the mile.

The memorable last section of Auden's elegy ("Earth, receive an honored
guest") provides the model for the comparable finale of Brodsky's elegy:

> Apollo, fling your garland down.
> Let it be this poet's crown,
> pledge of immortality,
> in a world where mortals be.

While this is obvious homage to Auden (with George Kline's Shakespearean
echo), it also sets itself up for comparison—or contrast, for Brodsky does not
assert Eliot's significance against a background of political apprehensiveness, as
Auden does with Yeats. Rather, he asserts a trans-historical significance, which
is where, at this stage, he locates the significance of language. Perhaps
understandably, then, he does so with the help of traditional elegiac terms:

> Forests here will not forget
> voice of lyre and rush of feet.
> Only what remains alive
> will deserve their memories.
>
> Hill and dale will honor him.
> Aeolus will guard his fame.
> Blades of grass his name will hold
> just as Horace had foretold.

The elegiac traditions that Brodsky borrows here are classical, both in the sense
of ancient, specifically classical attribution, and in the sense of unrevised. The
reference to Horace's *exegi monumentum*, just as it represents one of poetry's
most audacious claims, especially from Shakespeare to Shelley (enclosing, too,
as Brodsky would know, John Donne), and comes uncomfortably close to a
claim of omnipotence (thereby resetting the author's mug into a countenance).
The same ode takes on a special resonance in Russian poetry, where it appears
also by way of Pushkin, whose own famous "Exegi Monumentum" claims
specifically, "I will not die completely. In my sacred lyre / My soul will outlive
my dust and escape corruption" [my rendering]. Having spent two sections
applying and extending the resources of elegiac devices, Brodsky now reverts
to many of the elegy's traditional conventions, along with the professions of
faith that underlie them. These conventions (sentient nature, "voice of lyre," the
procession of mourners, etc.) are then pressed into service to ratify the extended
claims from the previous sections. In other words, in "Verses on the Death of
T. S. Eliot," Brodsky does not attempt the wholesale revision of traditional

elegiac conventions themselves, but does attempt to put a new twist on them in support of his contention that words, as it were, develop lives of their own in the form of "spirit." This spirit he now associates with love:

> Thus it is that love takes flight.
> Once for all. Into the night.
> Cutting through all words and cries,
> seen no more, and yet alive.

Just as with the mystery of death, love is associated with language (and here poetry) by its ability to be transformed and to transform. Yet Brodsky suggests that the link is closer than that. Love is an aspect of poetry (words) in reach and scope, in its ability to set the moral tone that underwrites the desires of community.[17] Nevertheless, the link has been established as a similarity, not an identity, for love "cuts through" words (thus poetry becomes a substitute—or in the case of Eliot, a backup for faith). Brodsky speaks of love in the early poetry of Akhmatova as a metaphor for spirit:[18]

Throughout one's life, time addresses man in a variety of languages: in those of innocence, love, faith, experience, history, fatigue, cynicism, guilt, decay, etc. Of those, the language of love is clearly the *lingua franca*. Its vocabulary absorbs all the other tongues, and its utterance gratifies a subject, however inanimate it may be. Also, by being thus uttered, a subject acquires an ecclesiastical, almost sacred denomination, echoing both the way we perceive the objects of our passions and the Good Book's suggestion as to what God is. Love is essentially an attitude maintained by the infinite toward the finite. The reversal constitutes either faith or poetry. (*L* 44)

In a final reprise, Brodsky generates a cluster of details, both from conventional elegiac imagery (a star, wood and field, a "realm of gloom") and from Eliot's poetry ("that vast and hidden room" from "Burnt Norton"), as if by permitting these gestures another bow he might arrive at the elegy's final synthesis, the performative (and thus reconstitutive) duty of words to embody memory, even as they go their own way:

> Wood and field will not forget.
> All that lives will know you yet,
> as the body holds in mind
> lost caress of lips and arms.

Not forgetting is perhaps the first duty incumbent upon the traditional elegist. Brodsky extends the duty to nature, which is where lies, as we have seen, the democratic realm of things and words at their most permeable. "*All* that lives will know you yet" [emphasis added] is a prophecy, and thus the elegist becomes himself a modern version of the Magi whose whereabouts he has earlier queried. Since in that passage he asserted that Magi "read men's souls," we can now see that they do so in poems. And since the suggestion is that "All that lives" does not yet know the mourned object or his poetry, the prophecy is also coextensive with the elegist's ambition and is hence a measure of it. The image of lost love remembered in the last two lines, as a way of epitomizing the general case of poetic power, also recalls the dimmer shade of Yeats. Brodsky's elegy reaches both Eliot and Yeats by way of Auden (who will be the object of his own elegy in 1976); thus in the course of this poem, Brodsky has adumbrated a personal poetic canon whose distinguishing marks seems to be, not the fact that they are, in some sense, correct choices but that they are loved figures. In this connection, at the end of the poem Brodsky reinforces the similarity of poetry to love, a similarity that he extends as the only necessary justification for this particular canon by way of noting that love and classicism go together: "[L]ove as content is in the habit of limiting formal patterns. . . . After all, there are only so many adequate manifestations for truly strong sentiments" (*L* 45). Stylistically, Brodsky's synechdochal abbreviation of this credo suggests a shorthand series of equations with which we are now familiar: parts of a body = parts of life = parts of speech. It is to the latter that he will increasingly direct the main beam of his attention, and the inferences hidden in the term "parts of speech" will fuel the armature of his subsequent career as an elegist. It is also the latter term that, though seemingly an abstraction of the first two, for Brodsky subsumes all the plenitude they imply.

NOTES

1. Insofar as the elegy is a challenge, it is less designed to correct an earlier elegy than to set one's own elegy against a standard. Auden, by contrast, corrects Yeats, whose faults and lapses, it is hinted, put him in collusion with a way of thinking that dovetails with the dangers of the time in which it was written, with the Second World War looming just months away. Even so, Auden's elegy is the reverse of Brodsky's in one important respect, for it shades challenge into homage, and such charity as it generates is also the measure of its forgiveness.

2. Even a cursory reading of Eliot's poems reveals that poet as time-haunted and elegiac. Indeed, the High Modernist poet actively sought to retrieve the past's wholeness as a contrasting ground in consciousness against which to depict the "shards" that history had become. Even in the early poems, one need only look beyond the screen of ironic aestheticism to perceive the elegiac stance. Eliot himself maintained that *The Waste Land* was an elegy.

3. Jacques Derrida calls attention to Nietzsche's assertion that literal truths are dead metaphors; hence, the call to distinguish between the literal and the metaphorical is seen as a false distinction. This suggestion should not upset the poet—except perhaps one of Symbolist or New Critical persuasion—for it also bridges the gap between the poem and the history in which it occurs—a gap that, though of poetry's own making, required religion for Eliot to close.

4. In his massive formidable apologia, even Grossman (1992) finds poetry "an art that seems . . . virtually dead. It is an art which has been driven into a corner; which requires justification; it is an art which has more practitioners than readers; an art the

function of which is hard to discern" (8). Since Grossman is describing the state of poetry from the perspective of the northeastern academy in 1981, the situation would seem to be rather less bleak for the then-Soviet poet, whose role as bearer-of-truth was widely acknowledged. But we would do well to bear in mind the strictures under which the Soviet poet operated and the ever-present dangers of taking that ancient prestige at face-value. Even the term "Soviet poet" exudes an aura of contradiction: Witness the suspicion that clings to such a star as Yevtushenko.

5. For Bethea, Eliot also provides a mediation for leveraging *homo sovieticus* out of his spiritual anomie and into what Mandelstam referred to (and what would strike the Brodskyan ear with a certain wistfulness) as "world culture."

6. Sacks suggests that "reality-testing" finds its rhetorical counterpart in elegiac questions (e.g., Milton's "Lycidas": "Where were ye Nymphs . . .?"). It also represents the shock of encounter with the discontinuous person, which, because of discontinuity, not only requires a "test" to make sure but also rhetorically counters discontinuity itself by introducing redundancy, for to question reality is to bring it before us again (22-26).

7. Of course, by the time of his death, Eliot's poetic career had effectively been over for two decades, blurring the meaning of a stilled voice. Brodsky, who often practices what amounts to a posthumous ventriloquism to bring his own inclusive perspective closer to language's, would no doubt have relished the gradations from full voice to disseminated language as both the slyest and grandest of Eliot's escapes from personality.

8. While mythopoesis has many varieties, all have in common the wish to connect up with what is absent from lyric poetry, namely a narrative, which then provides both a framework and a way of reminding the reader that a poem is, first and foremost, a *curriculum vitae.*

9. Eliot himself faced the same problem, differently posed, moving from the position that we can understand a poem without subscribing to its content as a matter of belief, to the position that understanding must terminate in belief. For Eliot, this was the intersection of the eternal with the historical, the word with the Word.

10. The trope of the dead eye is expressed perhaps most memorably in this century by Italian poet Cesare Pavese : *Verrà morte e avrà i tuoi occhi* ("death, when it comes, will use your two eyes to see").

11. The trope of the poem as providing the model for conceiving historical epochs is an ideal dear to Heideggerians who wish to distinguish between scientistic (i.e., metaphysical) and nonscientistic (i.e, postmetaphysical) worldviews. Like most poets, Brodsky was not content to concede the image of epochs in succession within merely scientific (read: Marxist) paradigms.

12. Of course, nothingness is no aegis under which to denominate similarities and differences (it is no aegis at all), but from the perspective of the living, it ironically acquires the status of a democratic dimension—a fortuitous projection, perhaps, but a helpful one.

13. This is a view of the world that, in spite of its poverty, is somehow charitable and—for a poet who spent part of his childhood in the Siege of Leningrad—appropriately Russian.

14. In "A Part of Speech," Brodsky speaks of the river's origin in a tear. One needs simply to be reminded to roll the film backward (it can also be rolled forward). Brodsky's ability to play the accordion from evolution to devolution suggests that continuity belongs not to time (or not merely to time), but to imagination and ideas, that is, to words.

15. The view that the poet's words belong to language, rather than to the poet, was also a view held by Auden. It, of course, disturbs the notion of originality, and, obversely, notions of allusion, quotation, and plagiarism—varieties of appropriation of language much in evidence in Eliot. The point, in Brodsky's terminology, is one of "greater" and "lesser": The greater ("language is greater") cannot be appropriated in a personal manner.

16. Just as England and America "contain" the ocean/grave, this is perhaps another way of saying that the living "contain" the dead, and containment, as we learn from Sacks, assuages our fear by imposing a sense of control.

17. The "moral tone" that love establishes is often connected with a turning toward God, which would be here appropriately fitting for Eliot. In Brodsky's world, however, God's *sine qua non* is replaced by that of language (a fact that does not so much get rid of God as redistribute his aspects), which is another form of the Good. Iris Murdoch (following Wittgenstein rather than Plato) makes a similar, revived form of the Good the hinge of her attack on what she sees as the destructive, anti-artistic leveling of Derrida and his epigones.

18. Love also finds Brodsky entering the territory important to Keats's odes, particularly "Ode to Psyche," where love is an external facilitator for Spirit (Psyche), the Keatsian mind (in the best sense), or poetry (in the broadest sense). Love represents the invitation and the possibility of transcendence and communion with a whole-making otherness undoubtedly sharing similarities, but not as radical as death. As with so many of Brodsky's poems, there is the *post facto* feeling—often uncanny—of the presence of English and American antecedents, though these suggestions by no means hint that Brodsky had recourse to such (he made no acknowledgment of only selective acquaintanceship). Thus they are less a testimony to fortuitous eclecticism than to the similarity of generic unpackings in poetic thought.

4

Word within Word— and Minor Elegies

Because the poet's medium is the most common of artistic media, the pressures of commonality itself often excite retaliation in the way of exceptional self-regard. The poet either attempts to reconstitute some originary status or performs purifying rites to attenuate language's abuses on the tongues of the *hoi polloi*, to say nothing of the more conspicuous defilements of ideologues and moral persuaders of all stripes. That quests for origins and rites of purification are performed in full cognizance and in full view of their circularity is lost on few poets. This fact yields, in turn, two possible results: (1) The poet retreats into hierophant's tower; (2) the poet is ironized with respect to the circularity. If the first, the poet often goes along with the joke, realizing that all claims about language are claims *in* language. This poet leaves the claim for poetic uses on the hook of belief rather than of fact, which is to say on the sanctity of the metaphoric, rather than the literal. Alternatively, the priestly poet emerges in full sacerdotal glory, offering a cult of secret rectitude with respect to language. Brodsky the ironist is yet the last in a tradition of such sacerdotal poets and holds them—that is, Mandelstam, Blok, Tsvetaeva, and Akhmatova—in the line of his own descent, and in spite of the fact of a preponderantly ironic manner that tends to ironize them as well. To put the matter in a less florescent light, it would be hardly surprising to find one who reifies language, as Brodsky does, to have come out of a tradition that has made a place for cults and fetishes. However, we should not take his irony as constituting a rebuttal of special linguistic set-asides, like poetic cults. Indeed, it may provide just the demystifying defense the lack of which has often spelled grief to otherwise well-meaning companies and coteries.

Such cults—or fetishes—of the word—are phenomena that rear a logocentric head from time to time in Russian literary history.[1] Indeed, we can detect evidence of it in a number of the literary movements that have sought to preserve literature from (for example) the reductive effects of political coercion, both from the Left and the Right, both before and after the revolution. Nor is such cultishness reserved for literatures that have been informed by revolutionary struggle (e.g., Russian and French), as it is possible to trace antecedents to Dante's internecine intrigues, to say nothing of the archaic contexts of Greek and Roman literature. Nonetheless, the particular rise of the cult of the word in many of its Russian variants, from *fin de siècle* Symbolism to 1910's Acmeism (the Russian equivalent of Imagism), is perhaps best seen as a consequence of the Russian intellectual tendency to take on "extremes" of thought, as outlined by Isaiah Berlin.[2] Berlin is not the first, though doubtless he is the most eloquent, commentator to identify this strain, which runs through not only literature, but also philosophy (e.g., the irrationalist religious philosopher Lev Shestov, whom Brodsky has called the *"samii velikii stilist"*— "the greatest stylist" in Russian prose[3]), art (e.g., the Futurists), music (e.g., Scriabin), and so forth. No doubt the acceptance of intellectual and artistic extremity was aided by social ferment, but it is necessary to note that conspicuous ferment is by no means a strict requirement, as the cases of Poe and Mallarmé demonstrate. Two poets of the (largely) pre-Soviet era, whose works bear upon Brodsky's in this respect are the Acmeist-neoclassicist Osip Mandelstam and the Futurist Velemir Khlebnikov. Mandelstam had heroically sought to preserve Russian poetry from the linguistic deterioration of the Stalinist period and even in the depths of the 1930s could proffer it as a fit instrument for the re-membering of European culture; hence Ovid, Virgil, and Dante haunt his poems. Brodsky has observed in relation to Mandelstam: "A song is a form of linguistic disobedience, and its sound casts a doubt on a lot more than a concrete political system: it questions the entire existential order. And the number of its adversaries grows proportionally" (*L* 136). In an interview with Sven Birkerts (1982), he adds, "In a sense he gives you a feeling that Russian literature belongs to civilization—it is not parochial" (13). While Khlebnikov's nerdy whimsy and Futuristic flights bear little overt resemblance to Brodsky's saturation in European culture, nonetheless the similarities between their thought merit comparison. In taking the idea of time, especially in the elegy, and the idea of nothingness to what would seem their absurd but nonetheless generative conclusions, Brodsky follows Khlebnikov into the realm of Ideals which, for the latter is epitomized by the realm of numbers.[4] Khlebnikov understood that numbers, as signs, bested even words, and thus he preferred numbers, reasoning that "in the verbal thinking the basic condition of measurement is absent—the constancy of the unit to be measured" (Polukhina 162). Brodsky, too, often avails himself of the measure inherent of numeration: "In figures there is something which in words / does not exist, even shouting them" (quoted in Polukhina 162). And again: *"Numbers don't die. /* They only change order like / telephone *numbers. //* By the eternal pen their throng is grafted / on to speech, widens the mouth" (Polukhina 163). Khlebnikov's aesthetic and moral outlook can be summarized, as with so many of the avant-garde poets of the

1920s, as follows: "Coming to love signs like the square root of minus 1, which have rejected the past, we acquire freedom from things" (Khlebnikov quoted in Polukhina 166).[5] We might also add that such a rejection would have given one the appearance of not offending, if not exactly subscribing to, the future-gazing side of Russian philosophy.

In Brodsky's version of this cult, all is reducible to signs, most especially including people. Because it is coextensive with infinity, and so at the farthest end, with Spirit (a Spirit that is ironically, like the Christian irony, manifested first in inscription), it is appropriately "modified in the guts of the living." By providing a link between the material with the spiritual realms, the word is capable of transcending not only things but more importantly, as we have seen, time. It enables the human being to realize that there exists—and can further exist—something in life greater than ourselves, which "warms us without warming itself" (*O* 214). When we consider it from one perspective as material means, and from another, as an ideal whose embodiment is poetry, the word becomes the ultimate signifier of human life, including its numinous division that arrives with the onset of consciousness; that is, the word becomes the Word, even as it remains a thing.[6] In this sense, language is both self-identical and capable of identity with any member of the All. If the sea is someone's speech, we would be wise not to underrate the importance of language:

I see it with my naked eye that what I am concerned with, to be more precise, what I put on paper, is to a large extent prompted by language rather than by my attitude to reality and that kind of thing. In this sense it may be said that being determines consciousness—not my being but the being of language itself. (quoted in Polukhina 62)

Language, therefore, stands prior to us, as air does; it is not our creation. Brodsky typically extends the precedence of language over content in a way that is characteristic of another modern poet, Francis Ponge, by boosting the status of things, which, by contrast, shrinks the status of the ego.[7] Only in this way is the human "fit" for the transformation to words and, further, to an identification with words. Language also, we might say, inherently reflects the connection between matter and spirit, the product of that modification in the guts of the living, for it is language that both shows the way and provides the means to synthesize them.

Thus there is a further sense in which the separation between poem and poet is a necessary movement in the process. As we have seen, Brodsky downplays the role of people in this aesthetic: "I do not like people—their unwillingness to accept death; they cling to life like dead man's fingers on the hull of a sunken ship." And it is not, therefore, without a twinge of irony that the aesthetic model that best performs these feats is the elegy for a dead poet, which supervenes precisely at the point where the poet, honored, is buried, his words' umbilical severed. It is at this point that the elegist can announce the autonomy of language and its extension into the future—in his own accents. In other words, for the poet who makes a fetish of the word and reifies language, the dynamic engine pre-installed in elegy will make it the form of choice for tasks well beyond the merely conventional.

Of course, set against a background of widening empiricist dispositions, English poetic tradition provides little evidence that any such "cult" of the word per se was ever a salient feature.[8] Anyone can produce notable exceptions with respect to individual poets, and surely some would suggest that in retrospect the "outrides" to movements like romanticism amount, in retrospect, to little more than cultishness. It is tempting to suggest that the alien grafting of similarly "extreme" notions on English (or American soil) could not but put many readers out of joint. Indeed, Brodsky has been vulnerable on this point of importing an alien emphasis, as far as a number of English and American reviewers are concerned, as well as American poets, who have implied that failure to distinguish between homage and muscling-in—a distinction with obvious ethical overtones— has resulted in an obscure violation (see, again, the reviews of Robert Hass and Sam Hamill for two versions of this implied objection). Brodsky himself was aware of the difficulty that his crossbred linguistic project posed; though he insisted on the closest possible fidelity between Russian and English for his poems, he ruefully observed in connection with his own and with Russian poems generally that they tend to come to grief upon entry into the English language.[9] The disposition of the "word" thus reveals itself as a potential problem. It is worth noting that no such objection has been voiced by other European literati, for whom the flexibility or inflexibility of the English language, while it is a concern, is not an especially burning issue. The fact remains that for Brodsky the very idea of a world culture is situated on our understanding of the possible meanings of "word," and it therefore must follow that just as words interchange with things, they stand to interchange with each other—a fortiori between languages. On Brodsky's view, translation is not only possible, it is a demonstration in principle: The translated poem reveals the existence of the transcendent "word."

Brodsky's attempts to establish a tradition that points the needle west from Russia to England (and beyond to the United States) and to erect a bridge between two traditions of poetry (although, in terms of English, Latin, and particularly Italian and French literature, efforts to establish such bridges had already existed as far back as the Middle Ages) must, in another important sense, be seen in light of his temperamental classicism and pre-exile geographical and cultural constraints. Yet the mantle of cosmopolitanism and *weltschmerz* that he later acquired do not significantly alter this fact of mythical and metaphysical tradition-building. The path to any tradition leads by way of personnel, and the occasion for elegy always puts the poet on the scent. The task is to find a usable tradition (which may also be extra-poetic), and thus the poet quests after what amounts to a wobbling pivot, but a pivot all the same, knowing all the while that such is provisional, dependent always on the uses to which it is put. Moreover, it is provisional in another sense, for in order to locate this center, the poet must assume his or her own flight from the stylistic epicenters (to use, again, the familiar notion derived from Shklovsky, who was initially influential among the generation of writers preceding Brodsky), engaging in a mythopoesis that will advance the poet toward a new center. In other words, a poet of Brodsky's persuasion appropriates the advantages of defamiliarization and decenteredness in order to undertake a structure more to his own liking and to staff it with personnel of his own choosing.[10] In the absence of a relatively free exchange of literary influence, such as was the case for the early Brodsky, a tradition of the "poetic word" would serve the metonymic purpose of such a center, the later task being to find its useful representatives (read: think elegiacally). A correlative fact to the poet's writing so-called "professional elegies," such as the Eliot elegy, and one of the most obvious contrasts between this kind of elegy and traditional ones, is the fact that the object of mourning need not be someone with whom the elegist had a personal acquaintance. This fact can provide a service, for the dead poet (in this case) becomes, him- or herself, public property, just as his poems always were; the lack of direct ties takes the stress off mourning. Brodsky echoes Auden clearly in this, while attempting to radicalize the aesthetic process that makes it possible.

The "minor" elegies to be discussed in this chapter bridge the earlier stage of Brodsky's aesthetic thinking, which focuses on the question of poetic transcendence in the face of historical and natural depredation and the later, less monumental elegies, which consider whether "art" is powerful enough to last through what he calls "the whole blackout." Be that as it may, the notion of transcendence is inherently ill-at-ease with the notion of the monument—and not only in metaphorical terms. Brodsky's fascination with ruins clearly carries with it the suggestion of the imagination at work on the deconstruction of monuments; meanwhile, his desire to pursue the transcendent option at any length reveals not only a poet's curiosity with the tools of the trade but also figure in full flight from the body.

"ALMOST AN ELEGY"

The aesthetic that reduces people to the status of things can also reveal a kind of death-in-life (here it is worth recalling the poet's identification of boredom as "the most frequent feature of existence"). As far as Brodsky is concerned, this zomboid perspective is one of the main characteristics not only of existence as such but also more acutely, of existence as it registers itself directly to consciousness. Thus, the ordinary bloke (a category that includes himself and his myriad stand-ins) continually verges on opportunities for self-elegy: "Almost an Elegy," a poem of 1968, catches this note:

In days gone by I too have waited out
cold rains near columns off the Stock Exchange.
And I assumed that it was God's own gift.

It may be that I was not wrong in this.
I too was happy once.

                    (*SP* 93, trans. George Kline)

The title itself suggests that although no one is clinically dead, yet time, the process that enables elegy, remains always on call for the elegiac intention. Thus Brodsky suggests that the way we come to acquire face-recognition of the elegy is based analogically on death-in-life. The poem opens with a wistful, fairy-tale expression of "once-ness," which is our first encounter with a state of fallen condition of humanity: It is not that we have fallen away from God or perfection so much as the sense that we have fallen away from the coherent self, which then revives pickled as an object of memory and imagination. The figure of the human next to the columns of the Stock Exchange situates commonplace, shape-shifting reality in the form of a human (conditioned by sobering weather—"cold rains") next to an exemplum of the Ideal; here is weakness in puny contrast with strength.[11] The Stock Exchange is also meant to represent to any Leningrader the prerevolutinary era and thus itself qualifies as elegiac. But the "experience" of death-in-life is hardly sufficient, for opposing the speaker are the slow-chapped grind of time and the annoying *byt* (everydayness) of historical circumstance. This same historical circumstance sees to it that the "I" is shadowed by a "too," suggesting not only elegiac repetition but also an admonition against self-pity. Since death-in-life becomes an object of imagination by first installing itself as the matter of (self-) consciousness, it becomes all the more the wrong kind of self-consciousness for poetry, with the trite thematic introduction of romantic love, whose loss endows the human being with the most obsessive kind of self-consciousness. Thus, reality flaunts its tawdriness, and the poem tests this reality, inquiring which, between the actual human loss and the potential poetic gain, has the more power:[12]

At the main entranceway I lay in wait,
like Jacob at his ladder, for a lovely
girl running down the stairs.
                    But all of this
has gone, vanished.

Clearly, the struggle, recast in biblical terms, suggests that the hope of love is also the hope of attaining heaven, or rather with more poetic optimism, of marrying heaven and earth in the course of the poem's performative utterances. Poetry, then, will have contrived to offer a reward—or consolation, comparable to religion, for after loss, as this poem suggests, there are only words:

And gazing out the window, having written
the word "where," I don't add a question mark.
It is September now. An orchard stands
before me. Distant thunder stuffs my ears.

The speaker doesn't add a question mark because, logically speaking, "self-questioning" is not an instance of inquiry so much as a metaphor for the groundwork for change (since the self must already have contained—but not precisely engaged—both "question" and "answer" as components of an intellectual or emotional dynamic). Moreover, the image of the orchard is one of bringing-to-fruition, which, more abstractly, already speaks of something having been. Indeed, the orchard comes to fruition without its knowing so, and this orchard's growth is contrasted with the "growth" of the poet, who must, unlike nature, come to know it. The "distant thunder," of course, signals a mortality that we hear through Auden's ears.

> The ripened pears hang down in the thick leaves
> like signs of maleness. And my ears now let
> the roaring rain invade my drowsy mind—
> as skinflints let poor kin into their kitchens:
> a sound that's less than music, though it's more
> than noise.

By comparing the pears with "maleness" (a melancholy comparison, surely), the speaker draws attention to a question of potency. Ironically, pears acquire their use after picking; thus, in the comparison, potency is activated, not in sexual terms, but after the fact, that is, when sexual potency has likewise been removed as an issue. There is, too, the fact that the pears must be "picked," that is, consciously selected; otherwise, they drop and are also "lost." The realization of this paradox is like the rain, which is "now" let into the speaker's mind. It is not because he wants to let the rain in, but because he undertakes an obligation, in the sense that one is "obliged" to grow older and take in the full, cold, expropriating fact of death.

But it so happens that the lovely girl of the first stanza and the fantasy future associated with her represent a prospect that does not appear in the second stanza. Instead, the anticipation that she elicits, combined with the realization that she no longer will emerge from the male dream of a building, begins to crank the lever that will start the machinery that will result in writing, to words, which have here become a kind of completed work, even of consummation—and indeed marriage, by way of being transformed.[13] Thus, the girl represents an intimation of a kind of poetry, perhaps a prelude to future elegy—less than an elegiac poem now, but in any case, more than nothing. Interestingly, Brodsky uses a "less-than, more-than" rhetoric in the final lines, a device for assessing the extent of loss in the absence of absolute measures. If, then, we follow him in thinking of loss in terms of such a rough-and-ready measure (i.e., if we begin to concoct a rhetorical scale to register its impact), it would seem that we have broached matters pertaining to objectivity, by means of an objectively conceivable situation. To put the matter in simple terms, Brodsky arrives at the rhetoric of math—quantification, objectification: its measurements, ratios; its logic, tautological. The speaker confronts the realization that death-in-life, itself the kissing cousin of nothing, activates the need for a mutation into words ("it's with a zero that our woes commence"), but it does so, perforce, in the mode of irony, by "objectifying" (and then measuring) emotion. The pleasing *ex nihilo* tinkle is sure to resonate with the poet's pleasure at self-creation, but it is likewise hardly a sublime distance from here to self-elegy. There is also a lingering sensation that one is the dupe of wayward endeavors—a knight errant—a characterization likely to incline thematically minded readers to overlay a pathetic construction. Later, such instances and potential instances for pathos will be routinely dismissed or subjected to ironic reversal. While a perhaps an inevitable byproduct of his poetry—and a kernel intrinsic to elegies, pathos will not be allowed to decompress into an appeal.

"THE FUNERAL OF BOBÒ"

Before the Auden elegy of 1975, Brodsky experimented with the elegy as a species of satire. If the consequence of the elegy is to bring us to words, then the elegy itself is always, in some sense, a pretext, a prolegomenon to a later linguistic (and post-linguistic) condition. Because it aggressively seeks to transcend the occasions for mourning, it will find both wit and self-deprecation as suitable ammunition to undermine the traditional elegy's high solemnity. From the time of his exile Brodsky personally appropriated satire as the preferred instrument for this condition—substituting satiric wit for emotional effect, irreverence for reverence— in large part to maintain the emphasis on the presencing of words, although increasingly to this would be added an inclination to suppress the elegy's innate immodesty in tending to devolve more specifically upon the self than is desirable. "The Funeral of Bobò" is a case in point.

This 1972 "elegy" is a self-reflexive text that concerns transforming the attitude of one "Bobò,"[14] so obtuse to tyranny as to be immune, into the words of the poem and the attitude of the author, who wishes to evince and validate a similar attitude in the face of the State, which is identified both with imposing power and with nothingness, which are then collapsed into each other. Bobò is meanwhile identified with a butterfly (itself the subject of one of Brodsky's best poems):

> Bobò is dead, but don't take off your hat.
> No gesture we could make will help us bear it.
> Why mount a butterfly upon the spit
> of the Admiralty tower? We'd only tear it.
>
> On every side, no matter where you glance,
> are squares of windows. As for "What happened?"—well,
> open an empty can by way of answer,
> and say, "Just that, as near as one can tell."
>
> (PS 50, trans. Richard Wilbur)

The image of the evanescent, delicate, beautiful, inconsequential, "free," butterfly mounted on the Admiralty spire is absurdly disproportionate and violent. At least the Admiralty factors down the absurdity somewhat: The symbolic value, from Pushkin's *Bronze Horseman* onward, is positive. But the image bears more scrutiny. It is the (non-) mourners who would perform this display of their lepidoptery, but this is only to suggest perhaps that the anonymity—especially of a non-communitarian yet "social" variety—has seen fit to corner the market on all forms of expression, including mourning. Moreover, the dead must be mourned in terms of this anonymity, before which any individual, let alone a butterfly, is but a character in Gogol. Additionally, in Brodsky's myth-making, the butterfly, whose hold on life is so seemingly precarious, supplies the link between life and death; thus it directs our attention to the death-in-life perception necessary for an understanding of the elegy's inclination to expand to other linguistic and cultural regions. The role of the speaker in the poem is to object to the automatic response to death that the others implied in the "we" are conditioned to make. Still, the speaker admits, an almost superhuman feat is required even to reject such a meaningless rite of mourning: "We are too weak to follow you, and yet / to take a stand exceeds our energies." All the more, then, the extraordinary solution—of elegizing by means of a poem that states its refusal to elegize—seems called for, and not only a refusal, but a subversion of its principles through flippancy and anti-climax: "Bobò is dead. Something I might convey / slips from my grasp, as bath soap sometimes does." And since the dynamics of mourning employ their version of logic, Brodsky subverts this logic with something approaching tautology: "Today, within a dream, I seemed to lie / upon my bed. And there, in fact, I was." We should note in this context that if double-speak is the State's chief linguistic tool against its citizens, its refinement—equivocation—has traditionally been a tool in the poet's revenge against the State's sensibility-agent, the censor.

Meanwhile, what of Bobò? As she is identified with a butterfly, her response toward the conditions of her former existence have the same ambivalence (i.e., nonallegiance) as the butterfly's toward its conditions. An attitude of non-commitment and noncompliance, therefore, is the stance that merits the speaker's approbation, and it is the disappearance of one instance of this (rare) attitude that provides the occasion for the text, which is Bobò's only shroud. Bobò has already, in life, exemplified a diffidence that the poem will both praise in the inconsequential accents of Maurice Chevalier ("But neither Kiki nor Zaza, Bobò, / will ever take your place") and raise into a Lord Rochester-like archness that crumbles any remaining emotional struts:

Now Thursday. I believe in emptiness.
There, it's like hell, but shittier, I've heard.
And the new Dante, pregnant with his message,
bends to the empty page and writes a word.

In speaking of emptiness as an object of belief, the poet makes a thing of it, and in doing so, implies containment, yielding a triple meaning: emptiness contains the no-thing that Bobò becomes ("You are nothing; you are not; / or rather, you are a clot of emptiness."), as contrasted with the empty abstractions of State linguistic practice; emptiness is the ironic fruition that such a necessary attitude toward existence in the State has come to; emptiness is the starting point of the poet's labors ("it's with a zero," etc.). Apropos of emptiness, Polukhina notes, "Among the numerical metaphors, zero is a synonym for death; for time; for exile; for the underlying absurdity of existence" (164).

The "new Dante," we might suggest, is new because he must, so to speak, incorporate Beckett (whose Cartesian absurdities loom behind his long early madhouse dialogue, *Gorbunov and Gorchakov*,[15] and perhaps too for his later play, *Marbles*). The "empty page" to which this new Dante bends provides the starting point for the substitutive and absurdly transcendent word—absurd because, although it is a desired thing, it must come about at the expense of life. In Brodsky's by-now familiar assertion that art is a substitute for life, this implies that if life is to be accomplished, this substitution must take place elsewhere: for example, in words. Brodsky also works the traditional Russian inferiority complex toward the French by, as it were, "frenchifying" the characteristics of his object and holding her up as a cheerful paragon of the nihilism that the poem more seriously investigates. It is also a welcome *frisson* to the bulk of his elegies, suggesting a kind of youthful declaration of cultural independence as well as the existence of legions of such distracted youth as Bobò.

"1972"

The transformation of song to its riper manifestation as partner to silence is the subject of "1972," Brodsky's comically clinical and Swiftean, sometimes banal (he was 32) recitation of the effects of aging. Here, the power of song is tied ever more closely to the body's sense of biological self-authentication. While the poem proceeds as an inventory of debilities, it becomes increasingly transparent to itself, and the point is that this transparency is tied to its auditory equivalent, that is, to silence. In spite of the protracted bill-of-goods by which the speaker summarizes his situation with lovingly foul fascination, this is no Juvenalian satire, for the speaker rightly works the overripe grandeur of his own rhetoric into a problem, as a function of his increasingly vivid mortality. As always, birds figure in the Keatsian guise of emotionally unmediated songsters, but the poem begins, "Birds don't fly through my skylight nowadays." The gesture of denial, which starts in wide focus, quickly narrows to the speaker's person. The same cannot be said for the poet's metaphors ("As for my dental cave, its cavities / rival old Troy on a rainy day"), where the focus remains open, as if to suggest that all that pertains to Troy has replaced all that pertains to birds; that is, the metaphorical world has replaced the world of nature, or to put the same matter another way, the setting of history has replaced the "dreamwork of language" (to use Donald Davidson's apt term).

The year of the title is the year of Brodsky's exile to the West, and as if to naturalize the drama of that expulsion, the speaker refers to his new "strange place. The name hardly matters." Indeed, the name does matter, except within the poem's economy of somatically inspired erasures ("it's not a horizon I see but a minus sign / of my previous life"), alternating with the agglomeration of bits and snatches of language tailor-made for nothing, but serviceable to the consciousness faced with the need to spin out expressive cadenzas in the face of its own aging. Whereas the language is tailor-made for nothing, it can hardly be said that the same goes for nothingness, and this end-point, where the speaker finds himself flung forward while his commentary, as it were, stays behind, is "Frightening! That's it, exactly, frightening." Poetic advancement therefore stands in inverse relationship to the body's advancement, but the speaker's task is to seek a deeper accommodation with what is otherwise merely a droll truism.

The speaker's own access to this accommodation is difficult, however, for though "The man with a spade is now a fitting / sight," it is also "premature / to talk of the shroud." The ambivalence arrives as a natural result of one's treating language as a thing, which then stands, not as completion, but in a perhaps more daunting sense, in opposition to one. Exile then becomes both a pretext and a sign that one's attempt to submit to forms of bodily transformation in order to be consistent with the transformation into language involves a potential downside. It is all the same to language whether one's life takes this course or not. The decadent's ennui, which Brodsky's poems affect to such perfection, is, one might say, the poet's answer to the recognition that his poetry is not "his," after all. The lesson that the decadent thus carries about is a variant of that silence he fears and must in some way befriend, as one befriends one's shadow.

> Oddly
> enough, even a cuckoo's crooning in darkness
> moves me little—let life be vilified
> by her plangent notes, or affirmed and verified.
> Aging is growth of a new but a very fine
> hearing that only to silence hearkens.
>
> (PS 63, trans. Alan Myers with the author)

The cuckoo's "crooning in darkness" leaves the speaker unmoved because that darkness, like the cuckoo's song, lacks a metaphysical dimension. By contrast, the "hearing" that is perfected in silence (again, a Keatsian notion), can only, we might say, obtain existence in a metaphysical dimension, for "any erosion begins with willing." That is to say, only a subtle—ironic, knowing—complicity with darkness, silence, and insensibility can avoid the sense of failed transcendence that always await the post-Romantic bard:

> Lo! that's the point of my speech, I'm proud of making it:
> of the body's conversion into a naked thing,

object—against a vast, vacant, and
empty space.

Unfortunately, the poet does not follow out the implications of his "speech" to
the point where we can make out more than a hint of the deeper problem
involved in this complicity. Rather, he is content to allow the two movements
that make up the poem's rhetorical structure—body/words—to dance to their
own tune. Yet in the course of this unfolding dance, the rhetorical music of
apostrophe (in this case, corporeal address) has already consigned the body to
the status of a (mere) "thing," as if thereby preparing it already to adopt
something approximating the "crow's high vantage point"—that virtually
illimitable *jeté* that is imaginable for the poet only in terms of something like a
posthumous perspective. Moreover, the dream of a "dead" man is always a
dream about the living, and the living here—or what amounts to the same thing,
the will to live—is the will of words to stick at the very point where the body
is erased. The point of transition from body to words is one that, in spite of a
posthumous perspective, is not yet lived, only imagined. The imagination, for
its part straining to verisimilitude, only comes up with metaphors for
embodiment, whereas the body, for its part, can no longer contribute words
when words would count most. This is a matter of coming to grips with the
difference between knowledge that is prospective, of an inevitable nature, yet
unknowable, and knowledge of a retrospective nature that is useless because its
object is the past. But a different kind of knowledge is also in play, for knowing
that the point must and will be crossed opens the door to a certain pathos, which
we have already seen in Brodsky as constituting an unwelcome elegiac byproduct.

"ON THE DEATH OF ZHUKOV"

As we know, many poets in the 1930s and 1940s found themselves pimping
the Muse by scribbling paeans to Stalin, hoping to prevent the fate that befell
other fellows of their suspect craft. As many times as not, this ploy backfired,
and they earned not only banishment or death but the shame of having penned
flaccid, dishonest homilies. Brodsky's "On the Death of Zhukov" (1974)
considers the passing of the chief military hero of the Great Patriotic
War—World War II. It was Marshal Zhukov who not only orchestrated the
1812-style defeat of the Nazis and commanded the Soviet forces in the fall of
Berlin but also—and perhaps more importantly for Brodsky's purposes—
supervised the ignoble "repatriation" (i.e., imprisonment) of Soviet prisoners of
war. Brodsky's elegy is rife with equivocation, reflecting the general
ambivalence of the man who saved the Soviet Union from Hitler, only to
preserve it for Stalin. Nor was the official attitude toward Zhukov any less
ambivalent: fearing Zhukov's power, Stalin removed him in the 1950s, but
neglected to murder him, and Zhukov was resuscitated for a while under
Khrushchev, before the pendulum, once more, swung downward. Brodsky's

elegy, then, mimics in part the praise of the patriotic poems obligatory during World War II (Brodsky was born in 1940), thereby diminishing the iota of tribute to which the marshal is entitled, a tribute, moreover, he willingly consigns to oblivion. In the process, he produces not only an anti-elegy but also an anti-poem:

> Marshal! These words will be swallowed by Lethe,
> utterly lost, like your rough soldier's boots.
> Still, take this tribute, though it is little,
> to one who somehow—here I speak truth
> plain and aloud—has saved our embattled
> homeland. Drum, beat! And shriek out, bullfinch fife!

> (*PS* 78, trans. George Kline)

Gavril Derzhavin's elegy "Snegir" ("The Bullfinch"), an elegy for Field Marshal Suvorov (1729-1800), stands behind Brodsky's elegy for Zhukov and thus provides a lens through which to superimpose the image of the later hero onto that of the earlier. A figure of towering splendor who according to one foreign account was held to be "representative of the truths of war and of the military qualities of the Russian nation," Suvorov remains in Russian memory one of the "great captains" of national history, capable of heroic exploits unalloyed by the milder palliatives that may accompany national strife. The truths of war in question involve such things as the restoration of force, not diplomacy, as the signifying act of war, and of military qualities: a recklessness toward human life—including that of his soldiers. Thus Zhukov is seen as a kind of avatar of Suvorov, and though his mission is Soviet, his derivation is merely Scythian.

The Zhukov of the poem has thundered onto the stage of history, "making walls crumble, / [holding] a sword less sharp than his foe's." The irony is that this same history, lengthened, will see this Scythian warrior with his blunt sword not only as the savior of the homeland but also as the henchman of the Leader, saving life with death ("How much dark blood, soldier's blood, did he spill then / on alien fields?"), from death (Germans) for death (the Gulag). The accounts of these deeds must be squared with history before his real praise can be returned:

> Sleep! Russian history holds, as is fitting,
> space for the exploits of those who, though bold,
> marching triumphant through foreign cities,
> trembled in terror when they came home.

Because history is no friend of Roman pomposity, Zhukov is depicted as a fallen Pompey, his corpse proceeding through "[c]olumns of grandsons, stiff at attention." Throughout, his "brilliant maneuvers" that "set him with Hannibal" are contrasted with his last days ("like Belisarius banned and disgraced"), contrasts that reflect less a true estimation of Zhukov than the inconstant nature of Soviet political reputations. Brodsky's grudging praise must be gotten at, then, by viewing Zhukov as a Russian, not as a Soviet, combined with the realization that it was the Soviet military engine that ironically provided both the means and the occasion for his heroism. All the same, he is himself depicted as a killing machine, oblivious to the slaughter he directed; even in death, he is a figure of martial essence: "Splendid regalia deck out the corpse: / thundering Zhukov rolls toward death's mansion." Nor does the prospect of an afterlife relieve him of the burden of his deadly karma:

> As he lay dying, did he recall them—
> swathed in civilian white sheets at the end?
> He gives no answer. What will he tell them,
> meeting in hell? "We were fighting to win."

Thus, Brodsky calls into question the antithetical nature of epic heroism: The hero holds no other value than to conquer at any cost, and this means his greatness is founded first and foremost on the ability to kill. That this ability also includes sacrifice traditionally lends the hero an aura of pathos, and, given the twentieth century's breakthroughs in killing efficiency and mentality for sacrifice, Brodsky is naturally eager to prune the pathetic leaf of the marshal's laurels, exposing the theatrical—but authentically tragic—nature of Soviet national heroism and the populace's response, which is an equally tragic lip-service.

NOTES

1. Polukhina's admirable account of this cult is much fuller than the sketch I can give here.

2. See *Russian Thinkers* (1978).

3. In conversation with the author.

4. Such ideals, which establish cognitive certainty somewhere, are of course generally traced to Plato, particularly in his Pythagorean aspect. Despite his tacit affiliation with Khlebnikovian views, Brodsky was characteristically ambivalent in his approach to Universals. On the one hand, he could be seen as joining in the chorus of postmodernist thinkers who dismiss Universals as an illusion sustained by scientism. On the other hand, he was deeply suspicious of the kinds of erasures that often accompany "revisionist" historical thinking. After his arrival in the United States, he seemed to develop a personal rendition of "revisionism" with respect to the usefulness of ideals in verse; however, one suspects he would nonetheless have liked to leave a loophole for ideals generally.

5. Brodsky updates Khlebnikov by attempting to go this aestheticism one better: We acquire the freedom *of* things once we have put them on the same level as words.

6. We might distinguish this word from Eliot's Christian incarnate Word, by way of Stephen Spender: "The gap which divides 'the illusion of reality' created inside the poetry and the reality of philosophical truth outside it, at certain points at least, becomes closed. What is literally true outside the poetry is literally true inside it. The word coincides with the Word." (Spender, *T. S. Eliot*, 143).

7. Ponge's project was partly inspired by a desire to diminish anthropo-centrism, which had led, on his view, to the disaster of World War II (see his *Le Savon*, [1945]). A similar desire was evinced, in American poetry, in Muriel Rukeyser, in her response to the War in Vietnam (see "St. Roach," 539). The American precedent for this kind of reassigning of status goes back to Whitman (*Leaves of Grass*, 32: "I think I could turn and live with the animals . . . . they are so placid and self-contained . . .").

8. Unfortunately, the term "cult" is tinged with opprobrium in this century's self-identity as the Scientific Age, seeming to suggest various strains of disproved and irrelevant procedures for representing reality in the face of dominant empirical descriptions by recourse to the "supernatural." Nonetheless, many poets have seen the necessity for subscribing to dualistic accounts, leading Kathleen Raine to denominate this species as itself "The Tradition," which is the continuous record of poetic, "alchemical" interchange between word and thing, spirit and matter. But dualistic accounts do not in themselves add up to a "cult," nor has scholarship seen fit (*pace* the estimable Raine) to characterize or approve of such accounts with reference to the term.

9. This objection in no way vitiates the advantages of an elegiac tone that translation, as we have seen, necessarily entails. On the contrary, Brodsky's goal is therapeutic: his lament takes poetic aim at the terribly beset state of literary translation in order to raise the aesthetic level of individual translations of poems. Translations, as George Steiner reminds us, are hermeneutic models; thus poems in translation should not leave us with merely formal elegiac hauntings but reinvoke thematic content as well (*After Babel*, 296-413).

10. The process of which Shklovsky (and Derrida) speaks does not entail merely an alternative equipoise. In Brodsky's view, all such user-friendly notions, from "familiar" perceptions to vast conceptual "centers," would be provisional anyway—tactical, not strategic.

11. It is an image typical of meditations that contrast architecture with living beings; hence it has been an important source of imagery for twentieth century poets as diverse as Eliot, Seferis, and Jarrell, to say nothing of the "ruin-bibbers" (to use Larkin's phrase) of the English poetic tradition.

12. The question, of course, is Yeats' "what becomes a poet most, / a woman won or a woman lost?"

13. Other marriages made-in-poetry occur in the poems. For instance, in "A Song to No Music" (1970), we have, "[F]or Euclid sees / to it himself that spheres encourage / two corners, alias angles, with / a third one. And it makes a marriage" (trans. David Rigsbee with the author). Their wish-fulfillment aspect to the side, such marriages show that along with their legal counterparts they are performed courtesy of words.

14. With obvious echoes of Charles-Louis Philippe's *Bubu du Montparnasse* (1901), a novel about a French prostitute for the English translation of which, incidentally, Eliot wrote an introduction.

15. Although Beckett is the presiding spirit behind much of Brodsky's handling of the discourse of the mad, the model for *Gorbunov and Gorchakov* is Daniil Kharms.

5

The 1970s:
"The Butterfly"

Soon after his arrival in the United States, Brodsky wrote "The Butterfly," perhaps his most extravagant attempt to write a Metaphysical poem in the seventeenth-century mode. The Metaphysical poem is typically constructed around a "conceit," a comparison between unlike things (in this case, the speaker and a dead butterfly) sustained over the entire course of the poem, yielding new, even fantastic meanings. The Metaphysical treatment of the subject involves not merely the juxtaposition on which comparison is predicated but also an aggressive pursuit of the comparable features. Here the theme of pursuit is appropriate to the butterfly in a more direct sense. That the butterfly is dead only recasts the pursuit as a literary one and brings us to the speculative ground of elegy. In terms of scale, the miniature world of the butterfly is doubled by the speaker's embedding the miniature timespan of the butterfly within our own. The speaker's meditation leads him to magnify both of these dimensions and in the process to atomize himself into both demiurge—an old trope—and reader of creation. It is in the latter aspect that the speaker's rhetorical strategy revolves around a fortiori argumentation: what his speculations and readings of the butterfly uncover about it, endorses what, with greater application, will be the case for the speaker. The poem's organization involves a kind of stylistic magnification, too; the 14 twelve-line stanzas suggests an exploded sonnet, in which each of the traditional lines of a sonnet is unfolded into its own amplified discourse.

The poem begins with a query and indeed contains thirteen questions, suggesting that the ultimate line of a sonnet of questions will reveal an answer. The chief question of the elegy is the succinct *Why must we die?* The speaker ushers in the subject of mortality with the first line, "Should I say that you're dead?" Ordinarily, such a question, so asked, would seem to contain the possibility for a good deal of nonsense by way of reply, but the reader is being put on notice that this is just the sort of nonsense that the poem will engage. Other instances of this kind of nonsense will include the apostrophe as a means of inquiry (along with the logic and the ethics of such apostrophizing) and the problem of anthropomorphism. In addition, Brodsky will propose the "nonsensical" notion that we might recalibrate the line dividing death and life—or at the least, section death into such thin component parts that its seemingly monolithic totality may be challenged, and thus it may be claimed that some components belong not to death after all but to life, still.

Despite its ephemeral nature, the butterfly has proved to be a durable insect for poets, for beginning its journey as a wormlike being, incarnated within the very grossness of materiality, it shape-shifts its way to winged, angelic evanescence. It moves by way of wholesale, intuitive transformation, defying the determinisms that beset consciousness and, by extension, appearing to overcome the springs of mortality. Brodsky applies his customary irony in the form of a gently sardonic apostrophe, since the butterfly in this poem is dead. Its death engenders the further irony—amounting to astonishment—that such an abrupt end could still coincide with its tiny magnificence. So the question would seem to be the extent to which time or its lack helps or fools us into distinguishing between magnificence and insignificance. Could they somehow be the same, and if so, what would the mechanism be for collapsing each into the other? For indeed, it seems as if all is a matter of perspective: The butterfly's insignificance to the human could certainly be made to stand for the human's insignificance with respect to something higher, whether God or language (or, again, the two collapsed). As we have seen, it is characteristic of Brodsky to pose questions in such a way that he imagines or appropriates higher perspectives than the biological eye allows. Some might argue that this strategy amounts to the vain illusion that one has climbed out the top of one's head, but this argument fails to take into account imagination's propriety. To be sure, we witness equivalent, logically impossible assertions with nearly every major poet—indeed with the fact of poetry itself, which seeks to reconfigure time in its own image and so quibble with Terminus.

Nevertheless, there is a headiness to Brodsky's inquisition, as if he can't quite believe the good luck of his own exemplary subject. The speaker questions his ability to "comprehend" such a brief life, since for humans life involves the unpacking and encountering of things within the context of time (i.e., experience and memory), something that for the butterfly only happens minus time's entailments for human consciousness. With the initial question, we are already deep within Metaphysical territory, for it will be the job of the speaker to persist in his interrogation, an interrogation that will function as a kind of lens to magnify the butterfly to human proportions. The deepening of his scrutiny, the questions that lead to other questions, will buoy and carry the conceit. Unlike seventeenth century Metaphysical poems, which tend to mechanize affect, Brodsky's poems often magnify pathos beyond, as it were, the point of affect, ironically not underscoring but disarming feeling by means of extreme perspective. Indeed, one of the recurring tropes in his poems involves magnification with the aid of tears, which then provide a convex lens.[1] In this case, for the speaker to comprehend "the words 'you've lived'," the butterfly's life span and finally time itself, must be re-scaled to the comprehensible, if predictable, human. Of course, in doing so, the speaker must reconfigure the butterfly's otherness into a thisness, but such a procedure describes precisely how the conceit will work and the comparisons be drawn. What the butterfly loses in otherness, however, it gains, for better or worse, in human terms, and this familiarizing reflects upon the speaker, who provides the context:

> There's much that's sad in
>   the joke God played.
> I scarcely comprehend
> the words "you've lived"; the date of
>   your birth and when you faded
>   in my cupped hand
> are one, and not two dates.
>   Thus calculated,
>   your term is, simply stated,
>   less than a day.

> (*PS* 68, trans. George Kline)

The butterfly is indeed a creature of extreme transitoriness to the human observer, but the speaker's inability to comprehend the naturalness of such a brief span suggests that it is, not the butterfly, but we who are trapped behind the bars of understanding because of our own perception of time. The reversal by which the butterfly's life is unfolded will constitute a way to imagine that the trap is not real, before its human reality asserts itself once more. To understand what a day is, is to weaken its lethal claim on our lives, which it makes with diurnal regularity. A day can be literally fatal to the butterfly, and thus the speaker must adjust the scales to compare them. Only then can he proceed in questioning the butterfly and anticipate answers for himself:

> Whenever days stand stark
>   against white borders,
> since they possess no bodies
>   they leave no mark.
> They are like you. That is,
> each butterfly's small plumage
> is one day's shrunken image.

The butterfly, which speaks to our mortality through the intersection of its miniature integrity (of containment) and evanescence (paradoxically, both flight and death), is therefore subject to figure-ground reversals: against the oblivious white of days it disappears. It should be further pointed out that the "shrunken image" belongs as well to John Donne, where it is both a jest of "conception" and more profoundly a trope of momentary universal containment that signals a triumph over loss. Brodsky also updates Keats's nightingale in posing the problem of articulation in terms of signs rather than sounds:

> Since I'm a mumbling heap
>   of words, not pigments,
> how could your hues be figments
>   of my conceit?

How indeed? except that they mirror human fragments: "There are, on your small wings, / black spots and splashes— / like eyes, birds, girls, eyelashes." In order to construe the elements in this series as parallel, we must understand the egregious term—birds—as being that which is of interest to the poet, not to his grammar. Obviously, wings were not meant to draw birds. The speaker avoids the mere looking-glass affirmations implicit in this small inventory: "But of what things / are you the airy norm?" Once the "norm" is established for this Ariel-like figure, it will be possible to meditate, just as with Ariel himself, upon the predicament of what it means to be threatened with the trap of matter and what freedom would be like, once matter is no longer a trap. Since Brodsky frequently puts time and space at each other's service, it will be possible for us to ask, too, what freedom would be like once there is no trap of time. But first we are led to consider the issue of frozen time—in the form of art—and history as time gone wrong:

> As for your *nature mortes*:
>   do they show dishes
> of fruits and flowers, or fishes
>   displayed on boards?

>   V
> Perhaps a landscape smokes
>   among your ashes,
> and with thick reading glasses
>   I'll scan its slopes—
> its beaches, dancers, nymphs.
>   Is it as bright as
> the day, or dark as night is?

As a metonym for art, the *nature morte* seems itself merely decorative when juxtaposed to the blighted landscapes of modern history. Rather more like a soothsayer or Talmudic scholar than a lepidopterist, the speaker becomes a questing reader, interpreting the signs that history has scrawled across its landscape, instead of indulging in appreciations of the kind of art that Brodsky, no less than his mentor Auden, would find merely vulgar. Under the lepidopterist's eye, the butterfly becomes a placeholder for an historical existence,

and so the speaker pronounces it "a protean creature." The poet's delegation of
protean qualities to the normally insignificant and unexampled (as opposed to
metamorphic) being brings with it the question of design, and the speaker
doesn't shrink from asking the question:

> Who was the jeweler,
>   brow uncontracted,
> who from our world extracted
>   your miniature—
> a world where madness brings
>   us low, and lower,
> where we are things, while you are
>   the thought of things?

The creator of protean miniatures is less Jehovah than Fabergé, which is to
say it is the filigree artist who overlays the butterfly with qualities that will
never, for the butterfly, have been understood as such, though they are no less
qualities for that. In other words, we are our own deities, though only in the
magnification of miniatures can our projected creations be said to have
significance. Nor can we enjoy our momentary divinity unaware of both the lack
of godlike purpose we possess and the lack of *ex nihilo* creation ("a world where
madness brings / us low."). For everyone who is not a tyrant, the problem of
creation takes care of itself since tyranny means in a sense believing, without
benefit of irony, in the work of one's own hands. But the question of creation,
set in the context of a death-haunted world, is the question of elegy proper:

> To God's least creature
> is given voice for speech, or
>   for song—a sign
>   that it has found a way
>   to bind together,
> and stretch life's limits, whether
>   an hour or day.

Yet as the speaker says, "You lack even this: / the means to utter / a word."
If we accept the proposition that a querying of the butterfly will provide human
meaning, and moreover, that this meaning will take on an especial resonance for
the elegiac poet, then the poem would seem to stall at the point where words
become impossible. But the speaker moves antithetically to consider the burden
of words and thus shifts a metaphysical argument onto ethical grounds ("Sound's
burden, too, is grievous"). Words involve their users in responsibilities because
words are the result of choices—not sounds in a void, but sounds in the context
of a human community. Because the butterfly avoids this "curse," it also avoids
many of the human fears that come as a consequence of setting words forth into
time, though clearly, had the butterfly—or, for that matter, any creature—lived

long enough (though what constitutes "enough" is never clear), it would have succumbed to the advent, for good or ill, of "words." This is not to say that the butterfly has no use for communication, either—even dead, its form communes with the speaker. But words constitute a special case of communication. We might say that it is the case in which communication discovers a need for ethics. A butterfly has no such need, but here the poet makes a distinction between purpose and value, for to possess the latter is not to presuppose the former. Like all creatures—indeed, like all that language presents to the imagination—the notion "butterfly" results as a construction of meanings specific to the occasions at which it is encountered. In its life, the butterfly

> spin[s], motelike, ascending
> above this bed of flowers,
> beyond the prison space
> where past and future
> combine to break, or batter,
> our lives.

For the poet, the comparison is irresistible: "The sliding pen . . . has no sense of the purpose / of any line," and yet the result will be some "amalgam / of heresy and wisdom." The poet then "trusts" his hand that is full of "silent speech"; that is, speech that is in the process of appearing on the page, as is the image of the butterfly, which in spite of the heightening of its figure, is moving into nothingness. What is being described is a transaction between being and nothingness and silence and speech, the upshot of which is that though the poet "reaps no pollen, / [he] eases hearts." Unlike the butterfly, which formerly reaped pollen but now only contributes (as it perishes) its image to ease hearts, the easing is not a "goal," in the sense that

> [n]o butterfly collector
> can trap light or detect where
> the darkness dwells.

There are a host of reasons why easing cannot be a goal, but one point stands out: Easing is a process—one cannot be fully "eased," except in death (and it requires no Hamlet to speculate on the terrors of that). In any case, to reflect on such complete easefulness would cause the process of easing to reverse itself. Hence the purpose of writing cannot be to do such things as make monuments (which only grow into ruins, the ironic savoring of which is a favorite poetic pastime that spreads far beyond Brodsky's connoisseurship). Moreover, words are things and eventually share the destiny of things: "Men's memories may wither, / grown thin, and fall / like hair." The past and its contents are not "shrinking files / backstretched"; the poet imagines in their place "huge clouds, circling together, / of butterflies." A past imagined this way has no more theme than the vectors of these insects, but for this reason they are "better," in that they are "akin / to nothingness," which is to say, if we substitute the idea of memory for the clouds of butterflies, they persist paradoxically "longer" by virtue of this kinship than by any attempts to make them into monuments would do—including presumably this poem. The finale of the poem brings the poet up and out of these airy meditations:

> Yet while you live you offer
>   a frail and shifting buffer
>   dividing it from me.

"It" refers to nothingness (or more precisely, no-thingness), and the ending is appropriate, for on the one hand it transforms closure into a matter of turning. On the other, it commemorates the real life of the butterfly and confers on it a value different than have chiefly concerned the poem: It brings to mind the simple fact that living beings are themselves shields against oblivion. Thus Brodsky has accomplished the unusual feat of constructing an anti-monumental monument. He has used the butterfly as an emblem for the poem of which it is the description and abjured use by confronting the existential fact of a fellow creature, whose brevity, to say nothing of its other biological deficits, could be said to open on the phenomenal world of muteness, suffering, and death, as opposed to the noumenal world of the poet's thoughts. It also answers the poem's driving question, "Why must we die?" by tactically concluding on a note of dualism, the very fact of which—separation—is merely another name for human self-division.

NOTE

1. An image surely derived from his reading of Donne, but the sentimentality of the lachrymose is as absent from Brodsky as it is from Donne.

6

Fair Idol of the Lawn:
Twenty Sonnets to Mary Queen of Scots

The figure of Mary Queen of Scots seems an unlikely subject for a Soviet exile, but as Brodsky remarks, one could make the same point about Schiller, or indeed about screen actress Zarah Leander, whose 1948 portrayal of Mary first brought the figure of Mary to the poet's attention.[1] The twenty 1974 sonnets "to" Mary constitute one of Brodsky's most sustained meditations on the relationship between history and art. By extension, the meditation is situated upon the divide between the no-longer and elegy. Although "The Great Elegy for John Donne" also addresses this divide, its concern surrounds traditional issues for the elegy, such as the poem's task of carrying the image of the dead across temporal barriers. *Twenty Sonnets to Mary Queen of Scots* (another expressive instance of the poet's Anglophilia) modifies that earlier concern by focusing precisely on this question of "image," for in the many images of Mary that have come down to us, it is no longer clear what is being designated by this term, nor whether carrying an image without a clear feel for what the image involves is yet a thing that elegy ought to try. As a result, this elegy is compounded with love poetry (the poem is a love letter to, among other things, the existence of beauty in the world and to the serendipity of a world that can compensate, in some meaningful measure, for the evils of history). It is, we might note, Brodsky's closest brush with another unseen beloved figure, Shakespeare.

The derivative mechanisms of the elegiac form dictate that it must exist in the future relative to that which it elegizes. This is so even, paradoxically, in the case of self-elegy (of which this sequence is also a case in point), since self-elegy presupposes a later knowledge that passes judgment on an earlier constitution of selfhood. Indeed, one of the tricks of elegy is to seem to be in possession of some piece of (legitimating) knowledge that it knows by virtue of being in the future, and the poet, lest he become merely a kind of reformer in hindsight, must conceal as well as manage a predisposition toward this knowledge because, otherwise, all legitimation and authority belongs to the past, the claims of the dead on the present becoming preponderant. The "problem" of the past, as enunciated by Bate (1972), Bloom (1973), and others, is too familiar for me to rehearse, except to remark that Brodsky throws light on the problem by here treating the past as History and the future (this present) as Art. To put this another way, the past's authority is queried by virtue of its contingency (i.e., by the fact that it has passed) as that authority is reinscribed by a superior authority, which is the knowledge of transformations surveyed synoptically: Mary become legend, a statue, a screen figure—all manifestations of "Mary Queen of Scots" that the actual Mary could not have foreseen and of which she "herself" is but a pretext for these virtual transformations. Mary is herself "improved" by these transformations—even as the moniker "Mary" succumbs to the cerements of quotation marks.

Brodsky further distinguishes between History and Art as between fact and beauty.[2] Mary's beauty was, for purposes of Brodsky's poem, one source of her troubles. By the same token, art is inspired to carry beauty across time, transmuting it into Beauty. This means shaking it free of those remnants of history that are associated with mortality. But the fact of the matter is that all such "remnants" are associated with mortality—the entire context in which something was held to be beautiful, and thus the future's "rescue," far from restoring beauty to its proper context, must completely refigure that beauty into its artistic equivalence, which means recontextualizing it—which means, in turn, attempting to render it ahistorical. The mission of art, in short, is to overthrow the dictatorship of history and thus bring its own superior authority to bear against mortality, or as Milton memorably put, with reference to his own august self, "Attir'd with Stars, we shall for ever sit / Triumphing over Death, and Chance, and Thee, O Time." Of course, were it not for this same history and mortality, art would have no *raison d'etre*. Therefore, art owes death a debt, even as it seeks to remove its sting. It is perhaps in recognition of this debt that Brodsky chooses a subject whose life is so intimately associated with the fact of a specific death.

The opening sonnet in this sequence presents an abstract of these considerations, stressing first of all the burden of art's transformative obligations:

What generation of what clan in tartan
could have foreseen you'd step down from the screen
a statue, and bring life to city gardens.

(*U* 18, trans. Peter France and the author)

One of the things that the future knows here is that all those hungry generations, irrespective of clan, are dead, and that in the blindness of their death, which is also her blindness, Mary's image carries forward through time into the present (ironically, itself represented at the time of composition, by the past), first as a screen image, second as a statue that "bring[s] life." By insuring her "place" in history,[3] they have also opened a place for her in art—a consequence they could also not have foreseen. The series opens with direct address ("Mary, I call them pigs, not Picts, those Scots"), and the poet will later associate the intimacy that this insult implies with the figure of a lost love, ultimately conflating one with the other on the ground that resurrection through art (as opposed to memory) de-individuates and decontextualizes historical beings. Strolling through the Luxembourg Gardens, the poet looks about "with the dull eyes of a decrepit ram," himself a jaded figure of excess, and spots the statue of Mary. Quoting a nineteenth-century love song, the poet declares that what follows commemorates the meeting in the spirit that "all the dead past now lives anew in my cold heart." Such a commemoration will come about by way of the poet's "old gun full of classic grape- / shot, squandering what remains of Russian speech." In other words, Mary will have her "reign" in this "life" that the poet will create. While she is historically older than the poet, she is also older at the time of her death than is he at the time of composition (he was 34; she, 45). More importantly, while she is given the posthumous extension of her life on earth (at first made possible by history), he is likewise self-characterized as after-the-fact in terms of language (i.e., as an exile). The poet explains that his interest in Mary derives from an encounter with her image when he was a child, following World War II. During this period of renewed Stalinist—which is to say historical—persecution, Russians are depicted as flocking to movie palaces ("not an empty seat, I bet"), where the "plushy womb" of the theater offers momentary escape from horrors that are only lightly alluded to ("but something calls us, at the hour of gloom, / back to the Spartacus"). The images of cinema resurrect not only Mary but also in a sense the Russian populace, who "come to the surface from the pictures." The whole apparatus of death and, more importantly, resurrection becomes crucial to the meaning of his poem in another way as well, for after the second sonnet recalling the movies, the poem takes a bow toward the supreme bard of these subjects, namely, Dante, for whom resurrection provided the definitive retort to death—at the opening of the third sonnet. If Zarah Leander had been a childhood inspiration both for basic escapism and for inspiring fantasies of a greater something within the future's scope, the poet strolling through the Luxembourg, having "traveled half [his] earthly road," encounters the second transformation of Mary by way of this statue, situated among "the petrified gray curls / of thinkers and of scribblers." Unlike the character Dante, the poet is not morally "lost" but "in decline." Here we may observe that the two sides of Mary's significance—her youth and her death in history (or History) correspond to two sides of the poet's significance, namely his "decline" and his after-the-factness in terms of language (or Art). The poet establishes these as equivalencies by noting characteristically, "Whatever you may say, the axman's blade / equates the ditches to the lofty reaches" (II). Shortly after the speaker has introduced the subject of his lost love, he remarks, "I cut across another line-whose edge / is sharper than a knife

blade: the horizon." The equivalence of blade to horizon is not as far-fetched
as it may at first seem; in particular, both separate previous life from any future
manifestations, and thus both "level" desire (their own or that of others),
resetting its trajectory to zero. The poem hints that such "leveling" is subject to
"containment" because containment is more desirable than desire itself: Mary's
transformation into legend and a statue is more important than her historical
importance; the poet's "decline," combined with "what remains of Russian
speech," is more important than the past love ("we . . . did not make a happy
pair"), although the admission is grudging: the speaking voice of "sort of grateful."

The Mary addressed is very much the one least likely to coincide with the
historical Mary, that is, with the historical figure, not the iconic abstraction. Yet
ironically it is the historical person that fascinates ("A crown, alas, gets dented,
bent, / or lost between the sheets with some odd gent"), her very singularity in
some way enforcing her claim to historical attention. At the same time, by
pressing this claim, "Mary" cannot additionally lay claim to the traditional two-
bodies conception of monarchy to save her skin.[4] As for the Scottish lords,
"They wouldn't relent / in pressing their quite sordid argument" (i.e., that Mary
was a "slut"). From the unstartling observation that Mary couldn't have it two
ways, Brodsky draws a further, more compelling moral:

> That's why a monarchy comes to an end
> while a republic may be permanent
> (see ancient pillars or a monument).

A monarchy, deriving from a person, is only as permanent as the person,
despite the monarch's second, "spiritual" body. A republic, meanwhile, can
secure something of permanence by virtue of its decentralized, de-personalized
structure. What is interesting in the further assertion hidden within, namely, that
a republic is as permanent as a "republic of letters," which derives something
of its power and authority precisely from the fact that it is a decentralized
exchange, not the dispenser of ukases. Such a republic also promises, while it
does not guarantee, an afterlife of exchange—again, not of personalities, but of
selfhoods transformed through the medium of exchange, language.

The poet, siding with his republic, can number himself among her lovers; yet
in his superior historical and politically "superior" position, he knows that it
would reveal a lack of art's clarifying privilege to dismiss her on the basis of
her mere self. Unfortunately, the same clarifying principle also renders an image
only approximate to history (a fact that explains how he can briefly conflate
Mary with his own lost love), omitting detail and nuance to the new (and
literally so) figure, except as the imagination can offer those things that are
"likely" equivalencies:

> May God send you in others—not a chance!
> He, capable of many things at once,

won't—citing Parmenides—reinspire
the bloodstream fire, the bone-crushing creeps,
which melt the lead in fillings with desire
to touch—"your hips," I must delete—your lips.

To put the matter in its simplest terms, God will not send you, but merely
"you." Ought we then to decry the loss of the original? Brodsky does not seem
to think so. In the first place, even our notions of what constitutes originality are
colored by the present: In mourning our loss, we are mourning something
presently conceived. In this sense, we stand with respect to Milton's Satan in
wondering, in our self-consolation, "[W]hat God after better worse would
build?" If we accept any of the problem areas of selfhood attaching to original
persons, by what standard are we to assert that the original was ipso facto
superior at all? The poet must make the case in writing the poem that it is this
second life of Mary, unstable and devoid of both continuity and coherence
compared with the original life, that has the power to overcome the rule of
chance, not in spite of its likely equivalence, but because such disparate artistic
manifestations (as film, statuary, poem) declare (and will always be in a position
to declare) their allegiance to the republic of Art. In addition, because these
manifestations are determined by artists, they are subject to no other, less
generous determinisms (whereas "your Scots barons neither couldn't nor can't /
think otherwise" [i.e., again, than that Mary is a "slut"]). The ability to
reconfigure that which determinedly routes creation from the realm of chance
to that of the imagination figures as the poet's "love" for his subject (cf. the
relationship of "the Infinite toward the finite"). Consequently, he subjects other,
more traditional expressions of this motivating force to ironic treatment ("And
my love of you [it seems, / its only pain] still stabs me through the brain").

Nevertheless, the original person qua person exerts a certain nostalgic pull for
the poet with reference to her lost being, irrespective of these sophisticated
arguments for her afterlife as art and argument. The tenderness by which this
is expressed entails a sonnet of its own ("Paris is still the same. The Place des
Vosges / is still, as once it was [don't worry], square" [VII]), as if to be guided
through images of geographical continuity would in some sense console the spirit
of the absent being, whose own absence is primarily a matter of fundamental
discontinuity. The poet would not, therefore, address the embarrassment of
death (especially the death of an illustrious personage); rather, he would change
the subject in such a way that the unfolding of subsequent history and its
continuity (by way of his travel narrative) would strive to ameliorate Mary's
discontinuous destiny by situating her life (and especially her life as a
significance-bearing thing) within a trajectory, as it were, that is still in effect.

Faced with the reality that history enforces—in other words, that Mary and the
poet did not and cannot meet, the poet invites and "muses" on that very futile
thought, transforming it from impossibility to the second creation, which
constitutes the artist's special claim over History. Specifically and economically,

he muses on the irony that only a few words—another few of which do unite them in the poem—might have united them in life ("I muse how just a few words would have been / enough for us, if fate had crossed our paths"). Indeed, the self-begotten literary artist is the first to know, if not the first to admit, that "fate" has crossed their paths.[5] The point is—one point at any rate—that a poet would keenly know that even history is as much invention and interpretation as "fact." Indeed, this would be acutely the case for a Russian poet, for whom history is not an obvious chronological sequence of events, but a narrative, subject to many vicissitudes having nothing to do with empirical reality, subject, for example, to erasure and "resuscitation." It is precisely analogous to the cases of humans and words that provide its content, with the difference that history's narrative unfolds at the expense of lives; art, by contrast, largely does not. In this musing, the poet declares, "[W]e'd have met our fate / together, severed by a wooden blade." As it is, they have met a common fate, if the blade and horizon are, as he insists, equivalent.

Yet Brodsky is careful to distinguish between the narrative machinery that goes into artistic creation and the theatrics that often accompany commonplace history. Immediately following his imagined encounter with Mary, he contrasts their common fate with what we know of Mary's downfall. The contrast, as we might imagine, is invidious: History's causes certainly do not seem convincing to futurity:

A plain. Alarum. Enter two. The clash
of battle. "Who are you?" "And you yourself?"
"Us? we are Protestants, we don't observe . . ."
"And we are Catholics." "Ah, bloody Papists!" Crash!
And then the corpses lie about like trash,
the endless din of crows' first-come-first-served.
And later—winter, sleigh rides through the slush.
A shawl from Persia. "Persia! "Ah! what nerve!"
"A land where peacocks make their peahens blush."
"Yet even there a queen at night can shush
her shah." "Or mate him, playing chess up north
in a cute Hollywood-style modest castle." Slash:
a plain again. Time: midnight. Enter two.
And drown you with their wolfish who-is-who.

As this masquerade alternates between a tender-although-silly bit of répartée and confusing Shakespearean recognitions-in-the-dark, history—no longer merely theatrical, but with real consequences, intrudes upon Mary in the form of her arrest. Ironically, while history turns from farce to tragedy, it must be remembered that it is because of the role Mary plays in history that the poet first comes to know of her. That he is aware of the temptations introduced by the exchanges between history and art amounts to one of the chief perplexities of the poem and helps to account for what appear to be occasional pauses for circumspection, when the purpose of the poem is implicitly called into question:

An autumn evening. All but with the Muse.
Alas, not heeding the relentless lyre.
That's nothing new. On evenings such as these
you'd play for kicks even the army choir.

This complaint against not writing, which of course is writing, merely seconds the maddening interchangeability of the poet's imaginative and factual alternatives. Forward momentum seems on hold, for after all, what would be a point to the realization that fact and fancy can easily change places? Or can they? Their exchange seems to leave the artist poised on the edge of an infinite regress, except that coincidence, which hangs about art like a charm, must contend with commonplace history, which shuts down (and commences) with the definitive—death: "The door may creak: death, having failed to knock, / will stand before you in her moth-holed frock." Despite the poverty of death's image, it comes bearing significance, and the world, including history, becomes habitable because of it.

Brodsky takes up the thread of this thought in XI in quite literal fashion, returning to the ram-sheep imagery, appropriate to Scotland and appropriated in the opening sonnet by the poet himself:

A clang of shears, a momentary chill.
Fate, envying the sheepfolk for their wool,
knocks off our crowns and bridal wreaths at will—
quite indiscriminately. And the heads as well.

While in this image death is likened to sheep-shearing, the image is complex and, like death, threatens to undo its creation, for if the poet is the old ram offstage, then he is, as it were, responsible for engendering the very sheep that Fate has "sheared." Death is a strange connector, and yet one of the things this elegiac sequence seeks to do is to investigate the ways in which death is a supreme fact of connection (even as it is the supreme fact of closure and disconnection), linking tenses with a particular urgency, for which temporality alone cannot provide a universal justification. Hence what we might think of as the problem of connections becomes an important component in the second half of the series (and indeed in the second part of this sonnet). After Fate has been in charge of severing our heads, the poet makes an important aside:

The brain's like a skyscraper in whose still
tight shell each cell ignores another cell.
That's how the twins in distant Siam swill
their booze: one does it, but they both feel swell.
No one has shouted to you, "Watch out!"
Nor did you, Mary, know enough to shout,
"I am alone."

Forster makes a famous adjuration "only connect," but here we see some of the consequences of attempted connections that fail. Or to put the matter another way: We are connected, but it doesn't follow from that that we necessarily conjoin in some larger sense. Mary's inability to articulate her isolation and her friends' failure to register their caution are of a piece with the situation of drunken Siamese twins, whose predicament is both humorous and grotesque. One can hold truly to his denial, although the hangover he will feel the next day indicts him well enough. With this peculiar comparison still in sight, Brodsky takes up anew the distinction he would like to make between History and Art—at last promoted to the true subjects of this elegy by their capitals. The former is associated with the material ("Well, bodies"), and the latter, "a body that has lost its head," in both senses: That is, a body whose death, as in the case of Mary, is reduced to a theme by the manner of its coming to pass versus someone who has taken leave of his senses. Schiller is the poet's case in point:

> Take Schiller, say. Young Friedrich served his notice
> to History. You never dreamt, I bet,
> a Jerry'd get, out of the blue, so hot as
> to resurrect the ancient case, long dead.
> It's not his business to discuss your quotas:
> who had you or who didn't in a bed.

> But then, perhaps, like every other Hans,
> our Fritz was simply frightened of the ax.
> And secondly, dear Mary, let me stress:
> there's nothing, barring Art, sublunar creatures
> can use to comprehend your gorgeous features.
> Leave history to Good Queen Bess.

Perhaps Schiller's motive in writing his tragedy was the defense hinted at; a more important motive for Brodsky is the one Schiller underscores: the wish to convey to sublunary creatures a means of contriving, against forgetfulness, access to absent beauty. To borrow Allen Grossman's compelling vocabulary, Art (poetry), unlike History, carries the image—"your gorgeous features"— across time and across the barrier of death (1972: 6-10).[6]

A ram, as place-holder for the poet, eavesdrops on the scene of history surrounding Mary's execution. Here, "Glencorns, Douglases, *et al*." exchange commonplace and banal remarks, revealing their narrowness (and unreliability as narrative figures) by bringing their remarks to a close on a seemingly trivial detail: the shift Mary wore to her execution ("You could see through it. Shameless!"). The figure of the ram shaking out "his ringlets, alias fleece" and "inhaling lazily the scent of hay" is reminiscent of the figures in Auden's "Musée des Beaux Arts," who are oblivious to the fact that the most momentous event in history (in Auden's case, a human's fall from the sky) is occurring even as they, humans and animal, go about their ordinary pursuits. At least in Brodsky's poem, the exchanges of the clansmen show that though they appreciate the magnitude of the event (weren't they implicated in it?), they little know the extent of its significance (e.g., for a poem like this, in which they "reappear"). And though the ram shakes out his ringlets with the same nonchalance with which the torturer's horse scratches its behind on a tree in Auden's poem, we see too that whereas Mary has already lost her head, the ram is in danger of losing nothing but his fleece (in sonnet XVII Mary also loses her red wig). In short, the ram survives, and the poet whose place he holds likewise survives the executioner's horizon-blade: Only Mary does not survive (rather, she is both overcome by "Good Queen Bess" and transformed). Perhaps the talismanic "fleece" hints at what survives too, to be woven into a new, "warming" fabric, a customary elegiac trope we have already seen in "The Great Elegy for John Donne."

The transformation of fleece into a metonymic object (its "alias") serves to remind us, if reminder were needed, that every successful elegy pivots on the desire for metamorphosis. Whether the desire exhibits itself through the procedures that and others have outlined, or whether, as with Brodsky, it is made to exteriorize and underscore its features in an attempt to justify elegy on other grounds than that of the affective, the question remains the same: not simply "why must we die?" but given that we do, what procedures does art possess to increase continuity in the face of individual (to use again Sacks's phrase) radical discontinuity? In the present case, we can see quite vividly Brodsky's penchant for descanting on matters of Art (which some find memorably epigrammatic, others intrusive—a matter of telling rather than showing) and, too, the correlative habit of lightly spicing these pronouncements with—to hedge them?—self-effacing (and not always successful) irony and humor:

> Love is more powerful than separation, but
> the latter is more lasting. Plus, the greater
> the statue, the more palpably it ain't her.

Despite the sometimes dubious tonal results (exacerbated in English), we can perceive the wish to come back to the pivotal question to which this sequence gives rise:

> Her voice, her wits, smell, finally, are cut
> off. While one blames it on the granite that
> you won't kick up your legs to starry heights, for
> so many fingers' failure to decipher
> your petticoats, one has to punish but
>
> one's awkward self. It's not 'cause so much blood
> and so much water—equally blue—
> have flowed under the bridge, but since the brass
> bed screams at night under a lonely lad,
> I'd have erected, too, a stone for you,
> but I would cut it in transparent glass.

To put the matter simply, her beauty, which art carries across time, is art's invention, for the greatness of art must manifest itself in and through the greatness of its own form, not the greatness (or accuracy) of representation. Art therefore must also generate its own standards, and paradoxically one of these standards has traditionally been held to be mimetic fidelity (albeit not without much suspicion and disturbance in the back rows). Although Brodsky would erect a monument "in transparent glass," he is nonetheless aware that her "voice, her wits, smell," the "gorgeous features," the "beauty of [her] face" can only be re-presented by means of illusion (an illusion that smuggles in a touting of potency in the Englishing)—the master-illusion of transparency, for example, which is mimesis proper. The poet's transparent glass of course would window nothing, as do a fortiori his words. The illusion that obtains in this demystified setting is similar to the desire of Brodsky's early hero, Eliot, to construct an "objective correlative," that is, a verisimilitude of some prior *Gestalt*—an omelet, the taste of which returns us to the uncracked egg. There is no attempt at portraiture here, only a seemingly accidental accumulation of details from the life of the poet and from common history, added to which is a desire to exercise some control over time in order to make fantasy scenarios possible. Brodsky's audacity at theorizing (and to some degree burlesquing) the conventions of elegy by means of *obiter dicta* should equally embolden us to consider that such an elegiac attempt is predicated on a very troubled notion of self. There is a Mary who, as a person known to history, can be an object of cognition, but there is no historical Mary who can be an object of appreciation, and yet it is appreciation, not knowing, that the poet desires to offer in the form of a significance-bearing creature. Thus, both the Mary who is to be appreciated and the significance to be drawn from the appreciation are less inferences than constructions. Perhaps Brodsky intends this doubling to be understood as the expression of a "greater making" in his poiesis. If so, there are other implications that need to be considered. For example, such a poiesis suggests that Brodsky's revisionary traditionalism, far from reflecting a mere artistic conservatism, is a means of extending the reach of his own poem-making, since the poems in whatever tradition—Russian, English, American—offer a web of prior constructions and more or less agreed-upon conventions, offering at once an enrichment and a shorthand. Moreover, this is to take them as completely artifactual, offering in turn a possible explanation for the particular brand of jaded irony and irreverence with which he paints his artistic predecessors (e.g., Schiller). Certainly there is no supervening sense of a "burden" of the past, in any of the senses given by recent critics.

If "the beauty of your face" was "something to which they, in those old days, / could see no end," we are left in the same sonnet (XVI) with the superior fact that

> few among those things that once could cause
> a tear of pleasure have survived the passage
> into the humus shade, how little stays.

The truism of these lines belies the colloquial force of the phrase, "could see no end." Not only did they see an end, the same end swallowed them up, so they must here be equally fantasized in order to believe the truism, as well as to offer it as worthy of our belief. Even so, although the poet invents both the believers and the belief, that is no sufficient reason to conclude on a note of final disbelief; on the contrary, "The thing that dragged from . . . mouths a shout / of wonderment . . . still impels / my own two lips." It is desire for justification, which is to say, desire to "for ever sit / . . . over Death, and Chance, and . . . Time," that impels the poet to song before a judge he has created and who yet pronounces the Iron Law of the poet's own contingency.

The beauty of Mary's face is stripped, by death, of the matrices out of which an aesthetic response could arise. We "know" it was beautiful not in the sense that we know what beauty is now, but beautiful in the context of place, nature, time, legend, and the like—things whose very nature is contingency itself. Art, such as the transparent monument the poet would build, stands without this context. For its beauty to be redeemed, it must suffer transformation into something singular and different, although this something must also imply equivalence, which means something that also establishes an equivalent context undaunted by the imperative of the mimetic (by what standard would we, the future, know if it were?). In short, it must be imagined. After all, "between us lie / eternity and ocean." Mary, in the Luxembourg Gardens, becomes a "fair idol on the lawn." The final elegiac twist pushes us toward the possibility of unspecified belief, just as Zarah Leander, although acting out a remote tragedy, somehow filled the Russian moviegoers with belief in something better than their historical reality. But while the exact nature of the belief may be unspecified, we have come a long way from a process of escalating fictions, based on slight coincidence. The poet's success will be rooted in his making it difficult for us to imagine what there is in life that does not conform to this formula. Things that begin in coincidence and contingency have a habit, over time, of seeming the products of destiny. Destiny is thus an illusion, whether pleasing or grimly deterministic, belonging to a certain kind of retrospect. Indeed, as we have seen, it is "love [that] is more powerful than separation," and this is so, if we are careful to read "love" as the will to replace mimetic desire with something imagined and transformed, something that will have the *force* of history, which is to say, of contingency. Instead of seeking to justify his art by repeating that this is what History killed her for, his art says, in effect, that to the extent that History would kill, it (his art) would give life for (i.e., in exchange for) an equivalent beauty, a hymn for the "fair idol." The point is that one's life is no more justified in History than redeemed in Art: both are as much manifestations of imagination as empirical conditions. In terms of chronology, one is merely superseded, and while both History and Art attempt to give the lie to this feature of temporality, only art offers a way out by redistributing the energy of fate that is chronology's spirit.

NOTES

1. The Swedish screen actress Zarah Leander became a German film star in the 1930s. She reached the peak of her career during World War II, when her films were

widely distributed throughout occupied Europe. Her first screen appearance was in the Swedish *The Dante Mystery* (1930).

2. The problem for Brodsky is the familiar one that has confronted anyone pondering the divide between fact and value, namely, how does one derive the latter from the former? Like any poet, he wishes to narrow the divide in the name of his art, but in this series of poems he is confronted with the spectacle of undesirable value arising from misunderstanding in fact.

3. In one sense, the *Twenty Sonnets* queries the notion of a "place" in history, since history is not constructed through a medium capable of conferring *places*. In ironic reversal, the best place becomes the constant shifting to many places—that is, no place. The sequence makes another pass at Auden's "the poems of the dead are modified in the guts of the living."

4. In Kantorowicz's classic account, the "spiritual" body escapes corruption.

5. John Berryman performs a similar musing with regard to an historical figure in his long poem *Homage to Mistress Bradstreet* (1956).

6. Grossman's account often achieves its force by literalizing modern readers' metaphorically inclined presuppositions.

7

And Sailed into Muttony Clouds: "Lullaby of Cape Cod"

The crepuscular decadence that becomes a stylistic feature of post-exile Brodsky reaches a sort of epitome in "Lullaby of Cape Cod," although "epitome" here suggests a kind of dispositional zenith, whereas what I would like to suggest is that this epitome is manifested in what Gerard Manley Hopkins called a "Parnassian style." Hopkins' phrase describes a mode of writing that proceeds not by force of inspiration but, as it were, under the kindly auspices of prior inspirations, of which it, in turn, becomes a kind of metaphor.[1] The "Parnassian style" is distinguished stylistically by its recourse to a rhetorical *savoir faire*, where the burden of poetical achievement is shifted onto what words can do, rather than onto poetic intentionality. The feeling, therefore, is of something less, a kind of high-level poetic patter that substitutes rhetorical embrace, an all-round *sprezzatura* for directed intensity and not just the *mot juste*. It is the memoiristic chatter of the retired secret agent in his smoking jacket. The feeling of less, which is one of deprivation, is most acute in the presence of verbal abundance—an irony with cognates in the discourse of many literary folk and constitutes already something like "the literary," as distinct from the spiritual, the military, the businesslike, or any other language game that doesn't make rhetorical self-consciousness a prerequisite for admission. The feeling of deprivation prompts us to ask what there is that one is deprived of: In other words, is the posture sustainable in the thick of issues surrounding poetry, for example? The intellectual specializing in belatedness, as Harold Bloom (1973), for one, characterizes the condition, is likely to link the deprivation to the fact that the self, once touted for its recourse to wholeness—political, social, spiritual, now shrinks to a tiny, agglomerative subject position, menaced by everything, master of little. Poets, who frequently distinguish themselves from intellectuals by their willingness to transgress reigning agendas, in this case resonate with the intellectual self-shrinkage but differ in that the demotion does not relieve them from the responsibility of setting tasks in the name of language. Hence the Parnassian arises to deal with humbler, if more existential burdens, which, themselves being "less," compared to no-longer-available spiritual ones, are treated with an experienced yawn, if not with mild contempt. Nevertheless, it frequently manages to be a good-natured yawn, post-disillusioned and capable of hints of fellow-feeling (as distinct from campy bonhomie, which it decidedly is not).

In English poetry, this posture has already received its most familiar embodiment in the—at once—tweedy and Episcopal Auden. The insouciant bagginess to which such a style succumbs is a version of its theme: accommodation and humility. Here there stands, behind Brodsky and Auden, Eliot's "humility is endless." If humility is endless, its endlessness is at least the match for the outrageous infinity depicted in such a poem as Brodsky's "Lullaby of Cape Cod," which is not a cloud-speckled azure but, as one would expect by now, a hectic, thing-packed infinity. Not only thing-packed, but packed with trivial, wearing, or absurd things. Humility also serves didactic purposes (Brodsky: "Lessons in humility are always timely") because in its talent for inverting the designs of the human will, irony teaches, in a manner approaching Emerson, that the part of infinity to which we have access is itself edged with an ironic fringe in the sense that it is not great but humble, not truly "infinite." One sees in much of Brodsky's post-exile work the poet coming to grips with outrage,[2] but instead of letting this stance get the best of him, he seeks to overcome it by demonstrating the exfoliating motives for his humility ("The smell / of old body is even clearer now / than body's outline"), and the ultimate sign of humility is the willingness to cooperate not only with one's own demise, but also with the demise in the force of one's words. This seemingly melancholy assessment will follow Brodsky's poems through the next decade, culminating in the "Roman Elegies" (1985), and it will become his project to accommodate himself to the conclusion that words, too, are mortal. If language is tantamount to God, does this mean that God is destined to be—once more—dead? To what extent is the poet (again) guilty? Might he reinvent his language? What new, salubrious entailments follow from that?

The "Lullaby of Cape Cod" moves through eleven numbered sections during which the onset of night, underscored as a sign of temporality, swells into a kind of negative panorama, requiring the human light to monitor and illumine nighttime things, which would therefore seem to be things of importance. But of course human lighting, in too cleverly imitating daylight, illumines indiscriminately ("like the fiery warning at Belshazzar's Feast, / the inscription *Coca-Cola* hums in red"). It provides no hedge against triteness or triviality. Sound, touch, and smell take a more prominent role in administering sensory data, but they discover the same thing: that while night may rearrange the priority of thoughts, the lesser senses at night are no closer to "the important things of life" than was sight. Behind these stand abstract thoughts and dreams, a kind of second-tier of comprehension and speculation. Tied to sleep, dreams, especially, become linked metaphorically, both to poetry and, perforce, to the body's accommodation to the flow and erosion of time.[3] This is a significant realization, and its effect is to pitch us toward a naturalized conception of poetry, granting no exception to it in the general sweep of things toward oblivion, for the materiality of words stands prior to their transcendent possibilities. Words thus have the status of things and acquire the destiny of things—perhaps even more significantly than other, ordinary articles such as objects, since their (i.e., objects') effects are designed to "ripple outward" in series of consequences that play out their physical aspects and so become subject to laws of entropy and inertia. Words, at least, put up a fresh resistance; yet they too stand in danger of succumbing.

Meanwhile, in a way reminiscent of Brodsky's frequent—in the 1970s— reluctance to distinguish between the imperial offerings of the United States and those of the Soviet Union, the national and ideological distinctions so lovingly worn by partisans and patriots are collapsed under the single sign: "Empire." As a concept, that of Empire has the advantage over historical specificity in representing a *Geist*, rather than a position. It is, to be sure, the consciousness carried about by the victim, but this is important in its own right, for in the imperial scheme, all but Caesar are by definition subjects, quite literally subjected to forces and varieties of unfreedom no democratic lip-service can reach. Yet even in their sometimes unknowing subjection, the Empire's subjects acquire a kind of historically determined, ad hoc lifeboat democracy:

I always used to regard "infinity"
as the art of splitting a liter into three
equal components with a couple of friends
without a drop left over.

        (*PS* 107, trans. Anthony Hecht)

Which is not to say that this is not in any way desirable as an arrangement of persons, but it is to point out the contingent nature of the arrangement; "democracy," we might say, is as close to contingent an arrangement of persons as can assemble and remain this side of the chaotic. The poem opens with an acknowledgment of this contingency, preparing, procedurally, for the kind of poem that will eventually evolve. It is a poem that feels chaos at its back, to be sure,[4] the blurring of empires separated by nothing more than the sea:

The eastern tip of the Empire dives into night;
cicadas fall silent over some empty lawn;
on classic pediments inscriptions dim from the sight
as a finial cross darkens and then is gone
like the nearly empty bottle on the table.
From the empty street's patrol car a refrain
of Ray Charles' keyboard tinkles away like rain.

Here we have a collocation of random objects, but what is chiefly suggested is the contextual scope of the poem: politics ("Empire"), nature ("cicadas"), history ("classic pediments"), religion ("a finial cross"), personal loss ("the nearly empty bottle"), and American culture ("Ray Charles' keyboard"). If one index of a poem's ambition is the amount of reality it tries to bite off, "Lullaby of Cape Cod" manages to reveal a Rabelaisian appetite. At the same time, it should be noted that the poem also contains some of Brodsky's most conspicuously failed-risk lines. Even the hand of Anthony Hecht seems to falter with such a line as "Sleep as those only do who have gone pee-pee." Lapses like this have not escaped the notice of commentators who renewed their scrutiny of Brodsky's work following the awarding of the Nobel Prize. Indeed, although there is little that can justify the publication of uninspired gaffs, it should be said in the case of Brodsky that all such lapses (and this is not to minimize the nodding poet's effect on readers) occur in the context of larger operative schema, and their damage is to some extent mitigated by the undeniably powerful armature of imaginative construction. At any rate, the poet with a taste for high-wire metaphorics is naturally apt to hold the ground in contempt.

The poem opens in swelling darkness and heat (the leitmotif of "stifling" summer heat should be understood in the view of a native Russian's perhaps more ruthless interpretation of "stifling"), and its speaker superimposes these conditions on his own, a superimposition that must find a way to change to accommodation:

> It's stifling. The eye's guided by a blinking stop light
> in its journey to the whiskey across the room
> on the nightstand. The heart stops dead for a moment, but its dull boom
> goes on, and the blood, on pilgrimage gone forth,
> comes back to a crossroad.

The difference between the heart's weariness and its "pilgrimage" is similar to the difference between thoroughly exile-informed and assimilationist conceptions of the self: The one is inertial, the other made virtuous of necessity. Thus, the speaker admits, "It's strange to think of surviving, but that's what happened." The strangeness is a skeptical one in the sense that it hints at a phantasmagoric unbalance, for which the sine qua non of getting to one's feet takes on a highly metaphorical significance, with or without the lure of whiskey. Indeed, much of Brodsky's poetry could be seen as an attempt to get past something like skepticism in favor of something like pragmatic alternatives. In this, he has truly arrived in America, for as I argue elsewhere,[5] this movement between two philosophical orientations depicts a highway linking two destinations in much twentieth century American poetry. But American poets have bounced on Whitman's and Emerson's knee, and their progress up from skepticism is a result of a contemplative rebound from the century's horrors in favor of still-imagined, if attenuated, paradises. Russian poets cannot be said to have been imbued with the same education, though their experience with horrors needs no commentary here.[6]

The coming darkness the speaker witnesses in the beginning of the poem is a metaphorical feature that takes a swipe not only at age but also at Americanism. Night arrives first across the Soviet Empire but eventually blankets the American Empire too; thus every experience of darkness is like every other in that it is naturally total. The speaker's survival with respect to his own situation is linked to his adaptability, and this quality is linked, in turn, to the image of amphibious creatures, adept on land no less than in the ocean:

> Crawling to a vacant beach from the vast wet
> of ocean, a crab digs into sand laced with sea lather
> and sleeps.

This kind of creature is, in turn, linked to various fish that negotiate the oceanic vastness separating the two imperial realms. As a metaphor for the survivor and exile, fish "stitch" together the countries whose differences are, as with so much else, as much a matter of geography as of cultures.[7]

Insofar as the poem can, and should, be read as a poetic gloss on the downward career, disorganization, and threat of apathy of the exile (i.e., the personal equivalent of chaos), we begin to supply a narrative to the details behind the impressionism the poem creates. At the same time, it is the impression that is foregounded, not the reality—the implication being that the interpretive sense of the events of 1972 belongs to their respective poetic figures of speech, thus assigning importance not to the events, vivid as they were, but to words whose playfulness distracts and ultimately vacuums up any other interpretation (such as a political one) that would presume to explain the poet's fate:

> And then with the brine
> of sea-water sharpness filling, flooding the mouth,
> I crossed the line
>
> and sailed into muttony clouds.

These figures of the amphibious and the gregarious could be seen as the scope of transformational figures for the solitary speaker, providing him with a means to fulfill the desire for a language-based perspective on events that otherwise confound explanation, as in this otherwise deflationary passage in which an Isaiah-like flat earth is seen to be more graspable from on high:

> I beheld new heavens. I beheld the earth made new. It lay
> turning to dust, as flat things always do.

The joke, of course, is that the perspective from on high is an illusion: The figure of the all-seeing and prophetic poet is here not so foregounded as to erase the significance of the fact that the speaker achieves his new perspective only momentarily, in the mode of a desire, rather than an actuality, and at the expense of his being sent away.[8] Many such self-subversive figures crop up in the course of the poem and provide it, *ceteris paribus*, with a note of pathos; without these preemptive ironies, it is tempting to become dismissive of the rhetorical extravagances so abundantly on show here. But pathos is not a criterion for poetry, and it is more useful, therefore, to see it as a way of attenuating the rhetorical tensions the poem sets up. Only such a speaker whose figures both declare and fold back upon themselves can assume the prophetic template of "I beheld new heavens. I beheld the earth made new" and keep something of its archaic pathos along with its keener sense of absurdity. In a word, the speaker can keep his necessary ambivalence intact. As an avowed classicist, Brodsky was hardly one to shy away from implied assertions of poetic priority, which Allen Grossman (1992) associates with "the authority of prior life" (220), and indeed the fact of prior life, in the sense of "another" life, itself provides the contrastive engine for this poem.[9] Although Grossman is referring to prior life in the sense of authority derived archaically, his point nevertheless glosses Brodsky's stance, for the poet's ambivalence extends to (1) his dramatization of past life as past—beyond all power of actual redemption (with all its personal implications) and (2) the comedic and perspectivalist advantages he can derive from the use of a "posthumous" voice, a parody of authority that usefully deflects the objection that he is implicitly trying to claim the real thing. To be beyond redemption as well as authoritative is to require the aid of the Parnassian catwalk, lest we submit the poem to logic's scrutiny and so miss the point by perceiving the contradiction too clearly.

Rather than combining with a poetic past (which requires, as medium, a cultural stream more or less within stable banks—not, indeed, an ocean), here it is solitude that tutors the speaker: "Being itself the essence of all things, / solitude teaches essentials." Solitude is the condition that puts him in tune with things; and though it also suggests a certain repudiation of the human community, it more properly suggests the exile's desuetude—that reality principle that requests his assent, even as it exacts his compliance by means of his own inertia:

> Meanwhile, my arm, off in the dark somewhere,
> goes wooden in sympathetic brotherhood
> with the chair's listless arm of oaken wood.

The listless solitude of the person stands in ambivalent relation, even at night, with what we might call the environmental effects of his new venue, where "a strengthless breeze [that] rustles the tattered, creased / news of the world" is itself compared with a "weary, buzzing ventilator [that] mills / the U.S.A.'s hot air with metal gills" (note, too, the ease with which the poet, writing from a Massachusetts setting, nods to that state's most famous poet's—Robert Lowell's—most famous indictment of home, "For the Union Dead" through the use of "gills," even as he foreshadows the cod's appearance). It is as though the speaker's projections of weariness can somehow calm the milling and buzzing that take place in every sector of the (American) Empire.

What is perhaps a peculiar feature of the poem is the way in which the poet speaks of a "change" of empires, as though one had changed shoes. Certainly this is a key devaluation of a milestone event, and we can see in it the desire for some sort of continuation of purpose, despite the actual rupture and the dramatic weariness. The purpose moves all the more toward the center of this poem when we consider its ploys and verbal posturing as a species of anxiety directed toward the meaninglessness of not writing. There are plenty of reasons why, given the circumstances, one shouldn't write (the meaninglessness of forced exile, for one thing); the point is to become inoculated against these reasons, and that inoculation can take place, in Brodsky's view, only within the dimensional ambivalence of language. The kinds of lines and sentences, therefore, that are directed against the threatened meaninglessness of personal events have the quality of transpiring for their own sakes. They are not, nor is the poem, a record of the poet's exile, though the fact of exile is its incidental occasion. The poetic lines and grammatical sentences of the poem create their own occasion, which has both an aesthetic and ethical advantage over the force of personal circumstance. In this sense, all poems are desiderata, existing in the "ought" not the "is." They are not so much records as wishes, although they are not, for that reason, tied to didacticism,[10] for didacticism makes a general claim with respect to persons, and the only claim made by the poem here, for instance, is for himself. In this limited but legitimate sense, the poet can proceed to assert, "The change of Empires is intimately tied / to the hum of words." This sense of poetry's mission becomes all the more important in view of the reversals of fortune, when, indeed, the mirror's reflection discloses "that the part in your hair / that you meticulously placed on the left side / mysteriously shows up on the right." By the same token, poetry is also a kind of sight, contriving its own perspectives with a freedom that common reality, on its own terms, and deployed among obstacles, disallows. Even in its most playful manifestations, poetry inheres in a purposiveness that is greater than either "the poleaxe's sinister cold" or bombers ranging to their "precisely chosen, carefully targeted spot." That purposiveness is not a "realization" taking place as the poem unfolds, but one of which the poet is already and always reminded:

> the giddy pen
> points out resemblances, for after all
>
> the device in your hand is the same old pen and ink
> as before.

The pen's continuity (as well as the pen itself) represents the continuity of its purpose; their aims are coextensive. This coextension, a rhyming of purpose(es),[11] represents also a fortiori the only freedom the poet has any right to expect from his circumstances. Yet it is a peculiar, negative freedom, for its existence reposes both in potentiality—that is, as an inference arising from the subject matter—and in the form under review, namely, the "Lullaby of Cape Cod." The poem itself, it should be added, is directed outward from its nest of weary curlicues into the midst of our actualities—like bombers and poleaxes. It is a matter of "freedom" because it is a matter of potential—it has not yet committed itself to the actual, since it is not clear what the commitment would involve. All the same, as words spin their wheels, clocks spin theirs.

There is, then, a new sense here, which shelves in and qualifies the classicist, in which writing partakes of the same quiddity as things and has no legitimate claim upon any prior ordering authority. But at the same time, in an undertow, the metaphoric of the poem works in the opposite direction, for the poet links writing to the amphibious connecting figures of crab, cod, and herring. In this New England setting, the speaker muses upon origins and concludes that the towns seem "cast ashore." Their monuments to founders are made ironic by the lack of monuments to cod and herring:

> . . . a continent that was first discovered
> by herring and by cod. But neither cod
>
> nor herring have had any noble statues raised
> in their honor, even though the memorial date
> could be comfortably omitted.

A memorial date would be to place them in human time, of course. Yet in some less constricted sense, time is of central concern in the poem, for it is in the doubleness of its dimensions (human and supra-human) that sanctions the ambivalences we have earlier noted:

> Because watches keep ticking, pain washes away
> with the years. If time picks up the knack
> of panacea, it's because time can't abide
> being rushed, or finally turns insomniac.
> And walking or swimming, the dreams of one hemisphere (heads)
> swarm with the nightmares, the dark, sinister play
> of its opposite (tails), its double, its underside.

It is, so to speak, from the perspective of this deep time that Brodsky finds the desirable fifth angle, and though this is not the same as the synoptic view *sub specie aeternitatis*, it enables the poet to speak to questions of human perception from a new perspective. For instance, by reversing the emphasis on human time, he also reverses the emphasis needed to pose our familiar conceptions of the tragic:

> In genuine tragedy
> it's not the fine hero that finally dies, it seems,
> but, from constant wear and tear, night after night,
> the old stage set itself, giving way at the seams.

The "constant wear and tear" of time on itself reintroduces a metaphor we have encountered earlier, namely, a "theater of poetry." Looking through the proscenium thus created, the poet finds a kind of trans-historical basis for the wear and tear he observes in his new location and in himself. At the same time, the time of the cod and herring is out of phase with customary human attempts to establish a dimension of pathos, since that is reserved for time confined to meaningful moments ("it's too late by now to say goodbye / and expect from time and space any reply").[12] Nonetheless, time fulfills the request for a basis upon which to write, albeit on its own terms:

> I write these words out blindly, the scrivening hand
> attempting to outstrip
> by a second the "How come?"
> that at any moment might escape the lip,
> the same lip of the writer.

There are multiple levels at work here, for the "How come?" emerges in terse, colloquial accents allied to the poems's occasion—the exile of the poet. Yet it is obviously not a request for information, though it is in part that. The poet worries that this question, accumulating metaphysical credentials, might "sail away into night, there to expand / by geometrical progress." Only "the scrivening hand" prevents this progression ad infinitum by stitching consciousness together (or something not quite to be dignified by the term, viz., "I write in a sort of trance"), rather as fish weave the element that separates the continental empires. In this way, the poet finds himself metaphorically on the side, as it were, of the cod and herring, for whom no monuments are erected.

One of the by-now familiar features of this poem is its thematic and tonal oscillation between the poet's wish to stanch the flow of "How comes?" and the danger of aligning oneself too closely to the cod and herring (again, one is reminded of Lowell's "dark downward and vegetating kingdom / of the fish and reptile"). For the latter always conceals the *horror vacui* that lurks behind any such attempt at negative transcendence. On the one hand, the speaker is content to settle for the status of a thing and suffer a thing's destiny; on the other, he wishes to incorporate, if not himself, at least his poetry in a larger scheme. This is familiar territory for post-Romantic poetry, indeed, and Brodsky would no doubt reject this characterization as immodest, perhaps by suggesting that attempts at transcendence are not uppermost in the classicist's scheme of things.[13] However, it is just this tension between accommodation and nostalgia (and between life *en-soi* and "transcendence" proper) that generates the energies of the poem, as well as its truly pathetic note, typically disguised in terms of geometry:

> Only a corner cordoned off and laced
> by dusty cobwebs may properly be called
> right-angled; only after the musketry of applause
> and bravos does the actor rise from the dead;

> only when the fulcrum is solidly placed
> can a person lift, by Archimedian laws,
> the weight of this world. And only that body whose weight
> is balanced at right angles to the floor
> can manage to walk about and navigate.

The extravagance and convergence of these images upon the mundane image of the body barely conceals the fear, not of exile, but of vertigo, and behind them is the deeper anxiety ("When . . . and *only* when") that there may be finally no spots where the Archimedean fulcrum can be "solidly placed." Thus, while the speaker moves out along both branches of his ambivalence, neither puts him on the ground: He is constantly after the fact for one; before the fact of the other. Both branches, as it were, end in air:

> Thought loses its defined
> edges, and the frazzled mind
> goes soft in its soup-bone skull. No one is here
> to set the proper focus of your eyes.

Survival, without losing its troubling aspects, becomes more or less naturalized within the context of exile, just as writing becomes more or less naturalized within the context of mutually exclusive alternatives. That "no one is here" modifies the poet's earlier "solitude teaches essentials," for it suggests that the act of writing is an act of faith (for a poet already experienced in *auto da fé*), suitably discounted to take into consideration the fact that it seems to side with some absent interlocutor, even if that person is not specified. This lowering of pitch accounts, too, for the somewhat epistolary (Parnassian) tone of this poem, as it does in more explicitly epistolary poems. The probability that a reader will receive a message serves as a great enough incentive for the poet to continue the blind, amphibious act of putting words to the page. Therefore, the act of remembering, so central to twentieth-century Russian poetry, in what Carolyn Forché calls "the poetry of witness," becomes, as well, an act of preservation, and what is preserved reverts to, not a lesson in survival, for that is a matter not only of will but of chance (cf., "it's strange to think of surviving, but that's what happened"), but a recognition of surprise, self-surprise:

> Preserve these words against a time of cold,
> a day of fear: man survives like a fish,
> stranded, beached, but intent
> on adapting itself to some deep, cellular wish,
> wriggling toward bushes, forming hinged leg-struts, then
> to depart (leaving a track like the scrawl of a pen)
> for the interior, the heart of the continent.

Words, in this context, are amphibious and evolving. It is as though the poet takes seriously Darwin's claim that the organism recapitulates evolution from conception to maturity.[14] If that is so, then exile becomes the equivalent of destiny: the poet belongs in this new interior, which becomes, *contra* nothingness and the giddiness of things, his equivalent for a place to stand. (In an untitled poem dedicated to Mikhail Baryshnikov, he urges the dancer to adopt the same opinion.) As though to authenticate the idea, the poet gives the speech in which this accommodation is expressed to the cod:

> Time is far greater than space. Space is a thing.
> Whereas time is, in essence, the thought, the conscious dream
> of a thing. And life itself is a variety of time.
>
> . . . .
>
> At times, in that chaos, that piling up of days,
> the sound of a single word rings in the ear,
> some brief, syllabic cry,
> like "love," perhaps, or possibly merely "hi!"

If life itself is a variety of time, it finds its habitation more squarely in terms of time than of space. The surface that "will always be there" is as much a surface on the face of time as of space. As Brodsky puts it in a fine image, "man juts out into time." As for time's being a "conscious dream of a thing," it is so in the sense that a thing acquires a context in the course of its duration: only thus can it gain a destiny. Moreover, it is important that the poet stipulate a conscious, willful dimension to things; otherwise, as Kant would say, there can be no basis for freedom. Only if a dream is "conscious," in both common senses of the word, can things hope to exhibit a dimension greater than that demanded by their physical necessities. Needless to say, the argument for "the dream of things" applies all the more toward human things. The speaker gives us several manifestations of such freedom, which are of the nature of wish-fulfillments, and they are all the more fitting for being set against a new physical necessity: the fact of being minus the beloved:

> Behold: Aladdin says "Sesame!" and presto! there's a golden trove.
> Caesar calls for his Brutus down the dark forum's colonnades.
> In the jade pavilion a nightingale serenades
> the Mandarin on the delicate theme of love.
> A young girl rocks a cradle in the lamp's arena of light.
> A naked Papuan leg keeps up a boogie-woogie beat.
>
> Stifling. And so, cold knees tucked snug against the night,
> it comes to you all at once, there in the bed,
> that this is marriage.

We are apt to object that this is not marriage but separation,[15] but the point is that marriage is precisely this hope that the dream of another will take place in the dimension of freedom that the dream consciously sponsors. Here, as elsewhere in his work, Brodsky collapses time into a moment of epiphanic possibility, as the dreamer learns to dream through desire, unimpeded by brute actualities like chronology or the opposition of virtual and real. To some, this will seem very nearly a recommendation for daydreaming, but the poet is making a distinction between that a certain ordinary version of reverie and an active accommodation that has poetry, for one thing, as its vehicle.[16]

Having left the Workers Paradise, he finds himself in another ("Coordinates show / my location as paradise") no less subject to ironic reversal, but in this mode of accommodation, there is no call for paradise ("The paradise men seek / is a dead end"), which is another way of saying there is no call for the certainty that mobilizes ideologies and armies. Brodsky arms himself with barely suppressed derision at this point, for all quests for certainty, whether political, artistic, or private, are sure to be thwarted, and the quester driven into mere skepticism when cornered by failure.[17] Accommodation means coming to terms with the absence of certainty ("All you can tell for certain is the time"). Nevertheless, the poet's task of preservation and witness amounts to something like finding words to express what it is like to be something—in this case, a poet for whom the certainties have been wrenched away, leaving a record of the subsequent process of consciousness, of which the poem is the ultimate means of such a process, as well as its model. Expression is, then, creation and representation—presentation. The process necessarily involves a crush of sensations, predicated on loss, and it is characteristic of Brodsky to load the poem with details that correspond to these sensations and attitudinal fillips, even to the point of contradiction. Yet the affront that contradiction creates is absent here, for that contra-rational feeling requires a rationality to pervert. As poets know, rationality has a way of melting into rationale (the kind that justifies the exile of a poet, for example), and "Great issues leave a trail of words behind, free form as clouds of treetops." Siding strategically, then, with contradiction and "irrationality" puts the poet on the side of freedom—morally, too, as the friends of Bobò would no doubt add.

The poet has not only exchanged empires; he has changed pasts. As Nietzsche tells us, what is most intolerable to the poet's freedom is the fact of his antecedents, which is to say, his past. Overlooking the United States' past, which by being only another part of the Empire is no different in kind from his own past—that is, it is only a matter of resetting the cultural calibration—the poet can look to the past represented by the cod and say, "Thus I willed it." Hence it is no surprise to find the cod reappearing at the end of the poem, a reappearance that would otherwise strike us as merely whimsical in the wrong way. Even as we assent to the justice of this line of thinking, we still encounter the grotesque image of the cod "stand[ing] at the door." This grotesquerie hints at how ridiculous all this must look to the mind not yet acclimatized to the thought of deracination. It hints as well that to follow one's nose is not always to encounter a rose or to embrace at last the heart's desire.

The poem is in effect a circle, and because of its circularity, it brunts the force of circumstance, which would insist that only its muscle has force. Indeed, circularity is important to the poem in many other ways as well. The diurnal movement that the poem follows begins from a (new) dreamlike landscape and leaves us with sleep and dreaming. The poem that constitutes the bridge between these two states assimilates not only the first to the second but also subtly suggests that the accommodation between the two states is less a matter of inertial response than of Nietzschean willing, itself being its own case in point. To put this another way, the poem bridges two forms of sleep and dreaming— one reality-bound and historical, the other creative, and by comparison, ahistorical. The dichotomy is similar to the basic one we have already encountered in *Twenty Sonnets to Mary Queen of Scots.* If history is the nightmare from which we are trying to awake, this poem suggests that the awakening take the form of another dream, for "man is his own end," and the dreamer is cognizant that willful dreaming is the freedom of the body, as a thing, and that this dreaming manifests itself in time:

> And longer still than these
> is the strand of matching beads of countless days;
>
> and nights; and beyond these, the blindfold mist,
> angels in paradise, demons down in hell.
> And longer a hundredfold than all of this
> are the thoughts of life, the solitary thought
> of death. And ten times that, longer than all,
> the queer, vertiginous thought of Nothingness.
>
> But the eye can't see that far.

All the poem's effects dovetail in this vision, which we might note is a total vision in that it supersedes earlier visionary gestures (e.g., "I find myself, as it were, on a mountain peak"), for nothing is more appropriate to life, finally and ironically, than sleep, in which one declares one's thingness and trusts that in that state one will, to paraphrase the poet, be one with the earth that was the occasion for exile. At the same time, it is a nonvision ("the eye can't see that far"): We are still waiting to find out the destiny of vision and language.

Whatever else "Lullaby of Cape Cod" is, I would suggest that one of its efforts at accommodation pertains to the question of Brodsky's attempts to accommodate his poetry to American poetry—and not only through the Americanness of its details (one thinks here of instances of the use of American cultural details whose effect is not accommodation, as in Lorca's *Poet in New York* but also through the attention it gives to what Bloom (1973) has called the "American Sublime." This sublime is one of geographic vistas, of European time exchanged for American space. Strictly speaking, the idea is Emersonian; but although Brodsky seems to be buying into this aspect of the Emersonian poetic, he does so by containing it within an essentially European perspective: His expanses result from a dream vision, and in the vision it is duration (not History) that is seen in terms of—not exchanged for—space. After all, this is the coast of Massachusetts, not Kansas. Moreover, most of the actual expanse that informs the poem consists in the sea and the land left behind. Well understanding the exchange rates of such transactions, Brodsky tropes them; his recognition of the poetic use of expanses constitutes another instance of poetic ambivalence, which is to say, of poetic freedom—as if to say he could have it two ways. It is not difficult to see why this assertion of ambivalence has called up the equally ambivalent response of some American poets toward Brodsky's poetry.

NOTES

1. I wish therefore to distinguish this kind of writing from John Simon's "wit writing," cited earlier.

2. See Harold Bloom's (1992) humorous and illuminating discussion of "the aesthetics of outrage" as it relates to our appreciation of W. C. Fields in Rosenberg (151-156).

3. Brodsky therefore threads the somnolent environmental ambiance of "The Great Elegy for John Donne" with the somatic tragi-comedy of "1972" and *Twenty Sonnets to Mary Queen of Scots*.

4. The notion is mitigated by only the infantile security of its title.

5. See my "The Materialist Muse: Theory and Language Poetry," *Pembroke Magazine* 28 (spring 1996): 64-87.

6. David Bethea, however, presents a case for Brodsky as a "cross breeder" who "adopts a 'mourning tongue' and elegiac form from one Western poet . . . in order to speak of the death of another. He goes out of his native tradition in order, as it were, to reinvent it" (120-121).

7. The image of lacy foam and of stitching suggests—although perhaps more by way of imagistic felicity than design—Sacks's notion of the importance of the shroud image in the elegy (18-19).

8. The omniscient vantage from a hilltop has a less ironic but equally important place in English poetry, starting with Spenser; in American poetry, Whitman's use of the same trope in *Song of Myself* ushers in the theme of the American Road.

9. Derek Walcott, another poet of exile, and friend of Brodsky, joins the senses of "prior" with "another" in his autobiographical long poem *Another Life* (1973).

10. They may, however, be tied, as value-bearing and in their orientation to the Good, to the moral sphere, as Iris Murdoch has recently argued.

11. Elsewhere, Brodsky refers to rhyming as a poem's way of "passing a law," perhaps with the suggestion that such an equivalence between legislation and rhyming points up the performative aspects of verse, the pressure points at which the poem says a legislative "amen." Presumably, we can extend this notion to larger issues of rhyme, echo, and allusion.

12. A similar notion is conveyed in Stephen Crane's little poem: "A man said to the Universe, / 'Sir, I exist!' 'However,' replied the Universe, 'the fact has not created in me / a sense of obligation.'" ("A Man Said to the Universe," 1899)

13. It is not clear whether any useful critical distinction still clings to the difference between the "classical" and the"romantic" poet at all, let alone whether such a distinction turns on an idea as generally vague as "transcendence." Nevertheless, the terms are certainly still used to make tactical distinctions and provide a ready means of self-description. Carolyn Kizer's "a classicist is just a romantic without all the excess" seems very much to the point here.

14. We have already seen Brodsky's admiring mention of the devolutionary mimetic scheme in Auden's elegy for Yeats.

15. Without trying to make heavy weather, we should nevertheless observe the possibility of a similar Conradian comparison in the beat of the "Papuan leg" with Eliot's "Inside my brain a dull tom-tom begins" from "Portrait of a Lady," both suggestive of barbarity lurking below the surface of, for Eliot, "civilization," and for Brodsky, "Empire."

16. Gaston Bachelard makes the same distinction the basis for *The Poetics of Reverie* (1960).

17. The quester for linguistic paradises is likewise threatened with the prospect of failure, skepticism, diminishment, and so forth. Brodsky's task in this poem and the elegies following will be to test the walls to see whether they should be called "home" or "prison."

8

Destinations:
"Nothing So Dear as the Sight of Ruins . . ."

In an obvious respect, the elegy came to seem highly appropriate for Brodsky's poetic, for it stands to be the generic *ne plus ultra* for exile; to the temporal discontinuity that is the traditional elegy's given is added geographical disjunction—a no less final state of affairs. This addition—for the elegist, also a subtraction—corners the market on dimensions. Of course, exile provides neither a sufficient nor a necessary condition for elegizing, for the death (or absence) on which elegy is predicated is, strictly speaking, a matter belonging not to the spatial sphere but to the temporal one. Nevertheless, we have already seen the extent to which the addition of spatial concerns to temporal ones can become interchangeable quantities in terms of metaphors, taking care of each other's business while insinuating the desirable note of literary irony. With permeable categories, then, the poet can arm himself to speak elegiacally in terms of space, just as he can speak spatially in terms of time, since time contains a "distance" to the poet's "view." Historically, such a procedure has had strategic advantages for the poet faced with the prospect of the censor's stamp: permeable categories give the poet a certain deniability. Although he was no longer under threat of silencing, once he arrived in the West, Brodsky nonetheless continued to relish the deniability implicit in his metaphorical constructs, for as we have seen, what the dead know in common with the poet is that the shadow of death, as it were, also extends over words, which have been both the means and the model for any transcendent enterprise. Although transcendence holds the promise of resetting the degree lines that reveal death's dominion, such a resetting merely buys time. The question will be whether the cost justifies the amount of gain, and this question in turn brings with it that of readership, namely, whether the literary endeavor (call it virtuosity) can ever escape the curse of diminishing returns to the point that even the guts of the living—to say nothing of their brains—are none the better for the poet's negotiations.

The poet is not deterred, therefore, by a scholastic quibbling over categories such as "time" and "space." Rather, he invests his spatial disjunctiveness with elements of personally elastic, mythological time in which epochs are collapsed into days, days stretched into dull eternities, and so forth. Although such simultaneity suggests affinities with the Modernists' wish to hold the great past within the consciousness of the present, there is this difference, that the Modernists did so in order to contrast the fragmented present with the more unified past. Brodsky's aim is less diagnostic than therapeutic: The great Modernists, including the Russian variety, had already made the diagnosis. He wishes instead to suggest how a life might be lived in view of fragmentations both interior (consciousness and memory) and exterior (ruins), nevertheless keeping a cautious, if jaded, eye on the possibility of paradise.

Meanwhile, as the elegy, albeit in sometimes exotic formulations, grew into his characteristic post-exile mode, Brodsky seemed to expend vigorous efforts to suppress any self-important urge to abet its expansion into mere self-reference. As he was fond of noting in essays and speeches, the course of the exile, in the West at least, moves virtually always from "tyranny to demo-cracy," which has, among other myth-deflating features, "the last word on individual liberty on its lips."[1] Thus, rather than tie the elegy to the woes of exile, Brodsky expands it into the presiding atmosphere through which we survey, not the spectacle of figures mourning the loss of lives, still less the mourning poet, but the Ozymandian principle that ruins themselves record the march of humanity whose passage toward paradise finds, with stubborn persistence, death. Not presuming to give voice on behalf of this failed humanity, even as "witness," he nevertheless translates its artifactual properties, with the inevitable result that these properties fall short of poetry's alleged memorials, but with the new addendum that since both partake of the destiny of things, both peer, as it were, from under the shadow of death toward still unattainable utopias. Having historicized himself, Brodsky will, as did Lowell,[2] find consolation, not in poetry's self-propelling promises, but in having averted complete benightedness in the process of writing itself, a condition Brodsky depicts, not as minimal, but as "flooded with light."

As we have seen, by raising ambivalence to the level of a virtue, Brodsky allowed himself considerable thematic leg room as the dynamics of his career moved him alternately toward and against the elegiac and the richly extenuating, though to some extent fictitious, condition of his mostly representative exile. By expropriating poetic and cultural analogs that have been enshrined in the lingua franca of Western civilization, before experiencing consignment to its central warehouse, he proposes representations that alternate as both monuments and ruins. For instance, he is fond of ransacking classical forms such as the Virgilian eclogue in which to encase both political commentary and personal statement, a mummification that both proposes and denies the legitimacy of assertion, policing all within the quotation marks of form, just as Nabokov, referring to the ordinary use of the word "reality," advised with respect to literal quotation marks. Greek and Roman ruins are not occasions for indulging in digressive whimsy—a common flaw of autodidacts—but are the features and literary furniture of that suspension of place and time belonging to all Western political exiles, for whom classical ruins merely generalize often obscure particulars. At the same time, in Brodsky's view classical forms also belong to Russian poetry generally as a welcome means of restraint in a culture not always apt to hold this quality up as practical. Therefore, insofar as it functions in poetry, it does so in a way that suffuses poems with a sense of ethics, if not a sense of modesty:

Apart from her metaphors, Russian poetry has set an example of moral purity and firmness, which to no small degree has been reflected in the preservation of so-called classical forms without any damage to content. Herein lies her distinction from her Western sisters, though in no way does one presume to judge whom this distinction favors most. (*L* 143)

In real terms, this means that the political poet becomes more and more inclined to speak in terms of Herodotus than in terms of the State monolith. Still less are these subjects evasions of the historical conditions that have determined his particular condition. On the contrary, their very deadness, and the Cavafyesque deadpanness with which they disburden themselves in mock solemnizings and dyspeptic asides, appear to be means for scrutinizing precisely the contemporary *res* by conferring the requisite dose of alienating distance. Indeed, many of his poems secure their *savoir dire* by the contrivance of posthumous address, that most absurd yet triumphant of poetic devices. As we have seen, the trick of posthumous voicing suggests final words.

"TO A FRIEND: IN MEMORIAM," "THE THAMES AT CHELSEA," AND "DECEMBER IN FLORENCE"

Many post-1972 poems pick up the threads of these elegiac modifications that also feature elements of self-elegy. We will consider two that have been misconstrued as mere travel poems (Brodsky's "postcards"):[3] "The Thames at Chelsea" (1974) and "December in Florence" (1976). These two poems find the metaphor for exile in the speaker's peripatetic descriptions and, in each case, of an adopted (and literal) *locus classicus*. But the original site of exile is the Soviet Union itself, and thus we will begin with the personal considered also as a site of anonymity.

In "To a Friend: In Memoriam," a self-reflexive elegy to an Soviet friend "whose name's better omitted," the poet bids an "anonymous muted farewell" in verse that is clotted with descriptions and attributions, none of which add up to a traditional coherent matrix, let alone a portrait. But this is the point, for the "Man of sidewalks" in a "homeland of bottle struck livers" possesses the average anonymity of which this elegy is a reflection (though not for that reason a successful poem). Brodsky addresses the problem of anonymity right away:

It's for you whose name's better omitted—since for them it's no arduous task
to produce you from under the slab—from one more *inconnu*: me, well, partly
for the same earthly reasons, since they'll scrub you as well off the cask.

(Trans. Joseph Brodsky)

The "same earthly reasons" are alienation and exile, the latter state a
geographical expression and literalizing of the former. Of course, death is
obviously a kind of definitive "alienation," and not only for the ostensible
subject of the elegy. Indeed, part of the task of the elegy is to query the sense
that the dead are alien (though, as we have seen, with a good deal of ambivalence) and, conversely, to query the equally troubling but more hidden sense
that there may be something in our makeup that is alien to the absolute limits
death imposes on life, something that prefers to cling unnaturally to our paltry
moments, suggesting that we are, in fact, not out of line to ask why no one can
preserve us from death.

The assertion, "[I] am too distant for you to distinguish a voice," reverberates
with these difficulties. The speaker is too literally distant; likewise, he is
metonymically distant: His poem is not powerful enough to transgress the outer
frontier of life and reanimate the attention of the dead friend (even in the sense
of the virtual, tactical attention he attributes to the spirit of Donne). At the same
time, it is not that the dead friend can hear nothing at all: He simply cannot
distinguish a voice, and not any voice, but this voice, the voice that would
attempt to elegize. Thus, there is not only the reality-testing vis-à-vis the dead
friend but also an anxiety about the power of elegy to console the living, since
it cannot "even" reach the dead. Here as elsewhere, and increasingly in the
1970s, Brodsky uses physical distance to represent metaphysical distance. The
only applicable stance toward death, then, is to match its apparent indifference
with one's own indifference, a stance we have seen more mordantly enacted in
"The Funeral of Bobò."[4] The situation, which seems hopeless enough, is
nonetheless exacerbated by the intrusive presence of the State:

[Y]ou, a tramper through hell and high water and the meaningless sentence,
who took life like a bumblebee touching a sun-heated bud
but instead froze to death in the Third Rome's cold-piss-reeking entrance.
Maybe Nothing has no better gateway indeed than this smelly shortcut.

(*U* 4, trans. Joseph Brodsky)

The "Third Rome" (i.e., Moscow), which would succeed the others in order
and spirituality, possesses neither and moreover, in the poem is depicted as the
antipodes of any Rome. In such a setting, Brodsky dwells in conventional
elegiac terms on the marvel of his friend's ability to avoid total disintegration
("you drifted along the dark river in your ancient gray, drab overcoat / whose
few buttons alone were what kept you from disintegration"). It is possible to
detect a whiff of admiration for one who will succeed in making the transition

to death, having had considerable practice in life ("Gloomy Charon in vain seeks the coin in your tightly shut shell"). From the perspective of the exile, the friend's death can at least boast the small advantage of logical consistency, while the elegist merely perceives that "someone's pipe blows in vain its small tune." The elegist's farewell ("With a bow") ends ambivalently "from the shores—who knows which? Though for you now it has no importance." The sense of futility that attaches to this sentiment sidesteps a general feeling of futility to opt for classic ennui, hinting that the dead friend would have joined him in this attitude had the times been more propitious. It hints further that the times were such that they foreclosed even on the ennui of the *boulevardier* devolved into the "man of sidewalks," for whom "This will do . . . for the duration" was thought to be acceptable utterance: at least no objection followed from it.

Brodsky notes that the human lust for immortality betrays itself when the human tries to achieve the status of certain kinds of things—of a monument, say: "In his futile attempts to overcome time, man, in reality, has imitated its actions, erecting himself bronze and stone statues, marble busts, turning himself into a thing" (quoted in Polukhina 143). In "The Thames at Chelsea,"

> Thomas More aims
> his eyes with the age-old desire and strains his mind.
> The dull stare is itself more solid than the iron
> of the Albert Bridge.
>
> *(PS* 89, my translation)

The speaker characterizes Utopia's stare as "dull" because the only Utopia not a dystopia in disguise must include immortality. Moreover, immortality cannot be merely an extension of life, for we predicate the term "life" upon and against a ground of termination.[5] Yet the only metaphors we can understand pertaining to this state proceed as merely extensions of the present (or past) condition: either the sempiternal, or time-stopped, though each approach contradicts the other. What no-time is, is unknown. The poem, in fact, takes up the death-in-life theme of "Almost an Elegy" from a different perspective; indeed, the poem concerns itself with perspectives (Thomas More) and prospects ("The endless street, making a sharp slant, / runs to the river, ending with an iron arrow"). But all perspectives, including abstract ones ("a man able to see a century into the future"), possess the qualification that they are provisional, since all prospects encounter obstacles that mar the total view. The controlling irony, of course, is that they are the view, and this principle serves as a corrective to our well-meaning but misdirected desire to reverse Blake, so that we do not become what we behold but behold only what we have willed.

Meanwhile, all the temporal markers in the poem show that the clock, epitomized by Big Ben ("London town's fine, the clocks run on time. / The heart can only lose a length to Big Ben"), runs despite this desire and moreover runs counter to it. With the mention of such riverside monuments, it should surprise no one that this poem, coming at the zenith of Brodsky's reverence for *res Britannica*, nevertheless cannot suppress echoes of Petersburg, the "renamed city" of his origin. It is therefore tempting in spite of the perhaps too telling details—umbrellas, Big Ben, Prince Albert—to read Petersburg as a palimpsest for this London.

Brodsky may well have been aware of Wordsworth's "Composed upon Westminster Bridge" sonnet, but instead of discovering an organic city as a part of nature, he finds only discrete things and bodies more or less in motion, against which he eases into a desuetude that embodies the realization that desire or not, this life, this city, cannot connect with anything greater than the sum of its own events and things. Thus repudiating any holistic conception of the city, the poet views every street, like every life, as terminal, ending in an "iron arrow," an ambivalent image, implying both motion and terminal heaviness. Even the air, that "lives a life that is not ours / to understand . . . starts overhead and soars / upward, ending nowhere." Because the city and its inhabitants are the sum of past events and things, the poet moves toward the elegiac and the consciousness of death-in-life, the precondition for the change to elegiac thinking, but this movement is nevertheless as wayward and makeshift as his own walking. The emergent words come from an undetermined source:

> These words were dictated to me not by
> love or the Muse but by a searching, dull
> voice that had lost the swiftness of sound.

The "voice" speaks in a disjoined, Beckettian question-and-answer manner beginning with "How did you live in those years?" and ending, "Are you afraid of death?" The intrusion of death occurs in the middle stanza of this seven-stanza poem and serves to mediate the delivery of the speaker's response (at first meant to be flippant: "No, it's the normal dark") that recapitulates the imagery of the first three stanzas but transforms it with the knowledge that death is one of the component threads of life, a thought strangely more effective than any evidence of the speaker's desire, though it is a substitution still somehow counterinstinctual to humans that must, it seems, be realized ever anew, even by poets:

> There is no longer anything one can choose
> to believe, except that while there's a bank on the right,
> there's a left one, too: blessed news.

As we know, Brodsky speaks of this object of belief as a "kind of ambivalence, I think, [that] is precisely that 'blessed news' which the East, having little else to offer, is about to impose on the rest of the world. And the world looks ripe for it" (*L* 10). No one, it seems, is more underwhelmed than the poet by the

astounding logic that life and its more diffusive delegate, poetry, must be able
to think in terms of self-elegy prior to any authentic poetry:

And when you sleep, the telephone numbers
of your past and present blend to produce a figure—
astronomical.

That astronomical figure, of course, begins with a zero ("where all our woes
begin"), and the zero is figured in the moon, whose telephone-dial face returns
the news that it is "Engaged." The poet concludes that "this steady noise / is
clearer than God's own voice," suggesting that every view of language is first
a view of death, but none is Providential.

"December in Florence" (1976) is perhaps Brodsky's most successfully
realized self-elegy. In tone and imagery, it approaches another admirable elegy
having Italy as its setting, Steven's "To an Old Philosopher in Rome." Unlike
the somnolent London of "The Thames at Chelsea," the Florence here seems
from the first line animated by its own antiquity: "The doors take in and exhale
steam," exuding an ancient vitality that stands in contrast to the speaker, who
is immediately introduced in a self-estranging, second-person address: "[Y]ou,
however, won't / be back." Working many similar contrasting pairs in the poem
(longevity/brevity; sophistication/awkwardness; inclusion/exclusion; inside[rs]/
outside[rs]), Brodsky also employs cadenzas of rhetorical figures, particularly
the synechdochal, by which he intimates a scale of being that is worthy, in
complexity, of a Donne. For example, people are regularly reduced to their
sight attributes: A man in a doorway is an overcoat, faces are reduced to eyes,
eyes to pupils, a writer to the words on his page, two crones to figure-8s (when
horizontal, the symbol of infinity—a description Brodsky uses elsewhere), and
so forth. Meanwhile, these reductions are contrasted with simultaneous
crescendos, if not in terms of size (since it is more natural to the perceiver to
produce diminished figurations than augmented ones), then of effect: A glimpse
of blonde hair among "the kingdom of the dark-haired" becomes "an angelic
vestige," *palazzi* are "stuck in the earth waist-down," and "a chance ray of
sunlight splatter[s]" the palace and sacristy of Lorenzo the Magnificent,
"pierc[ing] thick blinds and titillat[ing] the veinous / filthy marble, tubs of snow-
white verbena." Sometimes the contrasting movements intersect: "In a dusty
cafe, in the shade of your cap, / eyes pick out frescoes, nymphs, cupids on their
way up." While the synechdochal reductions work on their own as terms of
contrast, Brodsky reminds us that the ultimate reduction involves being reduced
to a sign. Hence, in this mythopoesis, the "way up" is equivalent to the way
"down," and the visitor, a transient, is as much in charge of creating the city's
intimations of eternity, as he is of creating a more durable substitute for his own
figure. In other words, the movement toward eternity consists in learning to
prefer the profile to the full face, as in this telling stanza:

A man gets reduced to pen's rustle on paper, to
wedges, ringlets of letters, and also, due
to the slippery surface, to commas and full stops. True,
often, in some common word, the unwitting pen
strays into drawing—while tackling an
"M"—some eyebrows: ink is more honest than
blood. And a face with moist words inside
out to dry what has just been said,
smirks like the crumpled paper absorbed by shade.

(*PS* 119, trans. Brodsky)

The continuum, not to say triteness and boredom, of life, of which Florence
provides the occasion, becomes the poem. The poem, therefore, is not a
reflection of Florence. Indeed, with the pervasive presence of synechdochal and
metonymic figures, there is little here that a real mirror would recognize. The
poet must not simply be present at some magical place where time and eternity
intersect; he must create that intersection. Brodsky alludes finally to the physical
nature of that creation in the penultimate stanza:

Intersections scare your skull
like crossed bones. In the low December sky
the gigantic egg laid there by Brunelleschi
jerks a tear from an eye experienced in the blessed
domes. A traffic policeman briskly
throws his hand in the air like a letter X.

In this complex of images, the two intersections, or opposed ways crossing, are
balanced by an image of wholeness and birth (of Brunelleschi's "egg," i.e., the
dome of the Cathedral of St. Maria del Fiore) itself more coherent than any
cloud it may purport to replace. Moreover, it is a case in which art has penetrated
"nothing" (cf. "The Thames at Chelsea") and in the process made one of nature's
evanescent instabilities, namely, clouds, stable by contributing its own brand of
eternity to the sky—the abode, not of heavenly beings, but of zeroes.

For the poet, the city approaches eternity at the moment of the poet's self-
subtraction (foreshadowed by figures of reduction): "There the streetcar's
multitudes, jostling, dense, / speak in the tongue of a man who's departed
thence." Although Brodsky seldom refrains from homing in on this aesthetic
and, so to speak, recommending it, he is equally aware of the cost for which
there is "no proper sum," that is, the inestimable expense of life:

There are places where lips touched lips for the first time ever,
or pen pressed paper with real fervor.
There are arcades, colonnades, iron idols that blur your lens.

This expense, though no quantification can dispose of its existential residue,

nonetheless bewitches (as it does in "Almost an Elegy"), he suggests, for the
wrong reasons: "Oh, the obstinate leaving that 'living' masks!"

Although legend would suggest otherwise, Brodsky met Auden on only two
occasions: at Kirchstetten, where Auden's Austrian summer home provided
Brodsky with his first stop after being expelled from the Soviet Union in May
1972 (Brodsky stayed with the solicitous, avuncular Auden and Chester Kallman
for a week). Later, a few months before his death in 1973, Auden introduced
him at the International Poetry Festival in London. Despite the slim basis for
acquaintance, the Brodsky-Auden link is well-established in terms of poetry:
Auden wrote an introduction to Brodsky's first generally available selection of
poems in English translation (1973), and Brodsky returned the compliment by
publishing a lengthy exegesis—transcriptions of a class lecture—of Auden's
"September 1, 1939" in his first book of prose, *Less Than One*, as well as two
elegies. The first of these—Brodsky's first published poem written in
English—suggests, perhaps too optimistically, his debt to Auden and was
included in Stephen Spender's memorial volume (243); the second ("York: In
Memoriam W. H. Auden"), a more accomplished and considered piece, is the
final poem from the sequence *In England*. Others such as John Bayley have
perceived more than a fortuitous, if timely, link between the doyen of English
poetry and the Russian exile, and this perception is often directed to those
qualities of what we might call a serious *levitas*: "He perceives the way in which
the art of the poem—its humorous civilization—in fact tolerates and accepts the
didacticism and unease to which it gives expression" (210). This lightness
suggests not only a similarity of temperament but also a devotion to the moral
benefits of a civilized sensibility.[6] Bayley, for example, throws caution to the
wind in suggesting, "It would be tempting to say that Brodsky and Auden are
the only really civilized great poets of their respective generations, and of the
past few decades" (205). More importantly, though, Auden clearly served
Brodsky at this stage less as mentor, and more as role model, as Brodsky
recounts in his essay, "To Please a Shadow" (*L* 357). The essay is, among other
things, a most informative account of the ways in which poets read each other:

Because I was Russian, he'd go on about Russian writers. "I wouldn't like to live with
Dostoyevsky under the same roof," he would declare. Or, "The best Russian writer is
Chekhov"—"Why?" "He's the only one of your people who's got common sense." Or
he would ask about the matter that seemed to perplex him most about my homeland: "I
was told that the Russians always steal windshield wipers from parked cars. Why?" But
my answer—because there were no spare parts—wouldn't satisfy him: he obviously had
in mind a more inscrutable reason, and, having read him, I almost began to see one
myself. (*L* 377)

He notes disarmingly that he had stumbled on Auden "by pure chance": "This
time the anthology that I had was in English, sent to me by a friend in Moscow.
It had quite a lot of Yeats, whom I then found a bit too oratorical and sloppy

with meters, and Eliot, who in those days reigned supreme in Eastern Europe. I was intending to read Eliot" (*L* 360). The accident by which he did not led to the realization that Auden, above all, understood "what language does to time."

It would be rude to suggest that such youthful curiosity and subsequent allegiance to the "infinity" of language could have resulted in the mindset of mannerist art, yet undoubtedly "the train of thought . . . set in motion [that is] still trundling to this day" contributed to a distinctive manner, one that feels perfectly free to split linguistic as well as argumentative hairs, as the occasion warrants. To the critic who is perplexed or irked by the poet who is stylistically headstrong in just this way, the term is indeed mannerism. Doubtless, Brodsky is a headstrong poet, not only in terms of style, but also in terms of metaphysics.[7] At the same time, he seems undaunted by the philosophic "ghosts" that go haunting when the Big Subjects of time and language come into view, as they do invariably. Stylistic overemphasis tends to give rise to mannerism as its means of expression, and this has been widely perceived as the chief flaw in Brodsky's poems. But while mannerism as a term has mainly served as a put-down to designate a certain kind of discourse unruffled by the rises, dips, and swerves of description and argument (dips and swerves that mannerism can, like ideology, but contain), Brodsky became mannered in precisely the opposite way, by frequently overriding the implied contours of his own poetic thinking, as if sensing that these always lead back to the homeland of thought: the parallel, but improved, universe of language.

Be that as it may, Brodsky's poetic tutors have been as much displaced, Nansen passport poets as indigenous Russian ones. Within and without their languages and cultures, they have become arranged as a new linguistic architrave surveying, in their togas, the century's fortunes. The chief figure in this arrangement is, of course, Auden, and clustered to one side are the by-now familiar Eliot, Cavafy, Mandelstam, Milosz, Walcott, Paz, and Montale. We may further imagine that on the other side of Auden appear Virgil, Ovid, and Dante as charter members of a newly raised temple. And yet as Brodsky was acutely aware, as far as the rest of the world is concerned, the fate of any particular poet is not especially important except as it concerns language and the fate of words. After all, the millions whom political fate has sent upon pointless pilgrimage in this century abruptly snatch, to use Brodsky's phrase, "the carnation from the writer's lapel."

Of the poets whose countenances jut from Brodsky's artistic Pantheon, however, none is so engraved with telling features as that of Auden, whose very likeness reflects all significance-bearing roads leading to and from Clio's (and Urania's) shrine. Even from the distance of the Soviet Union, Brodsky monitored the unfolding Baedecker of Auden's face ("one starts to wonder about the appearance of writers"), but to my knowledge he is the first to rhapsodize over the earlier, unlined face of the socially conscious Auden, whose eyes,

directly corresponded to the formal aspects of his lines (two lifted eyebrows = two rhymes) and to the blinding precision of their content. What stared at me . . . was the facial equivalent of a couplet, of truth that's better known by heart. The features were regular, even plain. There was nothing specifically poetic about this face, nothing Byronic, demonic, ironic, hawkish, aquiline, romantic, wounded, etc. Rather it was the face of a physician who is interested in your story though he knows you are ill. A face well prepared for everything, a sum total of a face. (*L* 371)

Brodsky views his journey as analogous to that of Auden's, who also "switched empires" from England to America (and from there to Austria, and, again, from Austria to England) and intellectually from the domains of Marxism and Freudianism to a benign, bedroom-slipper Anglicanism. It is worth noting that if Auden's countenance is the most prominent in the architrave—the part of Zeus—and moreover carved from life, then Euclid—geometry's progenitor and hence its deity—bears the mistier, more allegorical role of a Titan:

It's strange to think of surviving, but that's what happened.
Dust settles on furnishings, and a car bends length
around corners in spite of Euclid.

("Lullaby of Cape Cod")

Euclid is additionally the Titan that we, millennia in the future, still contend with, tortuously in the case of cars, symbolically in the case of poems. He is thus a tutelary deity in this world of confines:

[F]or Euclid
sees to it himself that spheres encourage
two corners, alias angles, with
a third one. And it makes a marriage.

("A Song to No Music")

Sven Birkerts has suggested that the source of Brodsky's obsession with geography lies in his brief formal schooling: the schoolboy's proofs of Euclid enlarged behind the vapors of the mature autodidact's wizardry (*Artificial Wilderness* 139). Birkerts' perceptive comment does not go far enough, for the real danger of autodidacticism does not lie with obsessiveness per se, but with the poet's temptation to steer obsession in the public's direction in the form of didacticism. Matters of geography are mere matters of space. Poems exist in time, [which] "is far greater than space" because the distances are greater—that is, metaphysical distances, providing perspectives that would have pleased even Archimedes. Moreover, poems partake of the continuum of thought, which is also of time. Like time, they are the "conscious dream / of a thing," which dream is also in a manner "trapped" behind bars ultimately of Euclid's devising, since the space to which a thing experiences its confinement is itself a "thing."[8] Thus in the case of exile we discover this extra dimension: that to the poet, a thing primarily begins in space but ends in time, transformed and no longer the mere equal of the particulars of the exile. Laying aside the question of materiality, for something to "end" in time means that once the new dimension is broached—as, for example, in thought—there is no recourse to any "return" except in weakness, which is to say nostalgia. All this is perhaps a too obvious way of allegorizing humanity's fallenness, but it is perhaps helpful that we belabor the obvious point, since Brodsky's plastic maneuvers frequently depend upon our understanding that every note from the poet's lute in a sense confirms a key change as well. Be that as it may, Brodsky must begin by assigning discrete status to space and time; hence the exchange between them is of necessity approximate, with such approximations negotiated by metaphorical cunning and sometimes more than a hint of jerry-rigging. Much is lost in translation, to revive that tedious cliché, yet the very recognition of its truism is a recognition of the elegiac. Substituting one key for another, in other words, the poet already adopts the elegiac métier.

The foregoing is by way of reintroducing the fact that Brodsky's meeting with Auden comes long after the former had launched upon a topic as suitable to his temperament as it would be for his themes. For both Brodsky and Auden, geography provides a central, endlessly permutable metaphor. Both experienced the changed poetic requirements brought about by exilic circumstance. At the same time—and switching dimensions—both agree in deploring History's manners, especially in terms of its levels of discourse, social, political, and poetic. Of course, this is not a problem that stops at the linguistic level, for "manners" is the polite umbrella for behaviors in general, but if language is subject to debasement and, like mankind, to alienation, it is also subject to renascence. But to neglect the problem, once it has been recognized, is, for Brodsky, simply "treason."

"YORK: IN MEMORIAM W. H. AUDEN"

Employing a kind of poetic shorthand, "York: In Memoriam W. H. Auden" recapitulates much of Brodsky's previous imagery and tactics in the elegy, but it differs from earlier elegies by pressing aesthetic devices into the service of moral questions. Brodsky's boast that Auden was the "most civilized" person of the twentieth century would be an empty boast indeed were it to rest on assessments of taste. Therefore, Brodsky's aim in this elegy is to imagine what would constitute consolation for the loss of his role model; but with equal emphasis, he wishes to look through Auden's eyes, so to speak, at the matter of moral bearing. Perhaps on the theory that imitation is not only a matter of respect but also an occasion for respect, imitation also adds a new kind of elegiac repetition. It is also, more explicitly and urgently than the elegy for Eliot, a poem that seeks to legitimate a poetic inheritance in such a way as to include not only a poetic sanction-by-association from the English bard but also his moral equipoise. In this sense, it is a personal elegy heavy with professional overtones that wields elegiac convention, as Auden would have approved, in a businesslike manner. The poem both begins and ends on Auden's home turf, Yorkshire, and the geographical specificity, supported by indigenous natural details, reinforces the elegist's natural desire not to relinquish his friend. Thus, in one important sense, the poem evinces a dialectic between the friend-as-loved-one and the friend-as-poet, and this dialectic will ultimately have to be worked out in favor of the latter for the elegy to be successful, though it should be added that the difficulty in relinquishing even the store of details related to this desire constitutes much of the poem's emotional muscle. Thus, Brodsky will attempt to have it both ways: the elegy (words) and the life (as experienced through natural associative details, such as Audenesque limestone). The necessity of laying the mourned one definitively in his grave in order to accomplish the elegy's task (the transformation to signs) thus acquires a vividly *trompe l'oeil* quality, for in the final analysis, the vividness of Auden's "place" is already one of signs, not life. But the proximity of the dialectical terms is intenser than usual in Brodsky's poetry, suggesting that love (or the affective dimension that words open upon) modifies the elegiac process (a process whose supervision has heretofore been a Categorical Imperative for the elegist) and is thus a powerful quality of signification because it is also precisely the liability that could prevent the poet from accomplishing his elegy.

As a result, there is every good reason for beginning the poem with a familiar image of the proximity of life and death, the butterfly: "The butterflies of northern England dance above the goosefoot / below the brick wall of a dead-factory." The butterflies' "dance" above the "brick wall" of a "dead factory" verges on the absurd image of the butterfly mounted on the spire of the Admiralty in "The Funeral of Bobò" except that the image depicts a *fait accompli* (in terms of the image), whereas the brick wall and dead factory merely loom in view. From this image, Brodsky moves on to note the weather: heat, auspicious for England in general, but inauspicious in the particular case (it is too hot, suggesting the poet's stranded situation in "Lullaby of Cape Cod": "dahlias die of thirst"). While nature, except for the butterflies, parches in the heat, a memory of Auden's voice emerges, and its full-throated pronunciamento both contrasts with and seems appropriate to the rasping of nature:

And your voice—"I have known three great poets. Each
one a prize son of a bitch"—sounds in my ears
with disturbing clarity.
                    (*PS* 126, trans. Alan Myers)

The "clarity" is appropriately disturbing in terms of poetic inheritance, for the poet (the elegist) admits looking "in the outstretched hand's direction." The three poets that the voice of Auden refers to are Yeats, Frost, and Brecht, and it is characteristic of the revisionary nature of poetic inheritance that Brodsky considers Auden wrong, even as he cherishes the memory of his voice (Brecht, in Brodsky's estimation, was not a "great" poet). In spite of this voice, ventriloquized by memory, the scene is depopulated: all are either stopped short of death or dead ("Chester died, too—you know that / only too well" [Chester Kallman in fact survived Auden]; thus Brodsky asserts that Auden "knew" this posthumously). The heat and drought seem appropriately "timeless," suggesting, too, that the elegist's movements are somehow thwarted, and the anomie again reminds us of "Lullaby of Cape Cod," a poem whose mid-Atlantic consciousness would surely have appealed to the "minor mid-Atlantic Goethe." Meanwhile, "The white butterflies' dance is like a storm-tossed ship." As the butterflies flit like spirits in and out of the poet's consciousness, the dynamic of the death-in-life consciousness begins to reassert itself. At first, it is merely an intimation (the "dead factory"), but as the poem proceeds, it begins to gather oppressively on the optic nerve:

> A man takes his own blind alley with him wherever he goes
> about the world; and a bent knee, with its obtuse angle,
> multiplies the captive perspective,
> like a wedge of cranes, holding their course
> for the south. Like all things moving onward.

The first line of this passage rewrites a famous sentiment of another of Brodsky's (and Auden's) favorite poets, Constantine Cavafy, whose "Ithaka" admonishes a questing Ulysses:

> Laistrygonians, Cyclops,
> wild Poseidon—you won't encounter them
> unless you bring them along inside your soul,
> unless your soul sets them up in front of you.
>
>   (Trans. Edmund Keeley and Philip Sherrard)

Brodsky, indeed, quotes this idea in his essay on Montale: "In spiritual odysseys there are no Ithacas" (*L* 97). The line also alludes to similar passages of blocked perspective in Brodsky's earlier work, most notably in "The Thames at Chelsea." Meanwhile, the bent knee—not of captivity, but the weight of the body—is compared to "a wedge of cranes," an image that contrasts with the other aerialists, the butterflies, in that the cranes (and the knee) are purposeful, not willful, but bent with the necessity of "all things moving outward." This outwardness opens eventually onto death, the emptiness that even "swallow[s] sunlight." But for the elegist and the object of the elegy alike, it also opens onto words, whose profile is at least handsomer than a "bent knee":

> Subtracting the greater from the lesser—time from man—
> you get words, the remainder, standing out against their
> white background more clearly than the body
> ever manages to while it lives.

For Brodsky, as we have already seen, nomination and numeration are virtual synonyms, as nomination and (e)numeration denote the same event from different orientations. The degree to which the cult of the word predisposes him frequently to restate his principles in epigrammatic formulas and sweeping generalizations is familiar to any reader of Brodsky's verse. Repetition, as Sacks has reminded us, may be understood as a psycho-poetic means of averting catastrophe (22-23). Brodsky points out that for Mandelstam, poetry itself aims to avert catastrophe, and just as the brick wall stands as potentially catastrophic for the butterflies, so the thought of death becomes potentially catastrophic for the would-be elegist: Many things—including love itself—conspire to prevent the poet from the "extreme thought" necessary to elegize. The elegy for Auden enumerates many of these difficulties, principally through assertion ("Lately I've been losing my grip a little") and image ("Closing my eyes, I see an empty boat"), as well as with the fact that the pilgrimage to Auden's place of birth runs metaphorically counter to the necessity for accomplishing the same linguistic maneuver vis-à-vis the man he knew and loved, as opposed to one he simply admired (Eliot). But just as Brodsky incorporates the emptiness of the northern English scene into the poem, so nature, in a variant of the pathetic fallacy that mimes the elegist's necessity, rather than mourning his loss, finds that "[t]he absence of wind compels taut leaves / to tease their muscles and stir against their will." As "vacuum gradually / fills the landscape," so death-in-life fills the elegist's consciousness: "[T]hus the source of love turns into the object of love." The source of love here (the man) is transformed into the object (thing-poem) of love. The degree of transformation necessary to create the adequate elegy is dependent not only on the scale of transformation itself also but on the degree to which it asserts it own textuality (as against other texts). This, argues Brodsky, is a function of love, as in this characteristic generality:

> Nothing so much
transforms a familiar entrance into a crowd of columns
as love for a man, especially when

> he's dead.

Again, there is nothing Providential that would assist in his transformation: it is an entirely human affair. And while the "corps de ballet of nimble butterflies" seem "to take their cue from an unseen bow," their conductor is not God, alas, but Darwin.

"ELEGY FOR ROBERT LOWELL"

Although they had met once before briefly, Brodsky's first real encounter with Robert Lowell took place in Massachusetts two years before the latters death. And although Brodsky carried some initial apprehension about what he felt to be American poetry's more Dionysian (nonclassical) contours—with which

Lowell had been associated—he encountered an amiable, passionate, imposingly learned ("He knew Dante inside out"), and kind man, as seemingly secure in the history of postwar American poetry as his family was secure in the *Social Register* but, at the same time, flinching at every recourse to security—a natural maverick. In short, he found someone as imbued with culture as his beloved Auden. By way of embedding his elegy for Lowell with allusions to Lowell's poems, the elegy calls to mind some superficial resemblance to "Verses on the Death of T. S. Eliot," but the act of homage is more direct, for it is a virtual anthology of Lowellian passages. Moreover, the poems is one of the few Brodsky has attempted in English and stands as a testimony to his sometimes maligned ear. The poem is organized into four short, thematic sections, the final three composed in regular stanzaic patterns, the last two of these being composed of quatrains, preceded by a section (2) in *terza rima*. The poem begins by alluding to what is probably Lowell's most widely anthologized poem, "Skunk Hour." In that poem, the survivor skunk, undaunted by the waste of a culture it forages, parades "under the chalk-dry and spar spire / of the Trinitarian Church." In Brodsky's elegy, the scene is shifted from Nautilus Island to Boston, as if to bring Lowell's poem closer to home. While the skunk is changed into a no less mildly threatening porcupine, the season (fall) and the metaphorical color (blue) remain the same:

> In the autumnal blue
> of your church-hooded New
> England, the porcupine
> sharpens its golden needles
> against Bostonian bricks
> to a point of needless
> blinding shine.
>
> (*PS* 177)

As in "Skunk Hour," architectural images here provide indices of status and seem projections of taste: of a quietly menacing, Victorian hauteur or of its downscale equivalent—arriviste shabbiness. In Brodsky's austere, if not also superior—and threatening ("hooded")—neighborhood, socially imposing "Bostonian bricks" seem added for good measure. Against these impediments, the porcupine calmly sharpens its quills: Though a pariah, it is a denizen nevertheless.

More boldly than in his elegy for Auden, Brodsky shows a taste for rewriting and "correcting" Lowell, who was so thoroughly imbued with the values against which he was in constant flight that he often seems in love with his very antagonisms. Such rewriting, and indeed overwriting, becomes Brodsky's form of homage, and here he attempts to recapitulate the feat in this poem for which he praised Auden in his poem on Yeats, that of recreating a thumbnail sketch of the master's stylistic development. The second stanza moves thus to Lowell's early masterpiece, "The Quaker Graveyard at Nantucket," compressing its main dramatic image—drowning—in a metaphorical image of parishioners besieged at worship by the proximity of the sea:

> White foam kneels and breaks
> on the altar. People's eyes glitter inside
> the church like pebbles
> splashed by the tide.

The personal first stanza, then, is transfigured in the second by the opposition of chaos and belief: The porcupine—an image of Lowell himself—is superseded by a wilder world that contains the Leviathan. Less indirectly than in the other elegies we have seen, the elegy for Lowell is willing to reconsider the existential basis for the elegy that springs from the naked question: why can no one save us from death? Previously for Brodsky, this—though, as we have seen, fundamental to elegiac thought—had been an unvarnished and inappropriate question, for the point of elegy had been to transform things in retrospect into a prospect of things, namely, words. The seriousness of Lowell's attraction to themes of redemption, based on religious models, however extraneous to Brodsky's aesthetic, draws the poet's attention perhaps to the otherworldly aspect of Lowell, a religious nostalgia made acceptable in view of his personal authority and authenticity. The third and fourth stanzas allude to this nostalgia, as expressed in the title poem of Brodsky's personal favorite among Lowell's individual volumes, *Near the Ocean*:

> O Bible chopped and crucified
> in hymns we hear but do not read,
> none of the milder subtleties
> of grace or art will sweeten these
> stiff quatrains shoveled out four-square—
> they sing of peace, and preach despair;
> yet they gave darkness some control,
> and left a loophole for the soul.

Brodsky aims a like despair in the direction of Lowell's absence but reserves no "loophole," ironic or otherwise. After all, the loophole implies that we are guilty for desiring salvation in the first place, and thus our spiritual rescue can never escape the taint brought on, we might say, by the superego's perpetual (and, for both Brodsky and Lowell, demeaning) frown—a superego that in the first place gets its stamp, for Lowell, from the Puritanical God. In Brodsky's view, we have nothing to gain from the hypocrisy implicit in Lowell's sly term. Brodsky's counter to this sort of post-Puritanical anxiety is simple: "In my case, if I were to begin to create some form of theology, I think it would be a theology of language" (quoted in Polukhina 169). He also remarks that "the poetic conception of existence eschews any form of finiteness or stasis, including theological apotheosis" (*L* 204).[9] In short, Brodsky's consolation will not engage the specifically religious sensibility:

The choir, time and again,
sings in the key of the Cross
of Our Father's gain,
which is but our loss.

There will be a lot,
a lot of Almighty Lord,
but not so much as a shred
of your flesh. When a man dies
the wardrobe gapes instead.

The last two lines of this opening section, by way of putting a blunt point on the fact of personal discontinuity, borrow accents from Auden in which to do so, as if the elegist were stepping back from the consequences of a too-involved empathy. But instead of using this as an occasion for criticism, Brodsky moves directly in the second, *terza rima* section to a contrast between language and final human silence, a contrast depicted as a classical struggle for the significance of the quester Lowell's body:[10]

On the Charles's bank
dark, crowding, printed letters
surround their sealed tongue.

A child, commalike, loiters
among dresses and pants
of vowels and consonants

that don't make a word. The lack
of pen spells
their uselessness. And the black

Cadillac sails
through the screaming police sirens
like a new Odysseus keeping silence.

In his last volume, Lowell had written a long poem, "Ulysses and Circe," a meditation on the epic wanderer's return to his wife (just as Lowell was rejoining his wife at the time of his death). Here, the uninstructed children—his alphabet—change to Pirandellian "characters" in search of their author and, finding none, become merely orphans. The farthest echo belongs, of course, to Dante: the "dark, crowding . . . letters" on the Charles's bank are, as well, souls in limbo, awaiting Charon, while Ulysses himself "sails" silently by in his limousine. Dante's Ulysses belongs to the twenty-sixth canto of the *Inferno*, where the poet begins the story, not of Ulysses' return to Ithaca and Penelope, but of his last voyage at the point where he leaves the island of Circe (not having knowledge of Homer, Dante picks up the story where Ovid leaves off in *The Metamorphoses*).[11] As in the first section of the elegy, this newly created Dantean underworld, which is Boston minus Lowell, reminds us again of

Auden, whose elegy for Yeats looms as large behind this poem as it does in Brodsky's elegy for Eliot. The words' unawareness that the poet is dead and that they are destined permanently for limbo refigures Auden's "The death of the poet was kept from his poems."

The third section reinscribes the well-known images of civic recrudescence in "For the Union Dead," particularly the ending, where

> [e]verywhere,
> giant finned cars nose forward like fish;
> a savage servility
> slides by on grease.

In Brodsky's revision, the same damning conformity is stressed and made even a pattern for patriotism:

> Huge autoherds graze
> on gray, convoluted, flat
> stripes shining with grease
> like an updated flag.

A society configured only to appreciate the acquisition and exchange of commodities is one ipso facto incapable of appreciating the poet, although in the case of Lowell, the poet was as much a personage to the public as an artist and to a certain extent had capitulated to celebrity, even as he tried to turn it to responsible account.[12] In fact, Brodsky argues, it is not appreciable artifacts that the poet came to deliver to the commodity exchange, for

> In the republic of ends
> and means that counts each deed
> poetry represents
> the minority of the dead.

Equivocating upon the idea of "appreciation," Brodsky consigns Lowell to the "minority of the dead," that is, those who, thanks to the irony of their circumstance, produced no "deeds" appreciable by the living society. A "republic of ends and means" will strive against and come to dominate a "republic of letters," for the former vastly outnumbers the latter. The irony that braces the word "republic" is all the more resonant coming from an exile from the Socialist Republic, whose name fits within quotation marks even more snugly. Yet poetry is a kind of "regard," a term that resonated in Brodsky's classical ear and that includes, variously, the sense of vigilance, an attending-upon, and the "rewarding" of life. Indeed, one of his favorite phrases, the "plane of regard" upon which perspectives take their aim, is subjected to loving reversal and revision, like a sleeve, in reference to the puzzling dichotomy of regard/disregard in the span of American history that was Lowell's lifetime. In the logic generated by this regard/disregard dialectic, it follows that

you become a part
of the inanimate, plain
terra of disregard

In the last section of foursquare quatrains, Brodsky returns to a meditation on the meaning of identification, the equals sign that establishes a strict commonality and therefore a medium for the perfection of exchange. Of course, the exchange upon which most professional elegies would base themselves involves power, that puissance of authority that the elegist seeks both in exchange for and to manifest in the elegy itself. It is the matter of "inheritance": The poet "inherits" the dead man's mantle and returns the favor with an encomium that constellates, ratifies, and symbolizes the continuing power of the dead to exercise an influence in spite of death. Because Lowell lived in a moral as well as a physical universe (and because the physical divorced the moral in Lowell's life, thus becoming his subject), Brodsky asserts Lowell's superiority to death, an assertion that is cold comfort to the moral victor but tonic to the elegist:

You knew far more
of death than he ever will
learn about you . . .

This superiority becomes an important point, for in identifying himself with the dead, the elegist inscribes himself as capable of securing the very moral superiority that is actually the result of his own pronouncement, without seeming to have engaged in subtle or even outright self-aggrandizement:

Under this roof
flesh adopts all
the invisibility of
lingering soul.

If there is something in this that seems to notch the legerdemain of allusion closer to lyric theft, it is worth remembering that in Brodsky's terms, poetry, no matter how hard the poet's pen presses, is signed "Property of Language," not "Robert Lowell" or "Joseph Brodsky."[13] Nor should we make an exception in the case of those who have tried by whatever means to warm to a closer, more personal (read: "transparent") relationship with language, such as the so-called "confessional poets," of whom Lowell was designated by M. L. Rosenthal as a founding member.

"ROMAN ELEGIES"

As befits the Neoclassicist who is also a (self-) elegist, Brodsky was fond of underscoring his interest in the emblematic possibilities of classical architecture, especially as that devolved to ruins. Both references to actual architectural ruins and metaphors of ruins as applicable to one's condition abound; indeed, much of the "uneven numbers" that mark many of his later and last poems—in seeming contradiction to his aesthetic—can be accounted for by this penchant. This interest, of course, which has the benefit of returning metaphorical opportunities to any existential being, may stand as especially resonant for the exile. As for the "man of sidewalks," ruins come to seem the Enlightenment dandy's death's head writ large, and this typical democratic man, like the man before columns in "Almost an Elegy," finds his destiny inscribed on the face of public buildings, a tiny Aeneus musing on the Carthaginian walls (and minus the promise of any future Rome, including a Third). Post-Romantic, plucky, but prim, he not only is confirmed by ruins but also projects them in his turn, finding them useful, a kind of visual lingua franca.[14] For example, in "Lullaby of Cape Cod," an infestation of cockroaches plus a homely wash basin become a kind of Circus Minimus:

> There's a cockroach mob in the stadium
> of the zinc washbasin, crowding around the old
> corpse of a dried-up sponge. Turning its crown,
> a bronze faucet, like Caesar's laureled head,
> deposes upon the living and the dead
> a merciless column of water in which they drown.

But most especially, ruins are applicable to one's person. The fact is not surprising, for ruins allow for the reversal of figure-ground relationships and so provide the poet sugar for his evaluative pill, a humorous property common to such reversals:

> The body repents its proclivities.
> All these singing, weeping, and snarled activities.
> As for my dental cave, its cavities
> rival old Troy on a rainy day. ("1972")

And this from "In the Lake District":

> [T]here I—whose mouth held ruins more abject
> than any Parthenon—a spy, a spearhead
> from some fifth column of a rotting culture
> (my cover was a lit. professorship . . .).
>   (PS 67, trans. George Kline)

We might note that the locus in both cases is the mouth, and quite apart from any intended commentary on the state of Soviet dentistry, the Pninian melancholy also points up a humble fact about the singer's indispensable orifice, with perhaps the suggestion that the songs issuing therefrom (in a magnificent pageant of disincorporation) are conditioned by the same association with ruin, as well as by the same association with classicism.

The 1985 "Roman Elegies" is perhaps Brodsky's most complexly satisfying elegiac sequence. Whereas Goethe's hexameters that go by this title perhaps too famously recount his tapping out the syllables of those very poems on the naked back of his mistress, Brodsky's dozen of sixteen-line sonnets à la Meredith's *Modern Love* find the poet solo, praising women, but mostly insofar as they "breed immortals" (i.e., successful poets). Thus the elegies are a speculative, post-amours,[15] account of a stay in the Eternal City; and just as his elegies are post-Goethean in terms of chronology, so they trade in Goethe's invitation-to-experience for an assessment of experience itself (that is, experience as it is manipulated by consciousness and reduced—or promoted—to its signs). It is also a sequence that dwells at humorous length on the body's—body which is satirically objectified and treated as a thing—inevitable descent into ruin. Most importantly, though, for all of the above reasons, it is a sequence of the eye's dialectical relationship with voice, as expressed in terms of light's relationship with dark. Brodsky has shown a fondness for singling out the eye in his essay on Tsvetaeva: "One of the basic principles of art is the scrutiny of phenomena with the naked eye, out of context, and without intermediaries" (*L* 265).

In the final poem of his last volume, Lowell complained of poetry that was "lurid, rapid, garish, grouped / heightened from life, yet paralyzed by fact," to which he opposed the thought of "something imagined, not recalled." Brodsky's "Roman Elegies" have the same snapshot quality as the object of Lowell's peevishness, his own poems. However, instead of seeking finally to accommodate himself, as Lowell did, to the accuracy of "fact," Brodsky attempts to conflate fact with imagining, on the view that "fact," for the poet, *is* an imagining, a thought that will be challenged by the contest between the body of the poet (and of the Beloved) and the poet's body of work. Thus, the sequence returns us to the familiar territory of his aesthetic agon as elegist, but with a new set of circumstances brought about by two expressions of the course of time. And yet this "progress," consequential as it may be to the particular person, shrinks to virtually nothing—a favorite Brodskyan size, accompanied by the diminutive ego, newly humbled—in contrast to the temporal scale of Rome. The Eternal City's own progress to its contemporary version is no longer so available to detection, although the evidences of it, for the time-haunted speaker, lie everywhere. For the city, time seems to unfold by glacial degrees (the poet is there in a "month of stalled pendulums"), refreshing the acceleration of the visitor's already evident deterioration ("I, the most mortal item / in the midst of this wreckage"). At the same time, as the greater contains the smaller, the poet feels that Rome's seeming "timelessness" ought to be able to contain any time, especially his own ("If somebody shouted 'Freeze!' I'd perform that marvel"). Brodsky uses the temporal disjunctiveness to set in motion the wry, recording camera of his own eye, trained first on the condition of himself:

Get busy then, faucet, over the snow-white, sagging
muscle, tousle the tufts of thin gray singes!

To a homeless torso and its idle, grabby
mitts, there's nothing as dear as the sight of ruins.

(Trans. Joseph Brodsky)

The torso (the word itself recalling artistic ruins), which belongs to the poet in
the beginning of the sequence, belongs to eternity towards the end, in a
complexly realized image ("Flesh that renders eternity an anonymous torso")
combining actual archaic torsos with a figure of human desire contained at its
moment of transformation. Yet containment, whether in terms of a torso or
events, is not only a temporal matter, but a spatial one too. The sequence,
therefore moves from the darkness of a "private Roman / flat" to a condition
"flooded by light." In spite of bodies, the chief trope of the poem involves sight
and seeing. As he says in "Lullaby of Cape Cod,"

In general, of all our organs the eye
alone retains its elasticity,
pliant, adaptive as a dream or wish.
For the change of Empires is linked with far-flung sight.

Thus, sight perception is not confined to the mere interplay between light and
eye, for Roman light possesses such a special potency for the elegist that its
various manifestations encompass even impermeable objects in a complicit
embrace. For example, "At sunset, the windowpanes pan a common / ground";
stones, too, have sight: "Thus the bold cobblestone eyes, like a happy sinner, / the
blue underthings of your leggy blond friend." Even ancient, "dead" things retain
the traces of this former ability: "And the Coliseum looms, the skull of Argus, /
through whose sockets clouds drift like a thought of the vanished herd." This
general attribution of the ability to see, at the level of things, becomes a fortiori
potent in the case of animate beings:

Cast inadvertently through the window,
a glance makes a bunch of blue jays flutter
from their pine tops.

As the Metaphysical poets did, Brodsky here revives Plato's notion, in the *Timaeus*,
of eyebeams that project light and so compete with light on light's terms. As far as
human sight is concerned, Brodsky brings us in close ("By nightfall, a blue eye
employs a tear, / cleansing, to a needless shine, the iris") with the familiar
Metaphysical trope of tear as lens, exaggerating and yet availing an almost scientific
scrutiny of the woes that gave rise to the tear. Synechdoche, as we have seen, is one
of Brodsky's favorite devices, not only for the reason that its more characteristic
substitution of part for whole begins the reduction of images to the "lower" level at
which we imagine that "things" dwell in their naked quiddity but also because it
simultaneously and therefore moves in for the closeup, as in this contrasting pair:

O, a dark eye is obviously more fluent
in brown furniture, pomegranates, oak shutters.
It's more keen, it's more cordial than a blue one;
to the blue one, though, nothing matters!
The blue one can always tell the owner
from the goods, especially before closing—
that is, time from living.

Brodsky uses this device, however, not only to magnify the potency of light which, compared with our ordinary diurnal variety, is already magnified and magnificent, but also to hint at another synthesis between light and eye. Since our familiarity with light takes its cue from the sun, solar imagery is traditionally associated, in the elegy, with the potency of the predecessor. As Sacks observes:

The sky god was emasculated and relegated to a remote height—a height thus ironically achieved by this very relegation. The figure of the sun thus functions like that of the phallus; and to lay claim figuratively (in contrast to Phaeton's literal attempt) to a solar . . . light may thus be understood as another aspect of the mourner's characteristic resolution. Such a claim involves an attempted assumption to one's symbolic legacy and an attempt to assert a figure that, like the other consoling tropes of elegy, offers the most paradoxical blend of absence and presence, of weakness and strength. (34)

Sacks makes the general case, but to suggest that Brodsky's sequence makes this exact investment would be pedantic for the simple reason that this is a self-elegy, and hence no specific precursor is in view, only hypostasized culture. Sacks is nonetheless interesting in this context, for Brodsky is in fact concerned with the various meanings of the "assumption to one's legacy." However, far from glorifying his own possibilities, he characteristically crops the poetic figure of himself to such an extent as to radicalize the problem:

        A bard of
    trash, extra thoughts, broken lines, unmanly,
    I hide in the bowels of the Eternal City
    from the luminary that rolled back so many
    marble pupils with rays bright enough for setting
    up yet another universe.

The droll but unflattering self-assessment as a "bard of trash" is yet consistent with the Chaplinesque figure of the modern intellectual who manages to survive "like a fish, / stranded . . . but intent / on adapting . . . then / to depart." The figure of the poet-as-garbage man also recalls an opinion of Akhmatova that Brodsky quotes approvingly in his essay on Tsvetaeva:

"If you only knew," said Akhmatova, "what rubbish verse grows from . . ." The farther away the purpose of movement, the more probable the art; and, theoretically, death (anyone's, and a great poet's in particular, for what can be more removed from everyday reality than a great poet or great poetry?) turns into a sort of guarantee of art. (*L* 202)

It is this same bard of trash who leaves "a track like the scrawl of a pen." (It is also consistent with a more Freudian self-directed ambivalence: note the self-burial implicit in "I hid in the bowels.") The imagery of light intersects with language at just this point: the "luminary"—that is, the sun, which is capable of setting up "yet another universe," is likewise capable of setting up an alternative life—from which it is but a step to suggest a capacity for setting up art: "For an inkpot glows bright whenever someone mentions / light." Light, then, deputizes humble luminaries in the same way:

Jig, little candle tongue, over the empty paper,
bow to the rotten breath as though you were courted,
follow—but don't get too close!—the pauper
letters standing in line to obtain the content.

Brodsky consistently underscores the sense of the humble scale of his enterprise in the context of Rome (the context of Western civilization itself): "A room in Rome, white paper / the tail of a freshly drawn letter: a darting rodent." To imagine such a thing as Western civilization at all puts us in view of the disparity between the scale necessary to "grasp" civilization and that required to apprehend the miniature scale of its avatar, the poet—symbolized here by the contrast between the sun and a candle. Brodsky is once more speaking of the difference between its time (which is "timeless") and his time. A common symbol for time, replete with its variations, is water, and Brodsky (following Eliot) associates its opposite—aridity—with spiritual depletion or emptiness: "water—the tutor / of eloquence . . . [that] split[s] / the face into rippling ruins."

In the face of this existential erosion, the poet will resort all the more to the redemptive opportunities of his alternative existence, knowing all the while that its redemptiveness will not actually be his, but language's. The striking familiarity of these themes reminds us that they comprise Brodsky's "country," all the more salient for being projected upon the grid of Italy. The rightness of the topological image should not surprise us, for in adopting Italy[16] Brodsky finds a topographical correlative of his exile's status in a manner similar to his revered (and exiled) Cavafy's adoption of Alexandria.[17] The city that belongs to no one provides, quite simply, a ground for metaphor (rather like language) and appeals, therefore, to the exile who would reinscribe his biography with origins more in line with his metaphysics. In this, Rome differs fundamentally from other cities about which Brodsky writes: Boston, London, St. Petersburg, and so on.[18] Self-elegy, for the translated man, would thus seem well-suited to the Eternal City, a city whose ascription of "eternity" seems to depend in some way on its inscriptions and revisions. Rome is the light-flooded eternity of the white page, even as it is the thickly worded page of Virgil:

I've never built that cloud-thrusting stony
object that could explain clouds' pallor.
I've learned about my own, and any
    fate, from a letter, from its black color.

Ironically, its "black color" is made visible by light; otherwise, it is simply a piece of the darkness that surrounds it. Hence the sequence ends with exclamatory utterance (although without the exclamation points): "I was in Rome. I was flooded by light." Clearly, this poetic sequence bespeaks a chastened happiness ("And we, too, aren't gods in miniature, that's clear. / That's precisely why we are happy: because we are nothings"), even as it caricatures the individual fate. Such intensification of a realization that life and art, as it were, move in opposite directions is not a heightening of the consciousness of death-in-life, which will facilitate the move to elegy (i.e., to words), as it is a realization that time—that a poem of time—exacts humility (and "humility is always timely"). The humility is compounded with the secondary realization that, from a more naturalistic perspective, life and art share the same destiny. The representative light, then, "pays off": "Golden coins on the retina are to stay—enough to last one through the whole blackout."

NOTES

1. See "The Condition We Call Exile," *New York Review of Books* (21 January 1988): 16-19. Originally a speech for a conference on exiled writers, where Brodsky was, tellingly, a no-show.

2. See Steven Gould Axelrod's comments on Lowell's *The Dolphin* in *Robert Lowell: Life and Art* (1977), 214-232.

3. Phoebe Pettingell's review of *A Part of Speech* provides a case in point.

4. As a stance, that of indifference, in effect, shows the lengths to which the elegist, deprived of consolatory devices, will go; but a larger theoretical question remains: To what extent is indifference (and ennui) antithetical to elegy's claims to remembrance? To what extent may it be contrived so as to fit its schemes? As a total retreat from pathos, an aesthetics of emotional refrigeration calls to mind Gore Vidal's aperçu: "you bring yourself to the point of indifference so that you can examine a situation with . . . as much logic and intelligence as you can bring to it."

5. Indeed, it must be completely reconceived to be self-consistent, self-referential, and originary—hence its impossibility.

6. Bayley goes on to assert that "civilization, in [Brodsky's and Auden's] context, is an affair of basic humour." (205).

7. Ultimately a question of "authorization," the Brodskyan manner has deep contextual roots. We would do well to remember the retort the poet made to the trial judge's question: "By what right [authority] do you call yourself a poet?" Answer: "God." See also Bethea (3-47) on the problems of authorization.

8. If abstractions like "space" are things, then words are "things" as well, for no abstractions exist apart from words.

9. Such statements tend to support the view held here that the career of a poem, like that of all things for which stasis is inimical, runs toward naturalistic, not transcendent, ends.

10. It should go without saying that the appearance itself of *terza rima* is meant to put us in mind of Dante, and of course, the Dante of the *Inferno*.

11. Appropriately for the author of "A Quaker Graveyard in Nantucket," Dante's Ulysses dies by drowning. Brodsky's Lowell/Ulysses combines this death-by-inundation with Ulysses' homecoming to Penelope.

12. Norman Mailer's description of the public, anti-war Lowell of the 1960s (in *Armies of the Night* [1970]) reveals a Lowell in the mold of Einstein, in that Mailer speculates on the liability of the poet's large head, which would be an appealing target for police batons during the potentially dangerous march on the Pentagon—a far cry from the kind of appreciations showered on the author of *Life Studies*. Lowell had become an icon, at least for the reading public. It is tempting to suggest that "public" artists in the United States have already succumbed to the level of cultural commodities: They are certainly liable to be viewed with suspicion by their fellow artists, as Lowell was.

13. Eliot, too, distinguished between the mediocre poet, who "borrows," and the superior poet, who "steals."

14. This man is the first cousin of the speaker in Philip Larkin's well-known poem "Church-Going," who imagines "some ruin-bibber, randy for antique" as his successor.

15. In fact, Brodsky notes that "all poetry is written post-coitum."

16. A number of American poets have felt the metaphorical aptness of the palimpsest that Italy provides, none more noticeably than James Wright, for whom Italy was frequently the layered, vivid heaven to which he opposed the monochrome otherworld of his origin, "dead Ohio."

17. See Edmund Keeley's *Cavafy's Alexandria: A Study of a Myth in Progress* (1976).

18. Perhaps more than any other city, including Athens and Jerusalem, Rome has established itself as a quotational city of the imagination. The capital of Brodsky's homeland, Moscow, was sometimes referred to as the "Third Rome," uncomfortably suggesting not only its claim to imperial *au courant* status but also echoes of the Third Reich.

Sister to Clio:
"To Urania," "In Memoriam," and "Elegy"

The consolations of the "Roman Elegies" are carried over to the title poem of Brodsky's 1988 English-language volume, *To Urania*. Because Urania ("Heaven") is the muse of astronomy, it is but a small extension of purpose to imagine her as the muse of nonterrestrial existence generally. In this light, she is therefore associated more closely with the project of poetry, as Brodsky conceives it; that is, she is associated with language and the absence of bodies:

> And what is space anyway if not the
> body's absence at every given
> point? That's why Urania's older than sister Clio!
>
> (Trans. Joseph Brodsky)

It is with this statement that we may say that Brodsky takes leave of Auden, whose own *Homage to Clio* declares him to be a child of History. And with this distinction in mind, Brodsky turns back to the effect of light—and all that it implies—in terms of the body: "In daylight or with the soot-rich lantern, you see the globe's pate free of any bio." The lantern's soot combines the residue of temporality with the metonymic eternity of light. The globe, meanwhile, tropes upon both the cranial and the terrestrial spheres. Thus, as elegiac repetition implies an improved continuity that seeks to restructure time, so the opening line, "Everything has its limit, including sorrow," demystifies repetition. With this poem, Brodsky seems to have gone completely over into language (a move that also suggests another way of understanding the often-repeated statement that he has "switched Empires"), but this, too, is a trope. The triumph of words always stands in contrast to the ruins from which they take leave, and each is a necessary reminder (or in numerical terminology, a "remainder") of the other.

The reciprocal nature of words and ruins is the subject of two late short elegies, entitled simply "In Memoriam" and "Elegy." Both titles imply an anonymity of objects, and just as the mourned objects are deprived of their names, so they lose the bias of their particularity. But since a name is not synonymous with identity, there is only a mild irony to the fact that "In Memoriam" is an elegy for the poet's mother. Although the mourned objects of both elegies may be stripped of their actual names, which belong to history more than to poetry,[1] the deprivation does not extend to their humanity, for the emphasis shifts to language—for Brodsky a richer measure of humanity. Even so, he goes so far as to begin "In Memoriam" with a whimsical cadenza, a stoic levity in the face of grief, as if to assert and remind that elegy is a matter of language: "The thought of you is receding like a chambermaid given notice. / No! like a railway platform, with block-lettered DVINSK or TATRAS." But the caprice of the railway metaphor gives way to the fact of the mother's human exit, and the fact that the son "travels" into the future where "odd faces loom in, shivering and enormous." Just as the dead mother signifies the poet's biological starting point, so she is also the first to give her son a perspective:

"Our family," you'd have put it,
"gave the world no generals, or—count our blessings—
great philosophers." Just as well, though. The Neva's surface
can't afford yet another reflection, brimming with "mediogres."

(Trans. Joseph Brodsky)

The no doubt well-meant counsel to accept one's fate becomes a perplexing conundrum for the son: "What can remain of a mother with all her saucepans / in the perspective daily extended by her son's progress?" A lengthening perspective must necessarily locate, in the mother, a smaller and smaller silhouette, and this, in turn, is no small reason for alarm, occasioned as much by guilt at this very "progress," as by grief at the actual death. The realm of words, of elegy, also gets a new obstacle: the poet's inability to mourn "properly"—that is, to consign life to words properly, since the throat is blocked "with the lips' nonstop 'She had died, she has died.'" From a Brodskyan point of view, the poem is not only a failed elegy but also an instance of how such a failure can happen despite the apparent stylistic confidence of the opening lines. The Word becomes, in Robert Hass's memorable phrase, "elegy to what it signifies," as well as by its own measure, a "ruin." But it would be an obdurate task to argue for an account of language that did not recognize the suffering entailed by the contingency of its origin.

In "Elegy," Brodsky notes, "A ruin's a rather stubborn / architectural style." By the same token, a ruin, conceived as an elegy, can be a rather stubborn poetic style, the closer one is to the mourned object. As its own ruin, the poem enforces anonymity throughout, only glancingly passing over many of the familiar effects of the conventional elegy (birds, sunlight, memories, voice) while describing "the place of battle" to which the poet has returned. This place is not specified, nor is the nature of the battle stated explicitly, but doubtless the battle has as much to do with contesting strategies as it does with psychological stress. The images that attach to the place are impastoed with seeming indifference to their relevance:

> Now the place is abuzz with trading in your ankles' remnants, bronzes
> of sunburnt breastplates, dying laughter, bruises,
> rumors of fresh reserves, memories of high treason,
> laundered banners with imprints of the many who since have risen.

(Trans. Joseph Brodsky)

But as we know, "treason" for Brodsky is a matter not of patriotic infidelity but of linguistic infidelity. Gradually the details of the poem, which seem to be shielding a personal privacy, suggest another interpretation: The poem elegizes the poet's faith in the ability of elegy to draw him into the necessary words because these are words that not only take leave of the loved one, but are at once the most necessary, psychologically speaking, even as they are the most in need of being turned out into the public thoroughfares. The fault that lies at the root of this incompatible mission, if fault there be, lies with the sheer fact of living as an contingent, historical being:

> All's overgrown with people.
> . . . .
> And the heart's distinction from a pitch-black cavern
> isn't that great.

In "In Memoriam," the poet writes, "None of us was well suited / for the status of statues," punning on his own eventual fame as a raiser of Horatian and Pushkinian *monumenta*. In "Elegy," he juxtaposes "wings" and "the shade of early twilight" with "stale bad blood." Abandoning the imagery of flight he sets out

> on foot to a monument cast in molten
> lengthy bad dreams. And it says on the plinth "Commander
> in chief." But it reads "in grief," or "in brief," or "in going under."

It may well be that each of these epitaphs is meant to be applicable, though none definitively, for no one is inscribed, either in terms of the way we view the common business of elegy or in terms of the metaphor (dreams).

Like his beloved Beckett, Brodsky specialized in paring away the traditional elegy's component parts in order to locate what remainder, if any, may be viewed as the *sine qua non* by which the form acquires its power to magnify the poet's voice on behalf of that rendered powerless, mute, even deprived of consciousness.[2] Brodsky's later elegies show an experimentalist's willingness to throw in matters of self-judgment beyond self-caricature, as if death's real sting—the deprivation of one's own consciousness—requires a contestation by one's whole mind, not just that portion the mind delegates by conventional literary means. The transformation from life to words, and from words to their further, unforeseeable destinies, is a tall order, perhaps even Utopian (which would, ironically, put Brodsky at the end of a long line of his erstwhile political foes); certainly it is a matter of responding to the call of an ideal, although the question of that ideal's complicity with Platonism remains to be worked out.[3] One of the things that may characterize poetic genres in general is their penchant for revealing inviting readers to peek under the hood, yet the elegy excels even this capacity for self-revelation because it gets us talking in Big Terms and figures such terms as the normative language game. For the poet, like Brodsky, who finds himself seemingly at every turn confronted with such occasions, the genre's pull will not finally relent until he has turned the spade of his talent in each occasion's checkered shade. The self-portrait the elegy makes reveals not only the forked self but the profile of that self's encounter with language. Hence, such self-portraiture is not just a matter relating to language more than to flesh, it is the portrait constructed by the light of non-being, which is a light in which any portrait reveals its debt to states of affairs hostile to its charms. To alter the metaphor slightly, it is a portrait constructed upon the ground of non-being, and any figure produced thereon is likely to acquire vertigo's grimace. The fact is all the more reason that the genre attracts poets' interest in excess of its occasions. In the process, each elegiac poet hopes to find what is most revealing, or at least most characteristic, in the life-to-word conversion. The sense derived from reading most of the great twentieth-century masters, from Yeats and Eliot to Akhmatova and Montale, suggests that plotting the graph of transmutation is never far from the poet's aims. Indeed, the sense of alteration, accompanied by the universal haunting of mortality, often calls for the poet's largest stretch, and in that sense, the elegy, as we have earlier hinted, could rightly be considered the modern successor to the epic in the old *curriculum poetae*.[4] Certainly, Brodsky's elegies provided many of the benchmarks of his career, and the advantage of a certain generic containment provides a chart as crisply telling as the ancient's progress from pastorals piped on oaten reeds (or "scrannel pipes of wretched straw," as the case may be) to epic grandeur. Brodsky used the elegy's generic flexibility to advantage by seeing in his exile a means of achieving the status of a Russian version of the Emersonian representative man (also featuring in this notion the disarmingly modest scope of the role).

The modern elegy (from the late nineteenth century until today) has differed from the traditional elegy chiefly in terms of refiguring what will constitute elegiac consolation, for, broadly speaking, the elegy has traditionally reserved religious consolation as its magic (in Daniel Dennett's term) "skyhook." Although religion's part in the work of consolation has been central, it is not crucial, since it is not a necessary constituent in the "work of mourning,"[5] The search for substitute consolatatory structures, with the setting aside or removal of religious belief, proceeds through the remaining three of what Ernest Becker identified as kinds of immortality: family, institutions, and art.[6] To this trio, we could follow the Romantics (themselves following, if with a certain literary inadvertence, elegiac tradition) in adding a replacement fourth: nature. For Brodsky, long solitary but at length married, exiled, urban, none of these had the availability of art, that is, poetry, although "naturalizing" poetry became an important late, if not a dominant, theme. But from early on in his career, he began to clear away the surrounding cultural debris to arrive at the level of poetry's "essence,"[7] simply, words. From here, he proceeded to replace many of the original parts, but suitably scrutinized and scrubbed, sensing, perhaps, that no modern artist was going to get anywhere in a secular age without first undertaking an inspection of means.

If language gives us the possibility of an alternative (albeit less than immortal) existence, as Brodsky frequently alleged, then it equally gives us the possibility for a moral existence. This aspect of his elegizing should not be overlooked. Although Brodsky is hardly a conventional moralist, he would have been the last to admit that the move to language relieves anybody of the responsibility to live a life with as complete a moral dimension as an aesthetic one.[8] Far from it, for in the last analysis, these things are aspects of a single, larger metaphysics that his poetry has intimated exists, or could exist, even if, approaching Berkeley (or Beckett), there are only a few able to make it out:

> [P]ast all boundaries and all predicates,
> black, white, or colorless, vague, volatile states,
>   something, some object, comes to mind.
> Perhaps a body. In our dim days and few,
> the speed of light equals a fleeting view,
>   even when blackout robs us blind.
>
> (*PS* 76, trans. Anthony Hecht)

Brodsky frequently, if obliquely, alluded to the connection between poetry and the Good. His point seems to be that, *contra* George Steiner, the fact of poetry directs our attention to arenas where the Good—suitably discounted, to be sure—is still the operative idea. In other words, Brodsky stops short of being a thoroughgoing relativist: The "common sense" that Auden found in Chekhov intervenes. Thus, irrespective of its subject, irrespective of whether the Good is conspicuously present though tantalizingly out of reach, a "Universal" or merely some situational rule-of-thumb, something like it orients our discourse— including poetic discourse—about ourselves.[9] But leaving the metaphysics of words aside, we should draw the exegetics to a close by noting with Brodsky that every poet is a democrat in the sense he or she starts from the infinite zero of possibility and that the course of any career factors the admission of this beginning into its subsequent components. Aside from whatever else may be implied in this fact, it also means that the poet's primary responsibility to language is and remains an existentially human one—which is to say, in spite of ideologies that promote individual projects at the expense of the communal, a public responsibility.

NOTES

1. Brodsky does assert his mother's (and father's) name(s) in the autobiographical (read: historical) essay "A Room and a Half," suggesting that their names might fare better in the English language of the essay, since English disallows the degree of moral ambiguity available in Russian. Thus, "I want Maria Volpert and Alexander Brodsky to acquire reality under a 'foreign code of conscience,' I want English verbs of motion to describe their movements. This won't resurrect them, but English grammar may at least prove to be a better escape route from the chimneys of the state crematorium than the Russian" (L 360).

2. Brodsky's vocabulary contains frequent mention of the key word "consciousness," and it may be worth our making the suggestion that if "consciousness can both condition and ignore existence," then threats to that consciousness acquire a political tinge, or taint, since the acquisition of the consciousness in question begins in reaction to Marx's dictum.

3. A poem such as "Plato Elaborated" (PS 129) seems to suggest that the spell of the ideal, though disguised as amusement, is real enough.

4. Although ranking genres is not my task here, I would point out that though the epic retains its prestige as the work for a master, it has few modern practitioners apart from poets for whom length, regardless of "matter," is the key constituent. Derek Walcott appears the single contemporary poet for whom the term retains its original aims, conventions, and implications.

5. If we distinguish between the work of mourning and religious consolation, we may be led to see analogous attempts to distinguish between the roles of, say, communitarian spirituality and a supernatural deity, such as is propounded by Iris Murdoch in Metaphysics as a Guide to Morals (1993) and Don Cupitt in Radicals and the Future of the Church (1989). For Murdoch, a religious ironist, our recourse to the supernatural option is always a gamble, since our traditional presuppositions about God provide us no definitive access. Following Simone Weil, Murdoch considers the possibility of a radical via negativa in which God would also be identifiable with the néant, a route she finds more consistent with modern artistic approaches (here see also Anthony Libby's Mythologies of Nothing [1984], a consideration of just such negative spirituality in post-war American poetry). Cupitt, deconstructing orthodoxy, considers whether it makes sense to maintain traditional beliefs for a religion deprived of the supernatural. Although their purposes differ, what these writers have in common is a desire to ask what the furthest "god term" might be that can no longer be deconstructed. Brodsky's aesthetic route, since language is a "god term" leads him to reject history as the course language (i.e., poems) takes, in favor of nature, where language loses its ability to maintain intention.

6. Becker demonstrates throughout that art's role is less generally available than these others.

7. In using this term, I don't mean to imply an essentialist argument, nor do I wish to be perceived as smuggling one in on my own under cover of equivocation.

8. If pressed, Brodsky would no doubt have agreed on the one hand with Derrida that the literary may as well manifest as much of any good as we can hang our hats on, but on the other hand with Murdoch that aesthetic "play" does not constitute all there is to the literary.

9. The later, mystical Wittgenstein called it the "system," the struts and hinges that the world makes available to consciousness.

10

So Forth:
The Problematics of the End

In the words of philosopher Richard Rorty, we are "incarnated vocabularies."
The task that the elegist brings to poetry is to suggest possibilities for the
disposition of discarnate vocabularies—a course that proceeds, roughly, from
self to text. If this is so, then what better occasion for the discussion of
discarnate linguistic self-fashioning than death, even though, as Wittgenstein
thought, this seems to deprive all words of any fashion? As an elegist working
within a postmodernist model, Brodsky moves to the point at which he must
perforce wrest the duty of the elegist to provide spiritual consolation and
reconfigure the purpose of language as a new kind of consolation. But what kind
of consolation is it? If this were just another case of poetry as "spilt religion,"
it is unlikely that anyone would clamor for the kinds of consolation to be had at
religion's expense. The trajectory of Brodsky's elegiac thinking shows a
progress from the early, wary belief in some transcendent mechanisms, be they
religions or other configurations of words, to a later skepticism about the first
and a drastic revision of the latter (i.e., as a medium we might control). His
later thoroughgoing naturalism both competes with and in some cases replaces
the elegy's position as a stand-alone instance of linguistic transcendent
mechanism. A case in point is Brodsky's last (1996) collection in English, the
volume *So Forth*, many of whose poems were written either directly in his
adopted tongue or translated by his own hand. With the exception of "In
Memory of My Father: Australia" and the self-elegy "At a Lecture," the
volume seems in short supply of elegies like those that have been the subject of
this study.[1] Just as Brodsky seemed to have traded in the transcendent prospects
of language for disseminative meaning, so the elegy seems to have exchanged
something of the authority and integrity that attach to poetic form and
convention in exchange for a *Geist*. Disseminative meaning also suggests that
the poet's final concession to language amounts to a trade of intention for

unforeseen modifications, most especially including those that occur in the guts of the living and not excluding any modifications that might escape those guts.[2] Thus, Brodsky comes to eschew the traditional routes to transcendence in exchange for the naturalist's option. After all, it is naturalism that assists the poet in transcending the very form (elegy) that the naturalist pronounces incapable of providing the transformation it traditionally intends. This fact may account for the quality of the poet's irony. Deprivation of the hope of transcendence leaves one on the horns of a dilemma for which either irony or despair appears the only alternative: irony as the foreclosure on a promise previously so carefully articulated and despair at finding that this foreclosure also apparently leaves the imagination no rejoinder and no redress. The Brodskyan irony derives from the sense of satisfaction that is piggy-backed on this same despair: One can always enjoy a good cigar in the presence of ruins, for these offer another way of talking about the metastatic dynamics of culture. In other words, rather than bringing elegiac thinking to the kind of point that a poem is—that is, a monument—Brodsky suffuses the collection with ambient and stylistic tags— ironic distance, "posthumous" voicings (in which the poem manifests voice at the expense of its status as report), and pointed self-effacement ("Self-effacement is not a virtue / but a necessity")—that undermine monumentality. These underminings range from the initial disenchantment of the cry, "What's the point of forgetting / if it's followed by dying?" (6) to the symbolic consolation of "the pen creaking across the pad / in the limitless silence is bravery in miniature." This consolation is related to the dutiful realization that

> when you shudder at how infinitesimally small you are,
> remember: space that appears to need nothing does
> crave, as a matter of fact, an outside gaze,
> a criterion of emptiness—of its depth and scope.
> And it's only you who can do the job. (19-20)

Such adjurations clearly acquire their quantum of sincerity thanks to the preconditioning irony that underwrites and characterizes their delivery. Thus, "snowflakes float in the air as a good example / of poise in a vacuum." Such poise, the aesthete's relish on the verge of widespread self-overcomings or mere transformations (or deconstructions) is akin to Shakespearean and Keatsian ripenesses, which are in turn imaginative attitudes garnered from personal history. And they are the poet's realization that he has finally collapsed the exilic distance separating Brodsky from "Brodsky." In the naturalistic view, all such quotational separations, once thought to constitute the very identity of the poet, are seen as being out of phase with language's agenda in the face of tenses other than the present. Thus in "Fin de Siècle," a poem recalling "The End of a Beautiful Era," the speaker admits:

> I am ready to play a thing
> of the past, if that's so interesting

to time, eyeing

absentmindedly over its shoulder its measly catch—
which still shows some movement, though not much
else, and is still warm to touch.

I am ready to sink for good in those shifting sands. And I
am prepared that a traveler shambling by
won't focus the beady eye

of his camera on me, and that he won't succumb
to some powerful feeling on my account. (56)

The embrace of the "powerful feeling" gives way to the irony of letting go, which among other things ties the scattering of the self to the "love" of "Verses on the Death of T. S. Eliot." It is not by virtue of underlining one's self or one's poems that one brings love within the realm of possibility. On the contrary, it is by virtue of forgetting—the final, selfless emptying—that love achieves its perfection, namely the extreme thought that attends final selflessness.

To put the matter another way, not only our poems are modified in the guts of the living; all ways in which we are imprinted in the memory are similarly modified. This fact obviously has consequences for identity and personhood: Far from embarking on a project of self-growth at an original, irreducible point from which we derive the store of our expressions, we are aggregated out of our attempts in the minds of others and out of our texts (to Lacanians and others these are the same). To constitute other texts is to constitute other minds and vice versa, and the poem (a fortiori the elegy, because of its self-consciousness with respect to the place of discarnate texts) is the primordial constitution of such a text. When Rorty says that we are "incarnated vocabularies," for a poet such as Brodsky this is both something to which we can attach real, if peculiar, consolation, although to the creators of old-fashioned elegiac consolation this is of no account. In Brodsky's last stage, the grasp of elegy includes the construction of the traditional elegy as a parodic set piece. It also ironically holds the sense of being of "no account" as a virtue:

        Only the seas alone
remain unruffled and blue, telling the dawn, "Go on,"
which sounds, from afar, like "gone."

And upon hearing that, one wants to quit one's travail,
shoveling, digging, and board a steamship and sail
and sail, in order to hail

in the end not an island nor an organism Linnaeus never found,
nor the charms of new latitudes, but the other way around:
something of no account. (59)

As if to show sincerity as a null ground for generating the authority of elegiac composition (even as it is the ground for the work of mourning), Brodsky wrote "In Memoriam," his elegy for his mother. As we have seen, it is a poem that refuses to negotiate a discourse by way of the literary products of affect. At the same time, it is clearly a poem of immense emotional investment, and the struggle between the halves—artistic restraint versus a perhaps unintended emotional emphasis—provides one of its sources of linguistic energy. His "In Memory of My Father: Australia," by contrast, finds the poet dreaming, and it is in the description of the dream that he suddenly remembers the voice of his father, a voice that erupts from the accretions of forgetfulness that the waking world, as well as the intervening time, has offered. Instead of wondering how it would be possible to keep the emotional lid on, the poet finds himself first startled at the presentness of voice:

> The voice, with a triple echo,
> ebbed and flowed, complaining about climate,
> grime, that the deal with the flat is stymied,
> pity it's not downtown, though near the ocean,
> no elevator but the bathtub's indeed an option,
> ankles keep swelling, "looks like I've lost my slippers"
> came through rapt yet clear via satellite. (21)

Although on one level the poem concerns the unpredictability of memory and the provenance of the images in memory, on another it is an elegy in which the poet's memory comes to his father's aid by attempting to help in an escape: "You arose—I dreamt so last night—and left for / Australia." This escape is literally heightened by a more than bird's-eye view of the satellite that governs the ghostly seeming ebb and flow of the father's voice. As extreme, remote, and unreliable as this is for rescue, it is still "better this than the silky powder / canned by the crematorium," not only with respect to what carries forward (voice versus dust), but perhaps more importantly with respect to the manner in which death is handled by the state, that entity that has evolved from the common polis.[3] The voice/dust contrast arises in answer to the question, "What can we save from death," which is a variant to the familiar, "Why can no one save us from death?" The poet prefers the unreliability of a voice's memory to the crematorium's *memento mori* (the crematorium's point of view—that of smoke—is represented in "A Tale," where war-mad generals cry, "Who needs memento when we've got mori?" (113). Moreover, from the perspective of an urban Jew whose heyday was the 1940s and whose environment was Europe, no crematorium, especially including those that return a "silky powder," can do its job without first raising a cultural eyebrow. Even as the poet moves rapidly away from these cautions and qualifications upon memory, he cannot help underscoring them:

> better these snatches of voice, this patchwork
> monologue of a recluse trying to play a genie
>
> for the first time since you formed a cloud above a chimney. (21)

As genies are in the business of wish-fulfillment, this genie is damaged, not by virtue of having first appeared as a "cloud above a chimney," but by being "a recluse trying to play a genie." Nevertheless, one must speculate that the very thought that one could qualify as a cloud above a chimney would in turn provide incentive enough to any rescuer, let alone a son. One wonders whether any reciprocity is attached to the fact that the father's status is pretended: Might not the son who dreams (as re-memberer, as poet) of rescue be equally liable to the pretender's role? Such questions at least persist long enough to allow us to entertain the possibility that their implications and entailments may be intended.

Questions of another sort arise from "At a Lecture," one of Brodsky's sardonic self-elegies that seems also to have acquired the obligation of bidding farewell to his readership. Not unlike Edward Hopper's late painting, "Two Comedians," "At a Lecture" suggests that the artist is the equivalent of a theatrical performer (in Hopper, a clown; in Brodsky, a speaker who is also an academic con man) ready to take his bow, a characterization that underscores and teasingly undermines the melodramatic and performative dimension of Brodsky's art. The title hints that the poet is as much a member of the audience as lecturer and is, moreover, supremely aware of the legerdemain necessary to undertake audience management. At the same time, it also implies that the poet derives the same kind of enjoyment from the execution of poetical tricks as the audience. The love of the spectacle somehow overcomes the constraints of circumstance, the limitations of nature and history, and most importantly, the self's own diffidence toward the content of the spectacle:

Some mistakes are inevitable, I can easily be taken
for a man standing before you in this room filled
with yourselves. Yet in about one hour
this will be corrected, at your and at my expense,
and the place will be reclaimed by elemental particles
free from the rigidity of a particular human shape
or type of assembly. Some particles are still free. It's not all dust. (123)

Not only the poet's lecture, but also presumably all that brought him to the lectern is seen as a construction. Be that as it may, the poet declines to endorse his own or any other constructedness wholeheartedly—that is, to the point of conflating construction with determinism. The freedom of some particles is precisely the freedom to escape the designs of the poet, who in his role as gracious creator would represent a benign interpretation of the unfreedom of matter. Even the free particles, the poet suggests, share the fate of their less fortunate compeers; but the fact is that no poet, no matter how universal and totalizing, can prevent the escape of "some particles." This line of reasoning becomes an ironic, comic, postmodernist version of a Mandelstamian cultural idealism argued from an atomic perspective. The fact is, too, that the freedom of particles involves an imperative of matter that extends far beyond "some":

> So my unwillingness to admit it's I
> facing you now, or the other way around,
> has less to do with my modesty or solipsism
> than with my respect for the premises' instant future,
> for those aforementioned free-floating particles
> settling upon the shining surface
> of my brain. (123)

As we saw in "Lullaby of Cape Cod," the general sweep of things toward oblivion is another way of describing the future. In "At a Lecture," Brodsky describes the future not as that which includes an oblivious, fateful tidal wave that we scatter to avoid, but conversely as a rectitude of things as they are, the thought of which settles on the brain—like dust.[4] The image is more complicated: These particles settle "upon the *shining* surface" (emphasis added), making clear that the poet is comparing his presence (in terms of its surface) to that of furniture—a metaphorical alliance with things used elsewhere in *So Forth*.[5] This alliance is of course to things generally, and things like furniture are such that they move easily along the border that limns the dialectic of presence and absence. The fullness that one is stands in contrast to the emptiness that one becomes, not like a monument, but like a commodious thing itself compared to life. The transformation represents an emptying out; in portraying God's self-emptying into creation as a poetic retrojection, Bloom and other Cabalistic interpreters redescribe the prestige of originary poetic creation by aligning it with a divine (or daemonic) prerogative. It is hardly fitting to suggest that a like emptying out of self into text is the accomplishment of death, but it is unquestionably the business of the elegist to distribute some of the burden of meaning-bearing on death. The point is that in making this distinction, the elegist removes the initiative from death, as it were, in the characterization made familiar by Yeats, "Life and death were not / till man made up the whole." In this world-construction, the presence/absence dichotomy is of course a version of the fullness/emptiness dichotomy:

> The most interesting thing about emptiness
> is that it is preceded by fullness.
> The first to understand this were, I believe, the Greek
> gods, whose forte was absence.
> Regard, then yourselves as rehearsing perhaps for the divine encore. (123)

The poet, who has it on the authority of the Greeks that emptiness is the destiny of fullness, suggests that emptiness, perhaps as the complete expenditure of all action, is, as Bloom and company would have it, also allied with divinity. If the Greek gods preview our emptiness with the (non-) spectacle of their own, we complete ourselves in death in ways unanticipated without the theoretical lens of language. The future is self-emptying, and the self that is emptied is, in turn, subject to dissemination. To make this future come earlier is not to embrace death so much as to acknowledge and invite the justice of change. This will strike some as an ironic, unintended consequence of that self-fashioning we have come to expect of artistic intentionality, on the theory that what is fashioned is no longer "self"— but this is in part the poet's point. We might say that it is precisely this self that has always stood in the way of one's securing, as it were, the repose of ordinary furniture. Self-fashioning therefore gives way to self-effacement, its ironic double. Note that even within the contextual paraphernalia, the poem itself is substituted for the lecture. The poem as lecture: Brodsky could scarcely be tied to a more edifying objective. The Greek gods (and all subsequent gods) have made a specialty of absence; might we not gain some measure of their divinity in emulating them, in assuming our quiddity? Like the Christian, Brodsky's evangel depends on prompt affirmation: "We all act out of vanity. But I am in a hurry."

The haste that Brodsky confesses here is but one of similar expressions of apprehension that arise in *So Forth*. As he and his readers feared, the "pilgrimage" on which the poet's "dull heart" had embarked would one day soon fail to return to its "crossroad," itself an image carrying hints of an unspoken Calvary. This sense of renewed urgency is manifest, too, in the poet's undiminished and redoubtable capacity for making light of serious things: "[Y]ou can make it come / earlier." Brodsky concludes this clever, Pninian travesty of a lecture (and yet a significant discourse withal) on a note of seeming displeasure: "As the swan confessed / to the lake: I don't like myself. But you are welcome to my reflection." However, the point is more literal. The reflection, far from managing a pale imitation of the original, provides its improvement, and this improvement comes about precisely through its capacity for disclosing the "necessity" for shedding its selfhood in favor of the "reflection." Indeed, for the poet, the reflection *is* the self—at least such self as mortals are entitled to earn.

NOTES

1. In spite of the fact that one of the poems is entitled "Elegy" and another subtitled "in memory of . . . ," thus setting into motion readerly expectations that are met with authorial deflection.

2. The difference between those who believe that there is such a possibility and those who find the notion nonsensical is the difference between a skeptical position and a pragmatic one. In general, it is customary to align poets with such things as the "ineffable," but this is to align the poet with skepticism. Here the ineffable suggests not only that which is "beyond description" but that which can never be reached by description. The distinction is important. To propound some thought as extra-linguistic would have been absurd to a poet of Brodsky's linguistic beliefs.

3. It is tempting to speculate upon the changes that might have supervened with respect to Brodsky's poetry had that state evidenced a modicum of communitarian, as opposed to "class," responsibility.

4. It is a naturalistic rectitude constantly under challenge by Stevensian aesthetics. For Stevens, it is axiomatic that "things as they are / Are changed upon the blue guitar."

This change Brodsky identifies with "the rigidity of a particular . . . shape" in the poem under discussion.

   5. For example, in "A New Life," we find

   Stepping out of the tub, wrapped in a bedsheet's linen
   in a hotel in the new life, you face the herd
   of four-legged furniture, mahogany and cast iron. (12)

And in "Homage to Girolamo Marcello": "Nowadays I don't get / on all fours any longer in the hotel / room, imitating its furniture" (64).

Epilogue

In suggesting by precept—and less frequently by example—that poets transform their poems into impersonal machines made of words, Modernist poets were aware that what most distinguished the twentieth century from preceding epochs could be expressed in terms of velocity and the "hardening" required to make the jump to warp speed. An analogous "hardening" for the elegy carries with it a number of risks and indeed poses a paradox for the genre itself. Elegy, as we know, is a form layered with conventional devices and engages in ritualistic moves whose aim is to provide some sort of consolation or compensation, even as it memorializes the dead. If the elegy is to remain convincing as a form that provides the former, can it do so at the expense of its own inherent connection to pathos? The question has extensive implications, and Brodsky evolved both an awareness of these implications and a sophisticated means of unwinding them further over the course of his career. For example, if the Modernist's objectivity meets the perceived requirement for a hardening of poetic forces, can there even be such a thing as an "objective elegy"? In what sense does it engage the central generic conventions? Does the Modernist situation with respect to elegy end in contradiction? What of the postmodernist's attention to the puissance of textuality? These are the kinds of questions that we are left to consider in the wake of Brodsky's elegiac career from "The Great Elegy to John Donne" to "Roman Elegies" and beyond.

Henry Adams in his famous *Education* had contrasted the attentive, patient agenda of the Virgin with the indifferent power of the Dynamo, metaphorical images that pitted, at least, the claims of spirit and flesh against the prerogatives of steel. But Adams' image only made explicit what poets were already sensing, and after the Dynamo won, there emerged the sobering sense that the undoubted power of mechanization resulted in what Blake called "Newton's sleep." The darker implications of Blake's prophecies could hardly be taken at face value by his successors, but the nagging sense of the rightness of his diagnosis left the Modernists in ambivalent relation to the Modern. On the one hand, Eliot's "impersonal" poetry and Williams's call for a "cold, hard" verse, no less than Russian Futurism and Acmeism, reflected allegiance with the triumphs of applied scientistic thinking. Celebrations of the locomotive, Crane's transformation of the Brooklyn Bridge, the socialist realist's encomium to the tractor: All sought, as it were, to modernize Ovid. On the other hand, it became clear that as a technique of prediction and control, scientism would not stop at machines, that its ideological underpinnings—amounting to the replacement of nature—would bring it, with ever more efficient means, at last to consciousness itself. It did not take a Foucault to suggest that science was a discipline of the eye: Millions of Russians, for example, learned that for themselves.

Modernism, as a result, has been tainted with a complicity in the effects of the very pageant it also sought to diagnose. Eliot provides the most obvious case of one who countered *The Waste Land*'s sleep of Newton, not by embracing solidarity with the afflicted, but by retreating into a nostalgic classicism ruled by Church, God, and King (and thus paving the way for the shrunken and embittered, postwar Little England-ism of Larkin and company).[1] Be that as it may, the classicism of a Mandelstam suggests that the "classical" rubric meant different things to the different exemplars of international Modernism. Mandelstam's nostalgia for "world culture," shared by Brodsky, and Akhmatova's rhetoric of memory were attempts to bridge the Newtonian sleep (in its Soviet guise) by invoking a watchful continuity with the past[2]—a continuity that itself manifested poetic truth, as opposed to the revolutionary breach that sought to locate the truth in paradisal futurity and hence desacralized the past, including its poets. The speed of change and the electric efficiency with which historical intervals leapfrogged each other secured the elegy as one of the century's most important genres (to say nothing of the murders of poets, which, without further ado, kept the professional elegist in subject matter). Indeed, the very notion of time compressed requires something like elegiac machinery to decompress it.

It is tempting, therefore, to repeat, with darkening intonation, the argument that the elegy stands as the most sadly fitting twentieth-century genre, although the case of parody and satire often seems equally fitting for taking on the lunacy of mechanized death, to say nothing of the other kinds of discontinuity that frame human obliquity, about which the modern age, for once, has no historical precedence. For elegy requires a cosmological systematic rich in implication. Unfortunately, the modern age has excelled in demystifying all such cosmologies with the result that elegists must shift to the cosmological equivalent of language or be seen as anachronistic curiosities. Brodsky featured this shift as the move made by his own poetry, and his career asks us to consider what may be learned once the shift comes to be understood as a wholesale fact. His candor in this respect has helped to situate his elegies in two traditions: that beginning with Pushkin in Russian and that including Yeats and Auden in English. He is the most recent avatar of the metamorphic privilege of language both to assuage our mortality and to frame its effects in self-consciously value-bearing work. That this privilege has been under attack in recent years in no way vitiates the scope or variety of its manifestations in his verse. If anything, it has contributed to an impression of singularity, that of the individual poet clinging to his project in the face of extensive, if not catastrophic, erosion. The poet even lampooned this Romantic notion:

I vowed to myself that should I ever get out of my empire, should this eel ever escape the Baltic, the first thing I would do would be to come to Venice and rent a room on the ground floor of some palazzo so that the waves raised by passing boats would splash against my window, write a couple of elegies while extinguishing my cigarettes on the damp stony floor, cough and drink, and, when the money got short, instead of boarding a train, buy myself a little Browning and blow my brains out on the spot. (*W* 40-41)

The elegiac conventions engage language with a peculiar intensity because the elegy is predicated in the first place on death, that is, on the antithesis of everything belonging to (in the largest sense) the tasks of poetry.[3] Its intensity as literary text is guaranteed by this contest between the spread of what is no more (and what is not) and the poem, which is an act of assertion. The elegy's inscriptions are predicated on sound; death, which is its occasion, on silence. Thus the paradox on which the elegy stands gives rise to a series of ritualistic contestations: between the dead and the singer, between powerlessness and power (or acedia and anomie and energy), between the present and both past and future. Elegy dictates that the past has a claim on the present, and it is thus, in a Burkean sense, a conservative genre. At the same time, it is the poet's further task to manipulate this claim in such a way as to seize the initiative on his or her own behalf from the no-longer. One way to do this is to reconfigure time by means of symbols that stand for our various senses of time, ranging from simple duration to "history." The structure of verse, the very "turning" of the strophe, is itself such a reconfiguration, and we might expand the notion to enjoin the reminder that poetry as such arises by means of the principle of time folded (like a shroud?) upon itself.[4] We sense this when we notice that poetry features itself as verse (as opposed to something else): It has entered a contest with time, which is its most elemental context. Brodsky has shown unusual originality in handling the hoary subject of time, a subject whose very ubiquity threatens to fence it in clichés. He does so by linking (1) duration with "spirit" and (2) preterit time (which unceremoniously empties into more time) with the space necessary for the poet to initiate the move toward verse. Thus time for the poet, time which we punctuate by signifying the openings and closures within it, is both a richer and stranger dimension than the diurnal metric enunciated by the rational clock: "I always adhered to the idea that God is time, or at least that His spirit is" (*W* 42). If God is time, then verse, we might say, reconfigures or translates God from the medium in which we are ephemera into that where both the human and the supra-human are one. The poet, in other words, attempts to perform the marriage of heaven and earth. The poet is equally aware that such a mystical marriage favors neither party particularly: That which reveals the meaning of duration is subtracted, while humanity—the elegiac subject—is exempted from the inevitable degradation (which is the effect) of ordinary life (the cause). But while poetry flatters neither party, neither does it derogate from either's standing. Rather, it proposes a meeting place where the face of this god can share the dais with that of his creatures, a meeting place emblematic of possibilities foreshortened and actualities foreclosed, as well as the open-ended opposite of these, namely, possibilities and prospects. The construction of paradise always requires a blueprint, which is to say a reduction and an abstraction. But it must be said that such a paradise jibes with our sense of moral, if not political or aesthetic, justice, for such an afterlife as poetry, especially the elegy, carries with it a sense of the purgatorial, if not the purgative.

Because we are historical beings, our imaginings with respect to transcendence must always take the form of transformations, and we would lack subtlety if we did not recognize that the playing out of transcendent imaginings amounts to Frost's "diminished thing."[5] This fact has far-reaching ramifications for poems if we conceive of poems in terms of their self-proclaimed task as transcendence mechanisms. One such is that nothing of the poem as originally conceived can remain intact; that is, nothing can arrive as it began, neither form nor content, neither images nor the sounds of poems. When Brodsky compares Eliot's poems to dandelion seeds, this seems to be a tacit admission of the fact that transformation is but another name for transcendent projects. It's not just that transformation means that the poems will be differently read than written, that what is transcended is place or time into a different place or time, but further that we can't predict what form that transformation will take; hence, it becomes all the more fitting to subsume it under a idea like "dissemination," which in its current popularity as a term, makes for a fairly wide rubric, though it is a helpful one. It makes little difference whether the point is that poems become modified in the guts of the living or whether they go, like fodder, to generate further texts. Still, an imaginative push as forceful as Brodsky's will lead us to imagine a profounder level of perplexity for the fact that we don't know "what happens" to a poem once it is written (and in this way the poem may be said—mutely, as it were—to parrot its *raison d'etre*, death). One thing that such perplexity (and complexity) suggests is that all true interpretation of poems is directed retrospectively, but poems themselves achieve prospective transformations. It may be that Eliot had a glimpse of the problem with poetic transcendence (and opted for the Christian one) with his turnings of the stair, each turning reflective of a stage in the transformations a poem undergoes over time. When we refer to the phrase "reconfiguring time," as a way of getting at the elegy's business, what a "reconfiguring" is intended to do is to make us feel that we're in charge of something that in fact escapes our actual mastery's grasp, though virtually speaking, we can get a better grip.[6] Nevertheless, it would be uncritical for us to neglect to note that the term has something self-congratulatory about it.

What these reconfigurations seem to do, rather, is to delay a poem's demise by giving it many different ways in which to be transformed on the way to whatever fact of dissemination it is destined to undergo. Perhaps this is just another way of speaking of the Heideggerian *phusis* of poetry, the "dark" side, its physical nature that can't be brought under control of the "enframing of technology," namely, logic and theories that base themselves on logical inference. The fact is that poetry's transformations tend to take into account, and to take place toward, the physical, and that means toward nature. The final image of a poem's transformation would therefore be placed before us as a natural image—a seed, a thing that, in contrast to the knowingness of the poem, is encased in its own obliquity—from which we infer rebirth, no doubt prematurely, since as metaphorics, we shall then merely travel to survey the palm at the end of Steven's mind—itself a natural image.

Poems manifest themselves to memory in different ways not only depending on such things as the degree of formal devices or mnemonic setup but also depending on the stage in that poem's transformation at which we encounter it. In other words, one could scarcely imagine a religion that invents as rich a posthumous diversity as literature has secured for the afterlife of poems. Think, for example of the way that we remember "Dover Beach." When one thinks about it, there's nothing about this poem that seizes us with the overmastering virtuosity of the poetic art, either in the exactness of the language or indeed in the quality of its images, and yet the poem sets up shop in the memory and conditions consciousness, irrespective of the intended particulars that go into "reconfiguring time."[7] But armed with its *je ne sais quoi*, the poem, as every school-aged reader knows, becomes a general conduit of far-reaching reflection, worming its way into memory like a computer virus, and sets about deploying its own mirrors by which we see what we see differently having known the poem. Yet a poem like "Dover Beach" performs this feat differently than does another memorable poem, say Hopkins's "The Windhover," with its quite explicit theme of the joining of heaven and earth.[8] Even such a well-known recent poem as Rich's "Diving into the Wreck" appears capable of resetting whole zones of memory and consciousness, despite its rather ordinary language and its worn central image, which though perhaps vivid, is hardly fresh. What this business seems to mean is that we can't predict with any confidence how a poem will array its effects in future time, how it will affect others, or whether or how it will "survive." Indeed, we seem to have arrived at the point at which it is unclear what "surviving" means with respect to a poem, and it does not take an epistemologist to see that much of the confusion is inherent, not in *rerum natura*, but in the language that deals our categories. If we subscribe to the scheme that poems inherently attempt to reconfigure time, and if the heaven of the poem is the degree of its transformation, such that it bonds with the mind on mysterious levels, even if it bonds at first as literal "memorization," we must not forget—as Brodsky has shown—that oblivion has a strong poetry too, one that revises that reconfiguring back upon itself.

Harold Bloom, who has thought long about the business of poetic perpetuation, entails upon such reconfiguring the trope of "apophrades," a total reversal of time in which strong poets seem to have influenced their forefathers. But even Bloom's map doesn't chart the course far enough, for even if we are armed with a formula for what constitutes a strong poet, the same formula can't tell us say what constitutes strong poems (there are no "poems as such"). Of course, we can prune away a good deal of rubbish by way of judging strategy, perhaps even improve our chances as poets and as people trying to understand where poems "go." But it is not clear, at least within the history of English and American poetry, that we will ever discover or invent the principle by which we can, in the lingo of pragmatists, bring prediction closer to control. Even if we knew how, it would only mean that we had said something about the further and further disseminations of our poems. Or it might mean something "about" or "in" poems—in either case, something pertaining to their components, about which we already know a good deal. However, what we know of that level does not confer the right to make assessments of a holistic complexion. Be that as it may, the slippery sides of interpretation hardly inspire critics with a sense of modesty in the effort to scale down generalizations about poetry. Nor should they: as long as heuristics do not become set as dogma, the problematics of poetic transformation will continue to direct our attention to the mystery of fundamentals.

The properly agricultural image of language as sowing the seeds (of what?) suggests, among other things, that dissemination is the poet's way of naturalizing death itself, for death, which has an abundance of representations, is certainly a part of the picture of nature. One of its most obtrusive features is the very fact that it presents itself to our consciousness for representation. Imaginative consciousness ironizes death by reconceiving it as the most egregious thing about the rule of nature and hence something that we would want to eliminate from the natural picture, even though such a picture would be a conspicuous lie.

It is perhaps because the traditional elegy has availed itself of religious consolation, at the outside, so to speak, that one of the key questions for the postmodern elegist is the extent to which he or she can fill the vacuum left by the demise of the supernatural. Indeed, to many contemporary readers, such traditional consolations must appear, as we have seen, as trump cards to be played when naturalistic consolations come up short. By substituting language for the consolation of religious sensibility, Brodsky has opted for a no-trump hand, in which are held only human devices. Last among these devices is the disseminative one, whose effect is naturalistic reconciliation. Although the term "dissemination," armed with its current connotations of seed, scattering, semen, family, originates with Derrida, the idea does not.[9] Brodsky has appropriated the idea and ramified it conspicuously to—it is tempting to argue—its furthest conceivable direction, before it slips into the haze of indeterminacy. This seeding, with its equinoctial connotations, has about it a strong proactive dimension. For instance, like the body, the poem is planted—a "seeding"—but unlike the body, the poem in its farthest reach returns to the earth something both in defiance of and in exchange for that which was removed by death.

Death is also one of the things that makes us most want to escape nature—into aesthetics, for example.[10] Perhaps the greatest intuition of the elegiac poet is to suggest that nature leaves no escape, including aesthetics. The elegist's intuition further stipulates that death is rendered as outrage to our consciousness by pointing to the want of any consciousness on behalf of the dead person, that person with whom we can no longer communicate (if we ever could in life). The elegist's task enters into the domain of ethics at just the point at which he or she must attempt to reconcile words to this fact of silence, which is to say to reconcile us to ourselves. Yet, the final "wisdom" of the poem is somehow subversive to the poem itself,[11] since the poem is predicated on a transcendence that is, as it were, a turning back to the earth. It was this earth that caused the poem to arise in the first place, in response to one of nature's most salient features, namely, the fact that it kills off each of its organisms with complete consistency.

Without trying to make heavy weather out of the self-subversive part, perhaps we should understand the elegy as therapeutic in the sense Keats had in mind: It tries to help us to achieve the equipoise necessary to perceive our "transcendence" as an unpossessable heaven, for possession presupposes death, and elegists and their readers are the living. But such therapy doesn't dispense with heaven: it redefines it as reconciliation. If paradise is truly such a thing as this, then bringing heaven and earth together becomes one of the motives for the frequent images of marriage as the reconciliation of contraries already present, namely in the form of our destiny as mortals. Such images, direct or cognate, seem of a piece in representing marriage as a fantastic union. Nevertheless, the poet who perceives paradise in such terms is, in Brodsky's phrase, "flooded with light."

It may very well be that poets must start out as dualists, but the reconciliation is poetry's final benignant act, since reconciliation is itself a healing of dualisms. The Good in this case is not an unattainable idea toward which we are forever oriented in the shadowland of our lives; rather, it is something like this rapprochement. In Allen Grossman's universe (1992), poetry is the model of intersubjectivity, bringing persons into each other's sphere of attention. Such a model impels us out of the guilty, death-denying solitary consciousness into the light of poetic discourse. Whereas Grossman's model addresses itself to the origins of poetic address, the elegist concerns himself with the conciliating ends, whereby the silence that blocks interlocution with the dead, even as it continues to model intersubjectivity between poets and readers and readers and readers, atones for the hubris of singularity by raising our sight from the walls of the cave. This atonement, or at-onement, secures our basis, not in morals, but in nature.[12]

NOTES

1. But Eliot may be a special case, if we take his notorious conservatism, not as effect, but as cause.

2. Vigilance as "witness" may be said to be the reverse (or obverse) of vigilance as surveillance. Certainly, these poets were eager to contrast the "positive" effects of a poetry of witness, with its emphasis on memory, to revisionist attempts to "correct" history.

3. By "tasks of poetry" I mean to stress only its ontological implications, following Grossman.

4. It is important to note that whether we speak of time's "natural" configurations or as "reconfigurations" by means of poetry, we are speaking of figures existent within language only. It is, of course, this figurative knowledge that lends Brodsky or any other poet the wherewithal to entertain such notions as "transcendence" or the interchangeability of people, words, and things. Precisely by the same token, Plato's condemnation of the poet comes down to his ability to "say of what is not, that it is"—which is to say, to lie. But one's failure to distinguish between a lie and a "lie" condemns the auditor (in Brodsky's view) to the destiny merely of a material thing, since any such discernment entails the very existence of consciousness; and the absence of such discernment, the lack of consciousness. Hence, putting the religious imagination aside as a special case, the literary imagination remains the only means of securing a higher destiny than the dust that awaits the mortal coil.

5. Brodsky has in recent years evinced an interest in Frost and Hardy, two poets of this consummate theme.

6. Brodsky would thus solve the problem of the "untheorizable" nature of death by continually seeking to narrow, if not close, the gap between actual and virtual.

7. This is in no way to suggest that underdetermined poems or those low in formal intentional values will ever have an "afterlife" apart from the ephemeral reception of their first readers.

8. Perhaps all we have said is that different poems work in different ways and that generic considerations merely set up a grid of expectations, constraining interpretation. Yet we have enlightened nothing in leaving matters at such a general level: Even interpretive police actions provide weak interpretive matrices.

9. However, the aptness of these connotations for two postwar, exilic, literary Jews would surely be worth our notice, if for no other reason than that both cosmopolites can be credited with the irony of offering to supplant a natural—as opposed to the agri-cultural—idea on literary-text production, and in so doing lowering the artificer's pretense—remarkable, too, in light of Brodsky's debt to the source of the agricultural metaphor, Virgil.

10. Such customary escape routes have been held in bad odor, especially since World War II, both by theorists and by other elegists such as Celan.

11. At the same time, Brodsky's poetic has developed along lines that necessitate abundant instances of double-pulling: In brief, he mitigates the contingent aspect of the elegy with recourse to the transcendent armature of language, even as he naturalizes the elegy and therefore calls transcendence into question. This dialectical pull itself suggests at least the residual desire for yet an *Aufhebung*.

12. A good deal of romantic ideology continues to revolve around art in the form of "license," by conceiving of art not as model, but as object. Implied in this ideology is the sacrificial notion of art at any price. The objection to this was raised anew in the case

of so-called confessional poets, perhaps most vividly in the storm surrounding Lowell's *The Dolphin*, a collection in which Lowell violated the privacy of intimate letters for the sake of achieving realism in the poetry while at the same time explicitly relinquishing the notion of a transcendent purpose to the same poetry.

Works Cited

Axelrod, Stephen Gould. *Robert Lowell: Life and Art*. Princeton: Princeton UP, 1977.

Bachelard, Gaston. *The Poetics of Reverie*. Trans. Daniel Russell. Boston: Beacon Press, 1971.

Bate, Walter Jackson. *The Burden of the Past and the English Poet*. Cambridge: Harvard UP, 1972.

Bayley, John. *The Order of Battle at Trafalgar*. New York: Wiedenfield and Nicholson, 1990.

Becker, Ernst. *The Denial of Death*. New York: The Free Press, 1973.

Berlin, Isaiah. *Russian Thinkers*. New York: Viking Press, 1978.

Berryman, John. *Homage to Mistress Bradstreet*. New York: Farrar, Straus, and Cudihy, 1956.

Bethea, David M. *Joseph Brodsky and the Creation of Exile*. Princeton: Princeton UP, 1994.

Birkerts, Sven. "Art of Poetry xxvii: Joseph Brodsky" (interview). *Paris Review* 24 (Spring 1982): 82-126.

_____. *An Artificial Wilderness: Essays on Twentieth-Century Literature*. New York: Morrow, 1987.

Bloom, Harold. *The Anxiety of Influence*. New York: Oxford UP, 1973.

_____. *The Poetics of Influence: New and Selected Criticism*, Ed. John Hollander. New Haven: Henry R. Schwab, 1988.

_____. "The Fatal Glass of Beer, or The Aesthetics of Outrage." *The Movie That Changed My Life*. Ed. David Rosenberg. New York: Viking, 1992. 151-156.

Brodsky, Joseph. *The Great Elegy to John Donne and Other Poems*. London, n.p., 1967.

_____. *Selected Poems*. New York: Harper and Row, 1973.

_____. *A Part of Speech*. New York: Farrar, Straus, and Giroux, 1980.

_____. *To Urania*. New York: Farrar, Straus, and Giroux, 1987.

_____. *So Forth*. New York: Farrar, Straus, and Giroux, 1996.

_____. *Less Than One: Selected Essays*. New York: Farrar, Straus, and Giroux, 1986.

_____. *Marbles* (play). New York: Farrar, Straus, and Giroux, 1985.

_____. *Watermark* (prose). New York: Farrar, Straus, and Giroux, 1992.

_____. *Stikhotvoreniia i poemy (Short and Long Poems)*. Washington: Inter-language Literary Associates, 1965.

_____. *Konets prekrasnoi epokhi: Stikhotvoreniia 1964-71 (The End of a Beautiful Era, Poems 1964-71)*. Ann Arbor: Ardis Publishers, 1967.

_____. *Ostanovka v pustyne (A Stop in the Desert)*. New York: Chekhov Publishing House, 1970.

_____. *Chast' rechi: Stikhotvoreniya 1972-76 (A Part of Speech: Poems 1972-76)*. Ann Arbor: Ardis Publishers, 1977.

_____. *V Anglii (In England)*. Ann Arbor: Ardis Publishers, 1977.

_____. *Rimskie Elegii (Roman Elegies)*. New York, 1982.

_____. *Novie Stansii k Avguste (New Stanzas to Augusta)*. Ann Arbor: Ardis Publishers, 1983.

_____. *Uraniia (To Urania)*. Ann Arbor: Ardis Publishers, 1987.

Cupitt, Don. *Radicals and the Future of the Church*. London: SCM Press, 1989.

Derrida, Jacques. *Spurs: Nietzsche's Styles*. Trans. Barbara Harlow. Chicago: U of Chicago P, 1979.

_____. *Margins of Philosophy*. Trans. Alan Bass. Chicago: U of Chicago P, 1982.

Eliot, T. S. *Selected Essays of T. S. Eliot*. New York: Harcourt, 1964.

Felstiner, John. *Paul Celan: Poet, Survivor, Jew*. New Haven: Yale UP, 1995.

Freud, Sigmund. "Mourning and Melancholia." *The Freud Reader*. Ed. Peter Gay. New York: Norton, 1989. 584-589.

Ginsberg, Allen. *Collected Poems 1947-1980*. New York: Harper and Row, 1984.

Grossman, Allen and Mark Halliday. *The Sighted Singer: Two Works for Readers and Writers*. Baltimore: Johns Hopkins UP, 1992.

Grossman, Allen. *The Long Schoolroom: Lessons in the Bitter Logic of the Poetic Principle*. Ann Arbor: U of Michigan P, 1997.

Hamill, Sam. "The Shadow and the Light." *The American Poetry Review* 19, 1 (1990).

Hass, Robert. *Twentieth Century Pleasures*. New York: Ecco Press, 1984.

Heaney, Seamus. "Brodsky's Nobel: What the Applause Was All About." *New York Times Book Review*, 8 Nov. 1987: 1.

Heidegger, Martin. *Basic Writings*. Ed. David Farrell Kress. Trans. Albert Hofstadter. San Francisco: Harper, 1977.

Kantorowicz, Ernest H. *The King's Two Bodies: A Study in Medieval Political Theology*. Princeton: Princeton UP, 1957.

Keeley, Edmund. *Cavafy's Alexandria: A Study of a Myth in Progress*. Cambridge: Harvard UP, 1976.

Klein, Melanie. *Love, Guilt, Reparation and Other Works, 1921-1945*. Ed. Masud R. Khan. London: Hogarth Press, 1981.

Lawler, Justus George. *Celestial Pantomine: Poetic Structures of Transcendence*. New Haven: Yale UP, 1979.

Levinas, Emmanuel. *The Levinas Reader*. Ed. Seán Hand. Trans. Alphonso Lingis. Oxford: Blackwell, 1989.

Libby, Anthony. *Mythologies of Nothing: Mystical Death in American Poetry 1940-1970*. Urbana: U of Indiana P, 1984.

Loseff, Lev. "Chekhovskaya tema v poezii Brodskogo." Paper delivered at the Chekhov Symposium, Norwich, Vermont, July, 1985. See Polukhina, 151.

Mailer, Norman. *Armies of the Night; History as a Novel, the Novel as History*. New York: NAL, 1968.

Milosz, Czeslaw. "A Struggle against Suffocation." *The New York Review of Books*, 14 Aug. 1980: 23-24.

Murdoch, Iris. *Metaphysics as a Guide to Morals*. New York: Penguin, 1993.

Oakeshott, Michael. *Rationalism and Politics*. London: Methuen, 1962.

Pettingell, Phoebe. Review of *A Part of Speech*. *The Nation*, 14 Oct. 1988: 54-56.

Philippe, Charles-Louis. *Bubu du Montparnasse*. Paris: 1901.

Picard, Max. *The World of Silence*. Chicago: Henry Regnery, 1952.

Polukhina, Valentina. *Joseph Brodsky: A Poet for Our Time*. Cambridge: Cambridge UP, 1989.

Raine, Kathleen. *Defending Ancient Springs*. Oxford: Oxford UP, 1967. 105-122.

Ramazani, Jahan. *Poetry of Mourning: The Modern Elegy from Hardy to Heaney*. Chicago: U of Chicago P, 1994.

Rigsbee, David. "The Materialist Muse: Theory and Language Poetry." *Pembroke Magazine* 28 (1996): 64-87.

Rorty, Richard. *Contingency, Irony, and Solidarity*. Cambridge: Cambridge UP, 1989.

Rosenthal. M. L. and Sally M. Gall. *The Modern Poetic Sequence: The Genius of Modern Poetry*. New York: Oxford UP, 1983.

Rukeyser, Muriel. *The Collected Poems of Muriel Rukeyser*. New York: McGraw-Hill, 1978.

Sacks, Peter M. *The English Elegy: Studies in the Genre from Spenser to Yeats*. Baltimore: Johns Hopkins UP, 1985.

Shaw, W. David. *Elegy & Paradox: Testing the Conventions*. Baltimore: Johns Hopkins UP, 1994.

Shklovsky, Viktor. *Theory of Prose*. Trans. Benjamin Sher. Elmwood Park, IL: Dalkey Archive Press, 1990.

Simon, John. Review of *A Part of Speech*. *National Review*, Oct. 1988: 54-56.

Spender, Stephen, ed. *W. H. Auden: A Tribute*. New York: Macmillan, 1975.

_____. *T. S. Eliot*. New York: Viking, 1975.

Steiner, George. *After Babel: Aspects of Language and Translation*. New York: Oxford University Press, 1975.

_____. *Language and Silence: Essays on Language, Literature, and the Inhuman*. New York: Atheneum, 1967.

Walcott, Derek. *Another Life*. New York: Farrar, Straus and Giroux, 1973.

Index

transparency, xiii, 8, 124; as
measure of humanity, 134; and
time, 114; transcendent purposes of
xv, 141-142; as value-bearing, xiii,
42, 150-151
Language poets, xiii, 8, 102n.
Larkin, Philip, 40, 67n., 131, 150
Lawler, Justus George, xiii
Leander, Zarah, 77, 79, 87, 87n.
Libby, Anthony, 138n.
Lipking, Lawrence, 18n.
Lorca, Gabriel García, 101
Lorenzo the Magnificent, 111
Love, metaphor for spirit, 49; as
"moral tone," 52n.; and poetry,
49-50; similarity with death, 52n.
Lowell, Robert, xvii, 47, 94, 97,
106, 119-124; JB acquaintance
with, 119-200, 131n., 156n.
"Lullaby of Cape Cod," 6, 89-103,
115, 117, 118, 125, 127, 146; and
absence of certainty, 100;
accommodation to American
poetry, 101; and ambivalence, 94,
96, 98; and "American Sublime,"
101; and "Empire," 91, 93, 95,
103n.; and exile, 93-95; "fifth
angle," 96; and humility, 90; and
infinity, 90; life as variety of time,
99; and Robert Lowell, 97; and
naturalized conception of words,
91; and paradise, 100; Parnassian
style, 89-90, 98; and poetic
priority, 94; as poetry of witness,
98, 100; and skepticism, 92, 100,
103n.; and synoptic view, 96,
102n.; "theater of poetry," 97; and
transcendence, 97

Mailer, Norman, 131n.
Mallarmé, Stephane, 8, 54, 113, 150;
and elegy, 13
"Man of sidewalks," 107, 109, 125
Mandelstam, Osip, 9-10, 19, 35-36,
53-54, 114, 119, 145, 150
Marbles, 62
Mary Queen of Scots, 77-88
Marx, Karl, 14, 138n.

Meredith, George, 126
Metaphysical poetry, 19, 33n., 69-70
"Metaphysics of presence," xiv-xv
Milosz, Czeslaw, 17n., 38, 40, 114
Milton, John, 44, 47, 51n., 78, 81
Modernism, 19-20, 31; and elegy,
149-150
Montale, Eugenio, 10, 40, 114, 118,
136
More, Sir Thomas, 109
Murdoch, Iris, 52n., 102n., 138n.
Myers, Alan, 63ff., 117ff.

Nabokov, Vladimir, 14, 106
"Nature Morte," 32n.
Neruda, Pablo, 5
"A New Life," 148
Nietzsche, Friedrich, xix, 50n., 100
"1972," 62-64; and ambivalence, 63;
and exile, 63; omniscient
perspective, 64

Oakeshott, Michael, 33n.
"On the Death of Zhukov," 64-66;
and antithetical nature of epic
heroism, 66; mimicry of patriotic
poems, 65
"On Tyranny," 17n.
Orphic function of poetry, 15
Ovid, 54, 114, 122, 150

Parnassian style, 89-90, 94, 98
"A Part of Speech," 51n.
Paul (Apostle), 28
Pavese, Cesare, 51n.
Paz, Octavio, 5, 38, 114
Petersburg, 110
Pettingell, Phoebe, 130n.
Philippe, Charles-Louis, 67n.
Picard, Max, 32n.
Plato, Platonism, and Universals, xiv,
xviii, 13, 52, 66n., 127, 136-137,
138n., 156n.
"Plato Elaborated," 138
Poe, Edgar Allan, 54
Poetry of witness, 98, 100, 156
Polukhina, Valentina, xiv, 28, 32n.,
54, 55, 62, 66n., 109, 121

About the Author

DAVID RIGSBEE is Professor of English and Chair of the Department of Language and Literature at Mount Olive College in North Carolina. He has written seven books, including four volumes of poetry and has translated poems from the Russian. His work has appeared in publications such as *The American Poetry Review*, *The New Yorker*, and *The Georgia Review*.

ISBN 0-313-30419-X

90000>

9 780313 304194

HARDCOVER BAR CODE